The
Psychology
of Dementia

THE WILEY SERIES IN CLINICAL PSYCHOLOGY

Series Editors

Fraser N. Watts *MRC Applied Psychology Unit, Cambridge, UK*

J. Mark G. Williams *Department of Psychology, University College of North Wales, Bangor, UK*

Edgar Miller and Robin Morris The Psychology of Dementia

Ronald Blackburn The Psychology of Criminal Conduct: Theory, Research and Practice

Ian H. Gotlib and Constance L. Hammen Psychological Aspects of Depression: Toward a Cognitive-Interpersonal Integration

Max Birchwood and Nicholas Tarrier (Editors) Innovations in the Psychological Management of Schizophrenia: Assessment, Treatment and Services

Robert J. Edelmann Anxiety: Theory, Research and Intervention in Clinical and Health Psychology

Alastair Ager (Editor) Microcomputers and Clinical Psychology: Issues, Applications and Future Developments

continued on back end-paper

EDGAR MILLER
University of Leicester, UK

and

ROBIN MORRIS
University of London, UK

The Psychology of Dementia

JOHN WILEY & SONS

Chichester · New York · Brisbane · Toronto · Singapore

Other Wiley Editorial Offices

John Wiley & Sons, Inc., 605 Third Avenue,
New York, NY 10158–0012, USA

Jacaranda Wiley Ltd, 33 Park Road, Milton,
Queensland 4064, Australia

John Wiley & Sons (Canada) Ltd, 22 Worcester Road,
Rexdale, Ontario M9W 1L1, Canada

John Wiley & Sons (SEA) Pte Ltd, 37 Jalan Pemimpin #05-04,
Block B, Union Industrial Building, Singapore 2057

Library of Congress Cataloging-in-Publication Data:

Miller, Edgar.
    The Psychology of dementia / Edgar Miller and Robin Morris.
      p.   cm. — (The Wiley series in clinical psychology)
    Includes bibliographical references and index.
    ISBN 0-471-92776-7 (cased)
    1. Dementia.   I. Morris, Robin, 1958– .   II. Title.
  III. Series.
    [DNLM: 1 Dementia—psychology.   WM 220 M647p   1993]
    RC521,M55   1993
    616.89—dc20
    DNLM/DLC
    for Library of Congress   93–5046
                                                                    CIP

British Library Cataloguing in Publication Data:

A catalogue record for this book is available from the British Library

ISBN 0-471-92776-7

Typeset in 11/13pt Palatino from author's disks by Photo·graphics, Honiton, Devon
Printed and bound in Great Britain by
Biddles Ltd, Guildford and King's Lynn

To Lorna and Sally

CONTENTS

Series Editor's Preface ix

Preface xi

Chapter 1 Introduction 1

Chapter 2 Memory in dementia 16

Chapter 3 Language 36

Chapter 4 Other psychological impairments 53

Chapter 5 Subcortical dementia 68

Chapter 6 Assessment of dementia 91

Chapter 7 Management of dementia 110

Chapter 8 Psychosocial aspects of dementia 133

Chapter 9 Conclusions and future directions 154

References 167

Index 203

SERIES EDITOR'S PREFACE

Dementia is a condition which is all too common, and unfortunately increasingly so. It is also one where psychological and psycho-social methods of assessment and management are extremely important. It is probably true to say that the biological aspects of dementia have attracted most research interest in recent years. However, as Miller and Morris emphasise, this research has so far yielded relatively little in terms of practical clinical applications, and is not likely to do so for some time. In this situation, the clinical psychologist remains one of the most important members of a clinical team providing services to elderly people suffering from dementia.

There is an increasingly strong body of clinical psychologists specialising in work with such patients. This text provides an authoritative and comprehensive guide for all clinical psychologists working with the problems caused by dementia, whether or not this is their major specialisation. It will be of value to members of other professions using psychological methods in their work, or who wish to understand the contribution of psychologists. The book will also be a valuable reference source for research psychologists concerned with the psychological aspects of ageing.

The book that Miller and Morris have written here makes an ideal contribution to this Wiley series. It takes an important clinical problem, presents the relevant scientific research in a readable and accessible way, and shows what psychologists can do in clinical practice. I hope that it will be read and used as extensively as it deserves.

Fraser Watts

Series Editor

PREFACE

Interest in the problem of dementia has expanded considerably in recent years. Extensive research into the epidemiology, neuro-pathology, genetics, neurochemistry and other aspects of the dementing illnesses has been conducted. As a result, considerable progress has been made in understanding the mechanisms under-lying dementia.

Nevertheless, the very term "dementia" is primarily psychological in that it implies, above all else, a deterioration in intellectual func-tioning. The psychology of dementia is therefore a central issue in the overall understanding and management of the problems posed by the dementing illnesses.

This book sets out to review the present state of knowledge con-cerning the psychology of dementia. It starts off by examining the more fundamental issue pertaining to the nature of psychological impairment in dementia and then goes on to deal with the more practical aspects like assessment and management. What is also clear is that dementia has an impact on the sufferer's family, and the psychosocial issues are taken up towards the end of the book.

It is hoped that this synthesis of psychological knowledge in relation to dementia will prove useful to both students and those working in the field, as well as making a modest contribution to the furtherance of our understanding of the problems of dementia and how they might best be resolved.

Edgar Miller
Robin Morris

March 1993

CHAPTER 1   Introduction

In recent years it has become generally realised that the proportion of elderly people in the population is rising, at least in Western industrialised countries. For example, in Britain about 5% of the population were of what is now regarded as retirement age in 1900. By 1990 this proportion had risen to just over 18%, and present demographic trends indicate that the proportion of elderly people has not yet reached its peak. One noteworthy feature of this increase in the proportion of elderly people in the population is that the relative increase of the so-called 'elderly elderly' is even greater. At the turn of the present century, about 1% of the population was over 75 years of age. The proportion in that category by 1990 was very nearly 7% (figures produced by the British Government Central Office of Information). Similar trends have been recorded in the USA, The Netherlands and many other Western industrialised nations.

One inevitable consequence of an increasingly elderly population is a rise in the number of people with those types of difficulty that are particularly associated with the later stages of life. One major and particularly difficult problem encountered in older people is that of dementia, and this book is specifically concerned with the psychological aspects of dementia.

Dementia is of course a multifaceted problem which has biomedical, psychological and social aspects. As already indicated, the concern here is with the psychological aspects, and other facets of the overall problem of dementia will be considered only to the degree that they relate to psychological issues. This emphasis on the psychology of dementia is justified on two main grounds, apart from the fact that the authors are psychologists and therefore best equipped to deal with the psychological aspects. One reason is that such is the range of work now being published on dementia that it would be impossible to cover all aspects adequately in a single volume of manageable length. Some specialisation of treatment is therefore necessary. A second reason for focusing on the psychology of dementia is that the term 'dementia' is primarily psychological in its connotations. It implies, above all else, a deterioration in intellectual functioning. The psychology of dementia therefore has a central place in any overall consideration of the problems that dementia raises.

Despite the central importance of the psychology of dementia, it also has to be recognised that the biomedical and social aspects are also of great significance and cannot be neatly separated off from the psychological. A degree of overlap and interaction of the different elements that make up the overall picture has to be acknowledged, and for this reason some biomedical and social issues will impinge on the following discussions. It also has to be stated that the emphasis on the psychological issues of dementia should not be taken as indicating that the authors regard these other aspects as being of only minor consequence. Such an attitude would be plainly silly, since the consequences of dementia are of enormous social significance and the exploration of its causation, and hence possible prevention, depends on an understanding of its underlying neuropathology.

WHAT IS DEMENTIA?

Like many terms in present-day use in the general area of psychiatry and related disciplines, the term 'dementia' has a long history and its meaning has changed and evolved over time. A historical discussion of the development of the concept of 'dementia' has been provided by Berrios (1990).

As Lishman (1987) has pointed out, the term 'dementia' is currently used in two different ways. One use of the term is to refer to specific clinical conditions, such as 'senile dementia'. As far as this particular usage is concerned, it is more appropriate to talk about 'the dementias', since there are a number of dementing illnesses. What these illnesses have in common is widespread, progressive brain pathology with consequent intellectual deterioration; there is also, as things stand at present, a rather dismal prognosis.

The other current meaning of the term 'dementia' is to refer to a syndrome that can occur in a wider range of clinical conditions. Definitions of this syndrome vary, but that offered by Lishman (1987) is as good as any and contains the essential elements. According to Lishman, dementia is 'an acquired global impairment of intellect, memory and personality, but without impairment of consciousness'. He adds that 'as such it is almost always of long duration, usually progressive, and often irreversible, but these features are not included as part of the definition'.

There is clearly a considerable overlap between the dementing illnesses and the syndrome of dementia in that the former carry the features of the latter. The features exhibited by the dementing illnesses usually include the non-essential manifestations of the syndrome, identified by Lishman, of long duration, progressive nature and irreversibility (or at present, at least, a lack of any useful knowledge as to how the process might be halted or even reversed). Almost all psychological research into dementia has been based on subjects exhibiting the features of one or other of the dementing illnesses, and this will be reflected in the discussions in the following chapters. The extent to which this work can be generalised to the wider range of conditions that may exhibit the syndrome of dementia is not yet ascertained.

Before leaving Lishman's (1987) definition of the syndrome of dementia, a few further comments are in order. Dementia is an 'acquired' affliction in the sense that it has not been present for the whole of the individual's lifespan. The implication is that intellectual deterioration has occurred from what was once a higher level of functioning during the person's adult life. It should be noted that the term 'acquired' in this context does not necessarily mean that the basic cause was encountered some time during the individual's lifespan. In fact, dementia may be pre-programmed in the sense that it can be related to a genetically determined disorder.

The 'global impairment of intellect, memory and personality' indicates that a wide range of cognitive and other psychological functions are affected. A specific impairment in memory and language, or a change in personality with no more widespread features and without any appreciable general intellectual decline, would not qualify as dementia. Being 'without impairment of consciousness' distinguishes dementia from delirium and toxic confusional states where there may be clouding of consciousness. This is a point with important practical consequences, because delirium and toxic confusional states are often reversible and old people suffering from the toxic effects of over medication, or who are confused because of afebrile infections, are sometimes wrongly considered to be demented.

A relatively recent trend in the literature on dementia has been to try to fragment the features of dementia into a number of more specific sub-syndromes. One example of this is the distinction between 'cortical' and 'subcortical' dementias (Albert, Feldman & Willis, 1974). This distinction will not be elaborated here but will be picked up later (see Chapter 5).

THE DEMENTING ILLNESSES

It used to be common to distinguish between 'senile' and 'pre-senile' dementias depending upon the age of onset. The cut-off between the two was imprecisely defined but often occurred at some point around the age of 65 years. This distinction has been strongly questioned and largely abandoned because it no longer appears to make sense in its traditional form. Where the features of dementia do vary with age this most commonly seems to be a reflection of the pathoplastic properties of ageing, rather than any fundamental differences in the underlying pathological processes or the fact that some dementing illnesses (e.g. Huntington's chorea) have an earlier age of onset than others.

The main types of dementing illness are set out in Table 1.1. Some brief comments about the most significant of these disorders will be given below, but more authoritative accounts can be found in the standard psychiatric and neurological textbooks.

The most commonly encountered dementing illness is Alzheimer's disease. Since a firm diagnosis of Alzheimer's disease can only be made on the basis of a post mortem examination of the brain, any

Table 1.1 The major disorders associated with dementia

A. With a predominantly cortical pathology

Alzheimer's disease
Cerebrovascular dementia (ateriosclerotic or multi-infarct)

B. With a predominantly subcortical pathology

Parkinson's disease
Huntington's chorea
Progressive supranuclear palsy (Steele–Richardson–Olszewski syndrome)
Wilson's disease
Multiple sclerosis

N.B. The above are only the most commonly encountered disorders linked to dementia. More exhaustive listings can be found elsewhere (e.g. Peretz & Cummings, 1988).

diagnosis of this condition in life is inevitably presumptive. For this reason it is often referred to as 'dementia, Alzheimer type' or 'senile dementia, Alzheimer type' (AD, DAT or SDAT). The pathology of Alzheimer's disease cannot be described here by anything other than a few superficial comments, but greater detail can be found elsewhere (e.g. Esiri, 1989). It consists of cerebral atrophy on gross examination of the brain, with raised numbers of neuritic (or senile) plaques and neurofibrillary tangles being observable on microscopic examination. The past 10–20 years have seen considerable advances in understanding the neurochemistry of DAT and it is now evident that several neurotransmitter systems are involved. It was first demonstrated (e.g. Bowen *et al.*, 1977; Perry *et al.*, 1977) that acetyltransferase was grossly depleted in Alzheimer brains, thus implicating the cholinergic system. However, it has since been established that a number of other neurotransmitter systems are involved, including the noradrenergic and serotonergic systems as well as some neuropeptides (for a general discussion see Cowburn, Hardy & Roberts, 1989).

Aluminium has also been thought to have some sort of role in AD. For example, raised levels of aluminium have been found in the brains of those who have suffered AD, especially in plaques and tangles, and there is a weak association between the incidence of DAT and the levels of aluminium in the water (MacLachlan,

1986; Martyn *et al.*, 1989). Nevertheless, the exact role of aluminium remains unclear and there are arguments to the effect that its role may not be causal. Furthermore, the evidence that oral ingestion of aluminium can lead to Alzheimer's disease is very weak (Williams & Miller, 1992).

It is worth also noting that a possible biochemical marker for Alzheimer's disease in life has recently been identified (Ghanbari *et al.*, 1990), although it remains to be seen if this work can be replicated and, if so, just how useful this marker will prove in routine clinical practice. More rigorous clinical criteria have also been developed (see Boller & Saxton, 1990) which enable a more reliable identification of cases of Alzheimer-type dementia in life for research purposes.

Alzheimer-type dementia has a gradual onset and most commonly presents with difficulties in memory as the first discernible feature, although it sometimes happens that impairments in other psychological functions, such as language, offer the initial manifestation. Abnormalities of mood (lowered mood or even mild euphoria) are also not uncommon as early features. Other neuropsychiatric disturbances, such as hallucinations and delusions, can also be encountered (see: Burns, Jacoby & Levy, 1990a–d). Gradually the deterioration in intellectual functioning becomes deeper and more extensive, with emotional response being flattened.

It is not necessarily the case that AD is a single entity, and the variability in the early features raises the possibility that it really represents a mixture of different disorders with some common features. Some have attempted to make formal distinctions between different subgroups and, in particular, a group with 'frontal dementia' (e.g. Neary *et al.*, 1986, 1988). However, it is not yet clear whether such subdivisions really represent distinct entities as opposed to being just the extremes of a continuous distribution of features. An investigation by Kurz *et al.* (1992) looked at various cognitive features initially and again at a 12-month follow-up, in a sample of 90 cases of alleged Alzheimer's disease. Their findings suggested a marked but continuous variation between individuals, with no evidence of distinct subtypes.

The other common form of dementia is arteriosclerotic, cerebrovascular or multi-infarct dementia (MID). Here the underlying pathology consists of a number of small infarctions in the brain. The clinical features are more varied than in DAT and depend upon where the infarctions happen to occur in the brain. The clinical course is classically associated with a stepwise progression, each small vascular episode being the source of a further small but sudden deterioration in function. Pathological studies of people with dementia whose brains have been examined at autopsy have indicated that the majority were cases of DAT and relatively few were arteriosclerotic (or MID). Some also had a mixed pathology (Tomlinson, Blessed & Roth, 1970).

Possibly also requiring a brief description are the disorders associated with the 'subcortical dementias'. The most obvious manifestations of Parkinson's disease are in the motor system, consisting of tremor, rigidity and bradykinesia (slowed movement). However, it has long been recognised that Parkinson's disease also tends to induce psychological changes which include depression and a degree of cognitive deterioration. Progressive supranuclear palsy, or the Steele–Richardson–Olszewski syndrome (Steele, Richardson & Olszewski, 1964), is similar to Parkinson's disease in its motor manifestations and occasionally it is misdiagnosed as such. Its peculiar feature is a paralysis of ocular movements, whereby the patient is unable to elevate gaze to a normal degree. Cognitive changes are often quite marked (Albert, Feldman & Willis, 1974).

Huntington's chorea is a rare but relatively well-known disorder with an autosomal dominant inheritance. In addition to choreiform movements, it can be associated with marked affective and cognitive changes. Wilson's disease is also rare. It is caused by an inherited failure (recessive) to process adequately the small amounts of copper that are ingested in food. This results in deposits of copper, particularly within the liver and the brain. Within the brain it is the basal ganglia that are most readily affected. Again, the disease is associated with disordered movement and intellectual changes.

The remaining conditions listed in Table 1.1. are sufficiently rare to not merit any further comment here. There are also a number of rarer conditions that have neither been described here or listed in Table 1.1. Accounts of these can be found elsewhere, for examples see Peretz & Cummings (1988) and Walton (1985).

EPIDEMIOLOGY

An important issue in relation to dementia is the size of the problem and the factors that determine its extent within a given population. As was the case in the previous section, which outlined the clinical descriptions and defining features of the various dementing illnesses, no attempt will be made to give a comprehensive account. A basic outline of what is known about the epidemiology of dementia will be offered, and the interested reader is directed to other sources for a more comprehensive account.

A useful description of the epidemiology of mental disorders in older people, including dementia, is given by Kay & Bergmann (1980). This account is especially useful in that it has introductory sections describing the aims and limitations of epidemiological studies and it gives a brief account of the methods used in epidemiological research. Amongst other things, the problems of defining the population at risk and of specifying what constitutes an example of the condition being investigated (i.e. the problem of 'caseness') are major concerns in epidemiology. Defining dementia in operational terms is not easy, and this is particularly so for mild dementia, in which it is particularly difficult to discriminate between lifelong low mental ability as opposed to an early dementia.

According to the studies reviewed by Kay & Bergmann (1980), the prevalence of moderate and severe dementia in the over 65s (65 years being the most commonly used cut-off age to define the elderly) varies between 5.6 and 15.6%, with a median value of 8%. The vast majority of these are cases of DAT and cerebrovascular dementia. Estimates of the prevalence of mild dementia show much greater variation, with figures reported lying anywhere between 5.7 and just over 50% (Kay & Bergmann, 1980). This extremely wide variation reflects to a considerable degree the difficulty already mentioned of defining exactly what constitutes 'mild dementia'. More recent estimates of prevalence usually give figures within the range already mentioned (e.g. Rocca *et al.*, 1991). Where they do not, there are straightforward reasons why this might not be so. For example, the study by Kokmen *et al.* (1989) in Rochester, Minnesota, reported an overall prevalence of only 3.5% for dementia in the over 65s. However, this report was based solely on cases known to local services and is likely to have missed cases which would have been detected in a 'door-to-door' community survey as carried out by Rocca et al. (1991).

Kay & Bergmann (1980) also pool data from three reasonably comparable surveys that have further divided the prevalence of moderate and severe dementia according to narrower age bands (Kaneko, 1975; Kay et al., 1970; Nielson, 1962). The results are summarised in Table 1.2. As can readily be seen, prevalence increases with age (from an overall 2.1% in the 65–69 age group to 17.7% in the over 80s). Furthermore, there are apparent sex biases. Despite the overall rates for males and females being very close, there is an increased prevalence amongst males in the 65–69 age band whilst there is a lesser trend in the reverse direction in the over 80s (both these differences are statistically significant).

These differential effects of sex are related to the type of dementia. It is the increased susceptibility of males to cerebrovascular dementia during the late 60s that mainly accounts for the greater prevalence in males in this age range. Females do not appear to become really susceptible to this type of dementia until they are over 75 years of age.

Because it is a point of practical importance in the planning and organisation of services, it is worth noting that the majority of over 65s with dementia are living at home in the community and not in institutions. Again, Kay & Bergmann (1980) have pooled data from several separate studies and these suggest that only about 25% of those with dementia are resident in institutions of

Table 1.2 Prevalence (%) of dementing illnesses producing moderate to severe levels of dementia, by sex and age group (compiled from Kay & Bergmann, 1980)

Age range (years)	Males	Females	Both sexes
65–69	3.9	0.5	2.1
70–74	4.1	2.7	3.3
75–79	8.0	7.9	8.0
80+	13.2	20.9	17.7

any kind. Given the difficulties involved in looking after someone with dementia, this figure indicates that a considerable burden of care is being borne in the community, mainly by relatives.

Data relating to incidence are less easy to come by. A fairly recent American study (Schoenberg, Kokmen & Okazaki, 1987) gives estimates of incidence for dementia of all types as well as for DAT alone. These are summarised in Table 1.3. As would be expected from the prevalence figures, the incidence rises dramatically with advancing age, onset before retiring age being unusual.

The conditions principally associated with subcortical dementia are all relatively rare with the most prevalent being Parkinson's disease. Estimates of the overall prevalence of Parkinson's disease range between about 1.0 and 2.0 per 1000. The figure of 1.5 per 1000 given by D'Alessandro *et al.* (1987) is not untypical. Again, the prevalence of the disorder increases appreciably with advancing age, with the earliest age of onset usually being in middle age. Nevertheless, isolated cases of onset at an even earlier age do arise from time to time.

GENETICS

Of the diseases associated with dementia and mentioned in this book, Huntington's chorea is well established as having an autoso-

Table 1.3 Incidence of Alzheimer's disease and dementia from all causes, as determined by Schoenberg *et al.* (1987). Figures refer to number of cases per year per 100 000 population

Age range (years)	Alzheimer's disease	Dementia from all causes
30–59	4	19
60–69	96	130
70–79	531	741
80+	1431	2175
All ages		
Crude	56	85
Age corrected	52	79

mal dominant inheritance. Wilson's disease, also an alleged cause of subcortical dementia, has a recessive inheritance (see Walton, 1985). Of the other conditions it is Alzheimer's disease that has attracted real concern from a genetic point of view.

In addition to the problem of identifying cases of Alzheimer's disease in life, mentioned above in relation to epidemiology, a number of other difficulties arise in the study of possible genetic factors in this disorder (see Hardy, Owen & Groate, 1989). Amongst these is the fact that in a disease which affects people in later life, an appreciable number of those who possess the genetic predisposition and who would develop the disease if they had lived long enough may die before it becomes manifest due to other causes.

Despite these and other methodological problems, a number of conclusions appear to be justified. It is clear that the relatives of those who have developed Alzheimer's disease have themselves an increased risk of developing this disorder. However, studies showing this relationship typically show no clear pattern of inheritance, although suggestions of a multifactorial inheritance or a single gene with incomplete penetrance have been made (e.g. Sjögren, Sjögren & Lindgren, 1952). It is also the case that a few substantial family pedigrees have been documented in which several family members appear to have developed Alzheimer's disease and in which the pattern of incidence matches that expected on the basis of a dominant inheritance (e.g. Breitner & Folstein, 1984a,b). Despite this latter point, the majority of cases arise under circumstances in which there is no evidence of dominant inheritance.

Families that do exhibit a pattern suggesting dominant inheritance offer a means of trying to identify the location of the genetic defect. The fact that Alzheimer type pathological changes develop in the brains of those with Down's syndrome has led to the supposition that there might be a significant locus on chromosome 21 (see Hardy, Owen & Groate, 1989). This notion has been confirmed by St. George-Hyslop et al. (1987). What is not yet established is whether there is a genetic defect in all families in which several members appear to be afflicted with Alzheimer's disease.

In the majority of cases there is no clear evidence of dominant transmission but only an indication of increased risk when one family member is affected. What particular genetic influences, if any, are at work here remains to be determined. Familial aggregation is not necessarily because of genetic factors, but it does not seem particularly plausible that the mere experience of living in a family with a member suffering from dementia is going to predispose an individual to dementia. Familial aggregation could also result from family members being exposed to the same environmental influences, but again the increased risk in cousins, aunts, nephews, etc., who have generally lived apart from the proband makes this less likely.

Hardy, Owen & Groate (1989) conclude their review of the genetics of Alzheimer's disease by pointing out that, as in many other conditions with some genetic influence, what may be occurring is an interaction between a genetic predisposition and environmental influences. What may be the case is that genetic influences are but one factor in producing Alzheimer's disease and are possibly not sufficient in themselves, as in the majority of cases who come from families in which there is no indication of a dominant transmission. It is possible that a genetic predisposition may not even be necessary in some cases, and that Alzheimer-type dementia is but the final common outcome of a number of different causal influences that can operate independently. Nevertheless, the balance of evidence indicates that genetic factors do play some role in causation. The fact that some families with an apparently dominant transmission do arise, accounting for a minority of cases, is also consistent with the notion that what is now described as Alzheimer's disease may ultimately turn out to be more than one condition.

PROBLEMS IN STUDYING THE PSYCHOLOGICAL ASPECTS OF DEMENTIA

The previous sections of this chapter have attempted to set the scene by providing some background information about dementia and the various dementing illnesses. Another set of issues that needs to be considered in dealing with the psychological aspects of dementia is the problems that arise in investigating this area. Rather than referring to these basic points again and again in the following chapters, it is more economical and sensible to deal with them right at the beginning and leave it to the reader to bear them in mind in progressing through the following chapters. Discussions of the methodological problems inherent in research in abnormal psychology in general can be found in a number of sources (e.g. Miller, 1988; Parry & Watts, 1989).

The first problem lies in the identification of subject samples. As has already been indicated in discussing topics such as the epidemiology of dementia above, there are difficulties in identifying subjects with dementia or particular types of dementia. Older people who have always been of limited intellectual capacity can be wrongly regarded as having dementia, and dementia can be confused with other disorders, such as depression, the deleterious effects of polypharmacy on mental functioning and confusional states. The latter confusion is more easily prompted in older people because the illnesses (e.g. chest or urinary tract infections) are not only more likely to produce confusional states but often remain afebrile, thus making it less obvious that an infectious illness is present (see Habot & Libow, 1980). It is often cases of dementia in the early stages that are of most interest for research purposes and it is in early cases that diagnostic confusion is most likely to occur.

As with many other areas of abnormal psychology, the criteria used to identify cases in research studies have improved with time, and special research criteria have been developed for DAT (e.g. Boller & Saxton, 1990). There is therefore a tendency for the more recently reported research to have utilised the most carefully defined samples, although it should be noted that this correlation is far from perfect. One possible way of dealing with the problem of imperfect identification of subjects with dementia is to follow subjects used in investigations for some time (Miller, 1980), in order to check that the diagnosis can be maintained. This is a tedious procedure that has rarely been employed in practice.

A key feature of dementia is that it is a progressive disorder. A full appreciation of the psychological changes produced by dementia has to take this into account by looking at the development of impairments. This means that longitudinal investigations following the same sample of subjects over a significant time period are required. Unfortunately, longitudinal studies are difficult to carry out and very few investigators have used anything other than cross-sectional investigations, which examine subjects at only one point in time. The almost total lack of a 'developmental' perspective on dementia is therefore one of the major gaps in work in this field.

Another major difficulty in trying to make sense of dementia from a psychological point of view is the pervasive nature of the psychological changes that occur. It is virtually impossible to study any one psychological process in isolation from others, and performance on experimental tasks can be impaired for a number of reasons. One simple example is the failure of a subject with dementia to name a picture of a common object (presumed to have once been within that subjects capabilities): is this due to a disturbance in naming or a failure to perceive adequately what the picture is intended to portray? As will be seen in Chapter 3, there is evidence in favour of both these interpretations. Especially in the case of more complex tasks, might any failure be due to the inability of the subject to comprehend what is required? Ways of teasing out the basis of particular failures in performance do exist but are not wholly satisfactory, and especially so in situations where it cannot be assumed that any aspect of functioning remains intact.

Not only can the multiplicity of psychological impairments present methodological problems in teasing out what is happening; there is also the problem that dementia tends to occur most frequently in older people. Older people are also more likely to have physical and sensory impairments in addition to any intellectual deficits. These can interact with psychological performance. To revert to the example of picture naming, it may be that poor visual acuity, if undetected or uncorrected, could be a source of errors in naming. Similarly, tasks requiring any form of motor response might be adversely affected by motor handicaps, and deafness can present a major problem in ensuring that instructions are fully understood. Many research reports ignore these factors and it would be unwise to assume that the procedures used took physical or sensory impairments adequately into consideration (e.g. by screening out those with certain physical or sensory limitations).

A final complication in considering the psychology of dementia is that for most areas of functioning there is a lack of well-established and robust models of normal functioning. There are models of such things as language, memory and so on, which can offer some guidance, but these are rarely so well developed as to provide a really solid basis for describing the nature of impairments that appear in dementia and other manifestations of abnormal behaviour.

OUTLINE OF THE REST OF THE BOOK

The following chapters will first cover the psychological changes that are produced in dementia of the Alzheimer type. Memory and language will be covered first because these represent the major bulk of the work that needs to be described. Other basic psychological aspects will then be dealt with together in Chapter 4.

The fifth chapter will then move on to examine the issue of subcortical dementia. This has traditionally been contrasted with so-called cortical or Alzheimer-type dementia and represents an area of research into dementia that has attracted much recent interest.

Subsequent chapters then move on to the more clinically relevant aspects. Separate chapters look at the assessment of dementia, its management and the psychosocial complications. The psychosocial aspects of dementia are of considerable importance because the majority of sufferers remain in the community and are therefore looked after mainly by non-professional carers, almost always relatives. Looking after someone with dementia places a considerable burden on the carer, and so the needs and problems of carers should be taken into account in service provision.

The final chapter offers an appraisal of the whole field, as well as dealing with some issues that have not arisen elsewhere in the book.

CHAPTER 2   Memory in dementia

Memory loss has been cited as the most prominent aspect of dementia, at least in the early stages, and is rated as the most common problem (Teri *et al.*, 1989). It certainly has the most devastating effect on the life of a person with dementia, with an inability to keep track of daily events and adapt to new circumstances by acquiring new information. This chapter explores the characteristics of the memory impairment associated with dementia and experimental studies that have been conducted to investigate it. Many of the descriptions of memory disorder in dementia have concerned Alzheimer-type dementia (AD), so this syndrome provides the primary focus for discussion.

HOW THE MEMORY DISTURBANCE DEVELOPS

The onset of memory disturbance, like other aspects of AD, have an insidious onset and develop gradually (see Table 2.1). At the early stages, a person may have the occasional memory lapse and forget to perform a certain activity. Often the problem can remain unnoticed until the person changes their routine or is in an unfamiliar location, such as being on holiday. An inability to take in new information and keep track of events then results in temporal and spatial disorientation. At this stage it can be difficult to make an accurate diagnosis, and the distinction between dementia and reversible causes of memory impairment in the elderly can be unclear. As the disease progresses, the disorientation becomes more marked and may extend to familiar environments, such as a relative's home or a club that has often been visited. Forgetfulness may place the person at risk, for example by misplacing important items, leaving the cooker on or forgetting frequently travelled routes. At a more severe stage of the illness, disorien-

Table 2.1 Stages in the development of memory impairment in dementia

---

Stage 1. Mild Memory Impairment

Mild memory lapses occur, but cause only a few problems for the person and are often falsely attributed to other factors, such as the effects of normal ageing, stress or depression.

These include forgetting errands, failing to pass on messages, becoming disorientated in unfamiliar surroundings. Memory for episodes in the near distant past is poor, including memory for conversations with other people.

These types of memory problems do not necessarily indicate a progressive neuropsychological impairment, and may be falsely attributed to dementia.

Stage 2. Mild to Moderate Memory Impairment

Memory impairment is more pronounced and starts to have a significant effect on daily living activities. At this point, the person may seek medical help (usually prompted by a relative or friend) and is likely to become reliant on a carer.

Memory errors include forgetting familiar people or friends, becoming disorientated even in familiar surroundings, confusing the time of day or day of week, becoming increasingly unable to keep track of daily events.

Stage 3. Severe Impairment

Forgetting close relatives, marked signs become apparent, such as confabulation and paramnesia.

Memory errors become more severe and can present safety problems for the person, such as wandering, forgetting to turn off the gas stove. Loss of information about person may occur, for example details of personal information, such as relative's names.

---

tation may occur with the person forgetting who their relatives are and even their own name. Temporal and spatial disorientation can result in behavioural problems, such as nocturnal wandering, that are particularly upsetting for carers and place the patient at risk (see Chapter 7).

CONFABULATION AND INTRUSIONAL ERRORS

A characteristic feature of AD is the degree of confabulation associated with the memory deficit. These are memory errors in which the person fabricates material instead of recalling information, but without conscious awareness of the fact. Two types of confabulation in Alzheimer's disease have been described by Kopelman (1987), a spontaneous confabulation which involves grandiose and wide-ranging ideas that are false, and a 'provoked' confabulation that is elicited in response to a particular memory cue and is thought to represent the normal reconstruction of a 'weak' memory. An example of the latter is where a person fills in the detail of an incomplete memory of an event to produce a coherent account. The spontaneous confabulations have been linked with a deficit in frontal lobe functioning in Alzheimer's disease, whilst the 'provoked' confabulations are thought to represent an impoverished memory system (Kopelman, 1987).

Related to confabulations are 'reduplications' of place or person, which is a more common feature of severe dementia. Here, the person thinks that they are in a different (although duplicated) place or that familiar persons are 'different' or even acting as impostors. A recent case study by Morris (1991) describes a patient with arteriosclerotic dementia who thought she had two husbands. Interestingly, when her husband died, she was able to 'adapt' to the death of one of them, but could not remember that the other (the real husband) was dead. An explanation for these types of phenomena is an inability to integrate new information into existing schemas or knowledge about the world, combined with a partial perceptual impairment that distorts incoming information (Ellis & Young, 1990). In the case of elderly patients, prior memories of people which are retained more strongly may conflict with the existing information.

Alzheimer-type dementia patients also appear to make a high level of intrusional errors in story recall, either from prior stories or extraneous material (Butters et al., 1987). For example, when given the Logical Memory Test (Wechsler, 1945), which involves presentation of two stories, they are more likely to insert material from the first story into their account of the second story. In this respect, their performance is very similar to amnesic alcoholic Korsakoff's syndrome patients, but dissimilar to patients with dementia caused by Huntington's disease. An increase in intrusional errors appears to be a common feature of the performance of AD patients in other tests of memory functioning (Fuld, 1983; Fuld et al., 1982).

DELUSIONS

A feature of more severe dementia is the presence of delusions or disorders of thought content that relate to memory failure. These can take the form of grandiose or persecutory delusions (Cummings et al., 1987), but in a high proportion of cases the delusions concern suspicion of theft (Burns, Jaccoby & Levy, 1990a). An example of this is accusing a close relative of stealing money from the person. It is probable that this type of delusion stems partly from the memory disorder, where the person fails to recall an event or the location of an object but lacks insight into the memory disorder, thus attributing the loss to another person.

EXPERIMENTAL STUDIES OF MEMORY IMPAIRMENT IN DEMENTIA

The nature of the memory impairment in dementia has been studied in depth and, although the deficits are pervasive, falls into a specific pattern of decline that differentiates the various forms of the disorder. Alzheimer-type dementia has been studied most extensively and provides the main form of dementia on which to base other comparisons.

The neuropathological and neurochemical causes of memory impairment in Alzheimer's disease are complex. Clearly substantial changes in the medial temporal lobes, including increased numbers of senile plaques and neurofibrillary tangles, are a contributing factor (Hyman et al., 1984). Added to this is the depletion of neurotransmitter activity in specific pathways thought to be involved in memory processing, such as the ascending cholinergic projections from the basal forebrain and the noradrenergic pathways from the locus coeruleus (Candy et al., 1983). The more wide-

spread deterioration in brain functioning throughout the association areas of the cerebral cortex may contribute to memory loss,
if memory traces have a generalised distribution. The pattern or
presentation of dementia will depend on the underlying neuropathology. For example, patients with dementia associated with
Huntington's disease rather than AD have damage to the caudate
nucleus, a subcortical nucleus that projects anteriorly to the frontal
lobes and appears not to be as sensitive to the effects of pro-active
interference (Butters *et al.*, 1987).

Models of memory functioning provide a framework to study
memory disorder in dementia. The main distinction made by cognitive psychologists is between memory for personally experienced events or material (termed *episodic memory*) and memory for
information about the world, including rules, concepts and the
meaning of words (termed *semantic memory*) (Tulving, 1983). Other
separable memory systems exist, including *implicit memory*, the
facilitation of cognitive processing based on experience but without conscious retrieval of information, and *skill learning*, the development of perceptual motor skills (see Baddeley, 1990). These distinctions are mirrored in the following sections which characterise
the breakdown of memory in early dementia.

Episodic memory

'Episodic' memory can in turn be split into *short-term memory*,
recall of material or events after a period of up to 30 seconds,
and *long-term memory*, memory lasting for longer periods, minutes,
days or weeks. Although there is no clear evidence that short-
term and long-term memory are separable memory systems, the
distinction provides a useful heuristic for studying episodic memory. Short-term memory tends to have a much smaller capacity
than long-term memory and involves more active rehearsal mechanisms, such as articulatory rehearsal (Vallar & Shallice, 1990). A
vast amount of information can be retained in long-term memory,
but memory processing relies on more complex retrieval mechanisms as material is stored for long periods without rehearsal.

Short-term memory

Short-term memory functioning. A basic method for assessing short-term memory functioning is the memory span procedure, which involves immediate repetition of a sequence of items. With verbal memory span, the items are usually digits, letters or words, whilst with spatial memory span the task involves tapping out a sequence of moves on an array of blocks (the Corsi Block Span Test, cf. Cantone *et al.*, 1978). Memory span is found to be consistently reduced in AD, but the decline is only slight (see Morris & Baddeley, 1988). The deficit is more dramatic if a delay is introduced between presenting the material and retrieving the items, filled by a distracter task. For example, in the Brown-Peterson Task subjects are required to remember three verbally encodable items after counting backwards by twos or threes from a three digit number. This produces a very substantial deficit in early AD patients (R. G. Morris, 1986; Sullivan, Corkin & Growden, 1986). Even with a very simple distracter task, such as a manual tapping task, material is very rapidly forgotten by AD patients (R. G. Morris, 1986).

An immediate explanation of increased short-term forgetting of verbal material is faulty encoding of material, secondary to a language impairment (Martin *et al.*, 1985). It has been suggested that the stimulus attributes of the material are not processed sufficiently well to produce a strong memory trace. This type of deficit would undoubtedly produce a short-term memory deficit for meaningful material.

Other explanations for the short-term memory deficit have been proposed in a series of studies by Morris (Morris & Baddeley, 1988) and by Baddeley and his colleagues (Baddeley *et al.*, 1986). These follow from models of short-term memory that fractionate functioning into subsystems reflecting different domains of information processing.

Experimental studies of short-term memory

The concept of short-term memory as a cluster of interacting subsystems was introduced by Atkinson and Shiffrin (1968) and by Murdock (1974). More recently this view has been reinforced through the study of patients with circumscribed short-term memory deficits. Central to short-term memory is some form of central controller that can coordinate attentional resources and ensure that the subsystems operate in sequence, given the term 'Central Executive System' by Baddeley (1986). Peripheral systems have been characterised such as those responsible for auditory–verbal short-term storage and short-term visual memory (Baddeley & Lieberman, 1980).

Preserved articulatory rehearsal. Articulatory rehearsal makes a substantial contribution to memory span performance. If it is prevented by getting a subject to articulate some irrelevant information, there is a sharp decline in verbal memory span. Morris (1984, 1987a) has explored articulatory rehearsal in relation to AD using a variety of procedures. Firstly, the *rate* at which a person passes material through an Articulatory Loop System can be measured indirectly by measuring overt articulation rate (for example, getting a subject to count from one to 10 as rapidly as possible). Morris (1987a) measured articulation rates in AD patients and found no difference from normal subjects. A second aspect of articulatory rehearsal is the contribution to span performance. By suppressing rehearsal, as described above, and measuring the decline in span it is possible to estimate the contribution. Morris (1984) required AD patients and control subjects to remember strings of letters or words and concurrently repeat the word 'the' in a continuous fashion. The subsequent decline in span was equivalent in both groups.

Another facet of short-term memory for verbal information is that material is held in a phonological storage system, corresponding to the sound form of the material (Vallar & Shallice, 1990). An inefficient storage system would reduce the capacity of short-term memory and produce a memory impairment. The efficiency of phonological storage is reflected in the size of the phonological similarity effect, the tendency for phonologically similar letters (e.g. *PTCVBG*) to be recalled worse than phonologically dissimilar letters (e.g. *KWYRZQ*) (Baddeley, Lewis & Vallar, 1984). Similar letters tend to set up mutual interference within short-term storage and thus reduce memory performance. The size of this effect has been explored by Morris (1984) in AD patients, showing that it remains robust and equivalent to that observed in control subjects, allowing for an overall reduction in memory span. In summary, the evidence is that both articulatory rehearsal and phonological storage is preserved in early AD. This may account for why verbal memory span performance is relatively impervious to the effects of the dementing process.

The dysexecutive syndrome in dementia. Baddeley (1986) has coined the term 'dysexecutive syndrome' to characterise disorders of sequencing or planning, or the coordination necessary for dividing attention between simultaneous mental operations. A Central Executive System has been proposed as a unitary mental process that fulfils these functions. The precise mechanisms of the Central Executive are only partially understood (Shallice, 1988), but different types of dysexecutive syndromes have been described (Morris, Morris & Britton, 1990). Executive functions are used in most short-term memory tasks where there is simultaneous processing and storage of information.

Patients with AD appear to be particularly sensitive to the effects of divided attention in short-term memory tasks as indicated by the impairment in the Brown-Peterson Task. Part of the reason for this may be a weaker memory trace such that distracter task material is more potent at displacing from memory the material that is to be remembered (Bjork, 1975). It also relates to the diversion of attentional resources away from rehearsing the material. In this respect, an impairment in the control processes of short-term memory reduces the amount of attentional processes that can be used in rehearsing material.

Baddeley *et al.* (1986) have tested this notion directly by combining a memory span task with different forms of distracter tasks. One difficulty with the Brown-Peterson Task is that subjects can perform poorly simply because they find the distracter task more difficult, not because attention is divided. Baddeley *et al.* (1986) devised ways of matching the difficulty level of the task for each subject. The main distracter task was pursuit tracking in which the subject had to track a moving dot across a computer screen using a light pen. By varying the speed of the moving dot they were able to 'titrate' the difficulty level in a series of practise attempts. Similarly, the memory capacity of each subject was taken by measuring the maximum number of digits that a subject could repeat back in serial order (memory span). The 'titrated' tracking task was combined with recalling lists of digits, which were constructed to be one less than the subject's memory span. The performance of AD patients was compared with matched controls with the two tasks separately, and when combined. In the AD patients the combination produced a sharp deterioration in memory performance, much greater than in the controls. Conversely, the concurrent memory span task substantially decreased the accuracy of the AD patients on the tracking task. More recently, a follow-up of the patients included in this study was conducted to explore whether there was a tendency for dual-task performance to deteriorate more rapidly (Baddeley et al. 1991). The patients were tested after 6 and 12 months showing that, whilst performance on the single tasks was maintained, the dual-task deficit became substantially more pronounced.

Although an impairment in Executive Functioning predicts this type of deficit, other possibilities should be considered. One is the possible presence of abnormal 'structural' interference between the two tasks. The underlying physiological processes that support the concurrent tasks could overlap and, if functioning less efficiently, interfere with each other (Kinsbourne, 1980). This is less likely in the Baddeley et al. (1986) Task where the tasks are designed to use different mental processes, but it could provide a mechanism for increased forgetting in other tasks involving divided attention.

Visuospatial short-term memory. This shows a different pattern of impairment than the verbal equivalent. Spatial short-term memory has been investigated using the Corsi Block Span Test, in which the subject has to tap out a sequence on an array of blocks from memory. Alzheimer-type dementia patients are moderately to severely impaired on this task, remembering much shorter sequences (Corkin, 1982; Spinnler et al., 1988). This contrasts with verbal memory span, which shows a less severe impairment. Similarly, AD patients show a faster rate of forgetting from short-term visual memory even when no distracter task is used in the period between presentation and test. Moss et al. (1986) used a delayed non-matching to sample task in which a subject is shown an object (e.g. a spoon or pen), which is then taken away and replaced with the same object and a new one. The instructions are to point to the novel object. The accuracy of the AD patients fell much more rapidly than the controls, as the delay between initial presentation and the choice stage increased from 20 seconds to 2 minutes. More rapid forgetting has also been observed in an equivalent task using computer-generated abstract visual patterns, with rapid forgetting between 14 and 16 seconds (Morris et al., 1987; Sahakian et al., 1988). Their performance contrasts with that of patients with Parkinson's disease (those on medication for the disorder and those without medication), in whom visual short-term memory is impaired, but the forgetting rate is not increased. This type of deficit in AD would suggest a consolidation deficit, with a more rapid decay of the memory trace.

Nevertheless, Money et al. (1992) found that the forgetting rate was not increased in their version of the delayed matching to sample task. They used circles of varying diameter, with one circle presented, followed by a delay and then the same circle combined with a novel one. They suggest that this task is a 'purer' test of visual memory and not subject to verbal and other coding strategies. This is a potential criticism of both the Moss et al. (1986) and Sahakian et al. (1988) studies. Although Sahakian et al. (1988) claims that a verbal strategy is unlikely, Money et al. (1992) found in a separate experiment that similar material to that used by Sahakian et al (1988) did produce verbal encoding. Clearly, it would be far more difficult to adopt a verbal encoding strategy for the 'circles' task. If this is the case, then the visual short-term memory deficit would reflect an encoding or retrieval deficit rather than difficulties with consolidation.

Long-term memory

This can be defined as the ability to remember material for longer than approximately 30 seconds. Patients with dementia have been found to be impaired on a whole range of tasks involving long-term memory, including recalling lists of words, sentences and stories or recognising words, faces or pictures presented by the experimenter (Corkin, 1982; Hart et al., 1988a; Miller, 1971, 1975;

Wilson *et al.*, 1982, 1983). Similar deficits have been found on long-term memory for visual information (Morris *et al.*, 1987; Sahakian *et al.*, 1988).

Memory for events or material relies on three essential processes. Firstly, material has to be entered into memory (encoding). Secondly, it has to be retained in memory (consolidation). Thirdly, it has to be retrieved from memory. An impairment in memory functioning can take place in any of these three processes.

Encoding and retrieval processes in long-term memory. A prominent feature of encoding material in long-term memory is the degree to which the meaning of the material is processed (semantic processing). The formation of rich associations or semantic structures substantially increases the amount of material that can be recalled by increasing the strength of encoding (Craik, Morris & Gick, 1990). A breakdown of semantic processing would cause difficulties in encoding material with a subsequent reduction in the retrieval of information. In order to explore this possibility, the 'Levels of Processing' paradigm, developed by Craik & Tulving (1975), has been applied to patients with dementia (Corkin, 1982; Martin *et al.*, 1985; Wilson, Kaszniak & Fox, 1980).

With 'Levels of Processing' the subject has to remember a list of words. Each word is presented within a sentence frame, which encourages processing at a sensory, phonological or semantic level. For example, in the study by Corkin (1982) words were presented with the following types of questions: 'Does a man/woman say the word?' (sensory), 'does the word rhyme with ____?' (phonological) and 'is the word a type of ____?' (semantic). Normally the sentence that encourages semantic processing produces superior memory performance. Corkin (1982) found, however, that AD patients did not show any benefit from the 'semantic' question over and above the other types of questions, indicating that semantic processing was not improving memory. This finding was also reported by Wilson, Kaszniak & Fox (1980) in an earlier unpublished study. More recently Martin *et al.* (1985) used essentially the same method but with the inclusion of a test in which the patients had to demonstrate the use of an object (semantic-praxis condition), encouraging a richer and 'deeper' processing of the material. Both semantic and semantic-praxis orientations increased recall in normal subjects and AD patients, but the AD patients failed to benefit from the procedures as much as the normal subjects.

These findings point towards a failure in semantic processing at encoding which, in turn, reduces the strength of long-term memories. Another way to investigate semantic processing at encoding has been to determine the extent to which patients make use of spontaneous organisation of material to enhance their performance. Weingartner has explored this issue in relation to recall of lists of words (Weingartner *et al.*, 1981). Words were presented to the patients, either drawn from two semantic categories, or unrelated. Normal subjects tend to cluster semantically related material together to improve recall, but this was not the case for patients with AD. It should be noted that clustering or organisation of material is as much a feature of encoding as of retrieval. Faulty retrieval strategies, in which the patient fails to make use of the inherent structure of information, would also lead to the results described above.

How fast is material forgotten? At first sight it appears that patients with dementia forget events or material very rapidly as part of the amnesic syndrome. However, this issue is more complex than it might seem, partly because of the problems that dementia patients have in encoding material as indicated above. The question is, once material has been encoded in long-term memory, how rapidly is it forgotten? Specific techniques have been developed to compare the rates of forgetting in normal and brain-damaged subjects (Huppert & Piercy, 1979).

A critical feature of comparing rates of forgetting for amnesic patients and normal subjects is that performance should be matched at the beginning point of the forgetting curve (Loftus, 1978). Any divergence in performance as the delay between encoding and retrieval is increased indicates faster forgetting. In effect, this means boosting the level of the performance of the dementia patients to a comparable level with normal subjects. A way of doing this is to increase the time allowed to view material that has to be remembered for the dementia patients. A series of experiments using visual material has been conducted using this procedure. Corkin *et al.* (1984) reported that AD patients forget at the same *rate* as control subjects, between 10 minutes and 72 hours, when photographs of scenes or people are used to test recognition memory. This finding was replicated by Kopelman (1985), who found that once material had been encoded in memory the rate of forgetting was the same over slightly longer delays than those used by Corkin *et al.* (1984). Over shorter periods, the pattern appears to change, since Hart *et al.* (1988a) have found faster rates of forgetting in AD patients between 90 seconds and 10 minutes. Taken together, these studies suggest that most of the forgetting of material takes place very rapidly in patients with dementia, but the remaining material is forgotten at the same rate as in normal subjects.

Discussion. In summary, encoding or retrieval processes appear to be impaired in dementia, influencing the strength of long-term memory, and there appears to be very rapid forgetting over short delays, reaching a plateau over longer time periods. It is notable that Hart *et al.* (1988a) found more rapid forgetting of visual material between 90 seconds and 10 minutes. It is possible that a similar result could be found for verbal memory, but performance is complicated by verbal rehearsal processes that appear to be unimpaired. In summary, the pattern of deficit points towards an encoding/retrieval deficit superimposed over a consolidation deficit, which causes the more immediate forgetting. The underlying physiological mechanisms responsible for these deficits are considered later (pp. 34–35).

Remote memory

The prevailing impression is that patients with dementia tend to remember events from the distant past more clearly than recent events. Indeed, therapeutic approaches such as Reminiscence Therapy (see Chapter 7) can capitalise on the ability to recall distant memories (i.e. using *remote* memory as a way to enhance interaction with other people). Carefully controlled studies of remote memory in dementia, however, have not confirmed the general impression. These are studies that have used photographs of famous people from the past to test systematically for longer term memories. For example, Wilson, Kaszniak & Fox (1981) used the Famous Faces Test on AD patients, requiring them to name 180 photographs of famous people from between 1920 and 1975. The patients were consistently impaired across the decades on both 'hard' and 'easy' items.

More recent studies by Sagar *et al.* (1988) support this finding with a similar consistent deficit for recall and recognition of public events between the 1940s and 1980s. Autobiographical memory was also investigated by providing patients with single word cues (e.g. the words 'bird', 'tree' and 'car'). Patients with AD were less elaborate and consistent in the recall of memories from the past.

These studies do not necessarily invalidate reminiscence therapy as a treatment for dementia. Part of the reason why more distant memories appear to be better remembered, but are not so on objective tests, may relate to the type of memories recalled. In reminiscing, patients with dementia may concentrate on events that have been recounted many times and thought about over a long period. Such memories are considerably 'overlearned' and presumably more resistant to the effects of the memory impairment. In support of this is an intriguing study of memory for the name of the current prime minister by Deary, Wessely & Farrell (1985). They took consecutive admissions to the Maudsley Hospital in London between the years 1961–1962, 1963–1968 and 1983–1984. Patients in the 1983–1984 cohort were far more likely to produce Mrs Thatcher's name than were the others to produce Mr MacMillan's or Mr Heath's in their respective eras. The increased likelihood of recalling Mrs Thatcher presumably reflects her greater salience and memorability.

Semantic memory

Memory for personally experienced events or material occurs within a certain time-frame or context and so is said to be 'episodic'. In contrast, much of our knowledge about the world, including facts, rules and concepts, is independent of time and does not have to be personally experienced. This type of memory is referred to as 'semantic memory' and is thought by some researchers (Tulving, 1983) to represent a different type of memory system.

The breakdown in semantic memory in dementia is far less striking than the episodic memory impairment. Patients with dementia are able to recall knowledge, appear to remember the meaning of words, and apply rules and concepts. On formal tests of semantic memory, such as the Vocabulary Scale of the Wechsler Adult Intelligence Scale—Revised (WAIS—R) the deficit is relatively slight and even used to estimate levels of pre-morbid intelligence (see Chapter 6).

There is evidence for more subtle deficits, particularly on tasks that require more than just passive retrieval of information. Firstly, semantic memory deficits can be seen on matching and categorisation tasks. These involve subjects having to match the picture of an object with the correct verbal label or category. Schwartz, Marin & Sffran (1979) investigated a dementia patient with probable AD and found that she had difficulty in word-picture matching. The main types of errors were matching the picture with a word that was semantically related but not the same. The patient also tended to allocate items to incorrect but similar categories in a category matching task. In a follow-up study using 53 AD patients, Flicker *et al.* (1986) asked specific questions about pictures of items concerning their category, such as 'is this a kind of vegetable?' The patients were unimpaired on this task, but they were impaired when presented with an item and asked whether it was called a particular name, where the name given was either a correct one or a false one drawn from the same category. In all, the results suggest that AD patients can distinguish between major categories, but have difficulty distinguishing between members of the same category. Similarly, Hodges, Salmon & Butters (1992) report a specific impairment in sorting material according to subordinate categories [e.g. deciding whether a set of land animals were (i) native to the USA or foreign animals, (ii) larger than a German shepherd dog or smaller and (iii) fierce or not fierce].

This type of result suggests that AD patients lose the knowledge of specific attributes of items, leading to a blurring of category boundaries. Support for this notion comes from the finding that AD patients tend to make semantic errors on naming objects, substituting the name with a semantically related one (Bayles & Tomoeda, 1983; Hodges, Salmon & Butters 1992; Martin & Fedio, 1983). For example, when shown a picture of a trumpet, an AD patient might call it a 'violing', or a 'blow.' Also, when tested on the supermarket task, which requires the subject to recall as many items that can be found in a supermarket as possible, AD patients tend to produce fewer subcategories and fewer items in each category (Martin & Fedio, 1983).

The semantic memory deficit in AD has been explained in terms of degradation of information, rather than a failure of access. Thus Hodges, Salmon & Butters (1992) report that, across a range of semantic memory tests, errors occur with the same items or material. For example, AD patients showed a significant correspondence between the individual items they were able to name and those that produced errors on a test matching picture to spoken word. A similar specificity occurred between naming and the ability to generate definitions of items in response to the spoken name. Indeed, AD patients appear to fulfil the criteria for a semantic storage disorder defined by Warrington & Shallice (1984), with consistency in failure across multiple presentations of the same stimuli, a particular vulnerability to subordinate information and a marked item frequency effect.

Implicit memory

The types of memory considered so far all require the conscious and explicit recall of material. A distinction can be made between this type of memory and situations where performance of a task is facilitated without the deliberate or conscious retrieval of a memory episode. An example of this is skill learning, where the improvement through practise is not a completely conscious process. Other examples, to be considered below, include lexical and semantic 'priming' effects (Schacter, 1989).

Skills learning

This refers to the acquisition of a set of procedures or operations that are brought to bear on a particular task (Kolers, 1979). This type of memory is assessed by having a subject execute a task several times to see the extent of improvements or 'savings' from the initial presentation of the task. Skill learning has been investigated in AD using a pursuit rotor task, which requires subjects to maintain a stylus in contact with a small metal target on a rotating disc (Eslinger & Damasio, 1986). The patients were required to practise the pursuit rotor task over five learning trials followed by a trial 20 minutes later. Patients with AD were impaired in their ability to do the task, but their *rate* of learning was normal when compared to normal subjects. In a subsequent study, Heindel, Butters & Salmon (1988) used an initial set of practice trials to vary the speed of the task, determining a set level of accuracy for each subject. This had the effect of matching the difficulty level of the task between AD patients and their respective controls. Again, the increase in accuracy with practise was the same in the AD patients as in the controls.

Priming

Priming effects refer to the facilitative effect of the exposure of an item to the subsequent processing of that item. For example, in a semantic priming task, the naming of the written word '*doctor*' is more rapid if it is preceded by the word '*nurse*'. It has been proposed that this effect is due to a temporary activation of a pre-existing memory representation, with a spread of activation throughout a semantic network such that other representations become more easily activated (Anderson, 1983; Collins & Loftus, 1975).

Earlier studies of dementia have used lexical priming tasks in which either the whole word or parts of the word are used to prime the processing of the same derivative item. For example, Moscovitch (1982) required subjects to read a series of words and they were then shown the same words combined with nonsense words. The task was to decide whether a word was a true word or a nonsense word. Prior presentation of the word speeds up the decision. Moscovitch (1982) found that the priming effect was as great in AD patients as in normal controls and was even exaggerated when a lag of 31 items was introduced between the prime and the lexical decision. Miller (1975) and Morris, Wheatley & Britton (1983) used a slightly different task in which the subjects were shown individual words and then the first three letters of the same words. The task was to complete the word, which occurs more easily with prior exposure to the item. Originally, this task was thought of as a means to cue episodic memory until it was discovered that completion of the correct word could occur without conscious recollection (Graf & Mandler, 1984). In the studies by both Miller (1975) and Morris, Wheatley & Britton (1983), patients with AD showed a normal facilitative effect of prior exposure to the word. A more recent study by Downes (1988) has confirmed this finding using a fragment completion task, but Shimamura *et al.* (1987) have reported reduction in priming in their sample of dementia patients.

An alternative way of exploring priming is to use semantically related items (such as the combination of 'doctor' and 'nurse', cited above). This is referred to as 'semantic priming' and has been investigated in dementia in a series of studies by Nebes and his colleagues (Nebes, Boller & Holland, 1986; Nebes & Brady, 1988; Nebes, Martin & Horn, 1984). Nebes, Martin & Horn (1984) used single words, presented visually to prime the naming of subsequent words. They found the same magnitude of facilitation in the AD patients as in matched controls. In a second study, Nebes, Boller & Holland (1986) replicated this finding using complex concepts conveyed by an entire sentence as a means of priming, rather than a single word. In addition, they used three types of sentence, a neutral one that would not act as a prime, a positive one that would prime processing of the word, and a negative one that would inhibit production. They found that both priming and inhibition effects were as large in AD patients as in normal controls, if anything more pronounced. A similar result has been reported by Nebes, Brady & Huff (1989), using a lexical decision task in which the subject had to decide whether a string of letters was a word or non-word, primed by a semantically-related word.

Discussion

With the exception of Shimamura *et al.* (1987), these studies point towards a preservation of implicit memory in dementia, in terms of both psychomotor skill learning and priming effects. It has been argued that implicit memory represents a different memory *system* to episodic memory (Graf & Mandler, 1984). If so, then this system appears to be preserved in dementia, in comparison to a severely impaired episodic memory system. Another interpretation is that priming effects are part of the same memory system but represent more automatic *processes* in contrast to the conceptually driven processes such as encoding and retrieval of episodic memories (Nebes, Brady & Huff, 1989). The relative preservation of these processes may mean that they are less sensitive to the effects of a generalised brain damage that impairs episodic memory functioning.

DISCUSSION AND CONCLUSIONS

The memory impairment associated with dementia is complex and experimental studies have gone some way in determining the different aspects. In summary, in Alzheimer-type dementia, memory disturbances are characterised by preserved articulatory rehearsal processes, but marked impairment in short-term memory tasks that involve divided attention. In long-term memory functioning, there is an encoding and retrieval deficit, at least for verbal material. 'Implicit' memory appears to be preserved, at least in the early stages of dementia, with no reduction in skill learning or priming effects. Semantic memory shows a degree of impairment, particularly in the structure of semantic memory and classification of material.

This pattern of deficits can be considered in relation to the neurobiological changes associated with dementia. Firstly, it is clear that the widespread deficits associated with dementia must impair memory functioning. Deficits in language functioning or perceptual processing must have an indirect effect on the encoding of material. But, over and above this, a distributed representation of memory storage in cortical structures will also mean that generalised damage will impair memory in different domains of processing.

In addition, more specific aspects of brain dysfunction may contribute to the overall picture. A prime candidate for this is the damage associated with the subicular and entorrhinal cortex in the medial temporal lobe and the hippocampal formation, which are known to be severely impaired in AD (Hyman *et al.*, 1984). Damage to these structures has long been known to produce a faster rate of forgetting over relatively short intervals, particularly when using non-verbal material (Mishkin, Malamut & Bachevalier, 1984; Sahgal & Iverson, 1978). More rapid forgetting, between 90 seconds and 10 minutes in AD, observed by Hart *et al.* (1988a) is commensurate with this pattern. So too, is the more rapid rate of forgetting on the delayed matching to sample task used by Sahakian *et al.* (1988) with abstract shapes as visual material.

An alternative explanation for memory impairment is diffuse damage to the cholinergic system that provides cholinergic projections to the association cortex and hippocampus (Arendt *et al.*, 1983; Whitehouse *et al.*, 1982). Damage to this system is known also to produce delay-dependent forgetting on modifications of the delayed matching to sample task, which have been shown to be ameliorated by cholinergic grafting (Dunnett, 1991). Again, this is commensurate with the delay-dependent increase in forgetting seen in AD.

The characteristics of memory functioning in dementia are only partially described by experimental investigation. The effects of loss of memory on everyday functioning have yet to be studied in any amount of detail but may shed light on changes in behaviour associated with dementia.

CHAPTER 3   Language

Although memory impairment may often provide the first and most obvious indication of the onset of a dementing illness, it is clear that other functions also become affected. Contact with those suffering from dementia reveals, at the least, impoverished speech. There can often be indications of more specific language impairments, such as difficulty in finding the right words or in naming, similar to those associated with aphasia due to focal lesions. Eventually speech tends to become more or less entirely lost as the condition progresses into its more advanced stages.

As with memory, the key question is not whether language impairments exist but what is their nature? As has already been indicated, the nature of the language impairment tends to change with time, and evidence relevant to this point will be cited later. In addition, it has also been suggested that early as opposed to late onset of Alzheimer-type dementia (AD) might be a significant factor. Some evidence suggests that language impairments are more prominent where the dementing process begins at an early age (Filley, Kelly & Heaton, 1986; Seltzer & Sherwin, 1983), although conflicting reports do exist (e.g. Bayles, 1991).

In addition to the above, there are two problems encountered in trying to elucidate the nature of language impairments in dementia, which need to be mentioned at the onset. The first is that sensory impairments, particularly deafness, are common in older people. It might be assumed that these would be present to a similar degree in age-matched controls and so any bias due to sensory defects would be controlled for. This may not necessarily be the case. Mild degrees of sensory impairment may be more difficult to detect in those with dementia. Where present in dementia, sensory impairments of a given degree may have a greater impact on the language behaviour of demented subjects simply because their linguistic capacities are under assault from the dementing process as well and the two things could have a synergistic effect. It is unfortunate that few studies of language in dementia appear to have considered very carefully the sensory functioning of the subjects used.

Another problem arises out of the fact that language is an exceedingly complex process and that any way of subdividing or structuring the work to be described assumes, implicitly if not explicitly, assumptions about the underlying nature of language. Models of language also remain controversial. As it happens, investigations of language in dementia have been relatively atheoretical and largely built around a number of different language tasks (Miller, 1989). Because of this it is easiest to subdivide the work described under the headings of the different language-related tasks that have been studied. This may not be an ideal way to proceed, but it does have the advantage of reflecting the nature of the work that has been carried out so far.

NAMING

As has been indicated by Ernst, Dalby & Dalby (1970), amongst other difficulties, difficulties in confrontational naming of objects or pictures, are commonly encountered in dementia and it is this aspect of language behaviour that has been most extensively studied.

Several studies have not only demonstrated naming impairments in demented subjects but have shown that, like normal controls, those with dementia find it much more difficult to name objects whose names are less frequently encountered in everyday language. Barker & Lawson (1968) and Lawson & Barker (1968) have found that this word-frequency effect is more marked in those with dementia than normal controls. On the other hand, Skelton-Robinson & Jones (1984) reported that the effect of word frequency was similar for both groups.

One major approach to explaining the naming impairment, has been to suggest that it is secondary to perceptual difficulties in identifying the objects or pictures to be named. Stengel (1964) was the first to suggest that the naming errors made by those with dementia indicated possible misperceptions of the object, in contrast to subjects with aphasia due to focal lesions in whom there is every indication of knowing what the object is but of failing to provide the word to go with it.

Later investigators have found evidence consistent with this position. Rochford (1971) tried to manipulate the difficulties involved in recognising the object and found that, as predicted, this enhanced naming in a demented group but not in those with aphasia. In a study with a similar rationale, Kirshner, Webb & Kelly (1984) varied the perceptual difficulty of objects to be named by using the actual objects, photographs of the objects, line drawings, etc. Again the nature of the stimulus had a much greater effect on naming by demented subjects than controls.

Since dementia tends to affect most aspects of functioning, it would not be surprising if perceptual processes were to suffer and that this might affect naming, under at least some circumstances. That this explanation of naming impairments has both plausibility and some evidence in its favour does not mean that it can wholly account for all naming difficulties. There is good evidence that other, more linguistic, factors are also involved. Indeed, the evidence indicating that naming in dementia is influenced by word frequency is difficult to square with a purely perceptual impairment (Barker & Lawson, 1968; Kirschner, Webb & Kelly, 1984; Skelton-Robinson & Jones, 1984) unless it is assumed that there is a strong relationship between word frequency and the perceptual discriminability of written words.

Huff, Corkin & Growden (1986) screened their demented subjects using a test of perceptual discrimination and found that those who performed normally on this task still exhibited naming problems. Skelton-Robinson & Jones (1984) had additionally prompted their subjects by supplying definitions of names that they had failed to produce. This latter procedure did not enhance naming as might have been expected if failures were solely due to misperception.

There therefore exists appreciable evidence that is inconsistent with the notion that naming difficulties are solely the result of perceptual inadequacies. The question that then arises is the nature of the linguistic deficit underlying naming difficulties. One approach is by the analysis of errors made in naming. Both Bayles & Tomoeda (1983) and Martin & Fedio (1983) considered naming errors to be semantic in nature, but Bowles, Obler & Albert (1987) described errors as reflecting difficulties in concept identification and in selecting between possible responses. As Huff, Corkin & Growden (1986) have pointed out, a problem here is that errors can be ambiguous and difficult to assign to categories. For example, is the subject who says 'horse' when shown a picture of a donkey exhibiting a perceptual error in assigning the correct name to an object that he has misidentified, or is this a semantic error based on misnaming a correctly perceived object?

Other types of evidence also lead to indications of a semantic component. In a complex investigation designed to examine components of the naming process, Flicker et al. (1987) claimed that there was a strong semantic component with language impairment in early AD being secondary to problems with semantic memory. However, Nebes, Martin & Horn (1984) studied semantic priming effects in dementia, whereby the speed of naming of a visually presented word (e.g. 'doctor') is enhanced if it is preceded by a semantically related word like 'nurse'. In their experiment, Nebes, Martin & Horn found that demented subjects showed the same degree of semantic priming as age-matched normal controls, thus implying that whatever semantic factors were being tapped by this measure had remained intact.

Hartman (1991) similarly found intact positive semantic priming of the positive 'nurse–doctor' type in AD patients where the occurrence of the first word increases the speed of the response to the second. In situations where controls showed negative effects (e.g. where 'nurse' precedes 'baker', compared with it coming before a neutral response word), there was no similar effect in the AD group. Hartman argues that the negative priming situation is unlike the positive, in that it requires subjects to actively generate expectations and in that the AD group failed to do this due to attentional impairments.

While the evidence is not entirely clear, there does seem to be good reason to believe that perceptual inadequacies can lie behind some naming problems in demented subjects. Nevertheless, it also appears to be the case that a purely perceptual explanation cannot account for all of the naming impairment and that some truly linguistic processes are involved. The latter seem to involve semantic aspects, but it is difficult to be much more specific as to the way in which semantic processes are broken down. Hartman (1991) has also hypothesised that attentional impairments may play a role in poor naming.

WORD FLUENCY

Another language-related test commonly used with demented subjects has been word fluency. Word fluency measures have been used both as a general index of verbal functioning and as a measure of semantic memory. Here 'semantic memory' is being used in the sense proposed by Tulving (1972), to refer to knowledge of procedures, rules, meanings, etc., that are not tied to specific instances. Whilst semantic memory could be regarded as part of another functional domain, that of memory, it must have strong links with verbal behaviour because language has essential semantic aspects.

The essential feature of word fluency tasks is that they provide the subject with a category (e.g. words beginning with the letter 'F', names of flowers, items that can be bought in a particular type of shop) and then require the production within a given time of as many words as possible belonging to that category. Appell, Kertesz & Fisman (1982), in using the Western Aphasia Battery, found that word fluency was the subtest on which demented subjects did worst. A number of other studies have similarly reported that word fluency is affected by dementia (e.g. Flicker et al., 1987; Miller & Hague, 1975; Ober et al., 1986; Pendleton et al., 1982; Rosen, 1980; Storandt et al., 1984).

It is more generally recognised that subjects with focal lesions in the frontal lobes perform badly on tests of word fluency (e.g. Milner, 1964). In consequence, tests of word fluency are commonly utilised in neuropsychological assessments as indices of frontal lobe damage. Nevertheless, both Miller (1984a) and Pendleton et al. (1982) found that demented subjects were as badly impaired as those in comparison groups with frontal lesions.

Rosen (1980) employed only demented and normal control groups but required them to produce words belonging to different categories (names of animals and words beginning with certain letters). She found that it was the initial-letter form of the test that best discriminated between her two groups. With the demented group, degree of dementia was related to performance. Rosen has suggested that because animal names break down in a hierarchical way into different subcategories, such as felines, animals used as pets, etc., this makes retrieval easier. Words beginning with a given letter do not easily fall into subcategories in this way.

Ober *et al.* (1986) varied both the degree of severity of dementia and the type of word fluency test employed. Like Rosen (1980) they used initial letters and words falling into specific categories, such as fruits. In addition, they had another category of things that could be found in a supermarket. They had put forward the notion that demented subjects were selectively impaired in accessing low-dominance semantic category members, or even less frequent words in general. Only with the supermarket test was there any indication of a restriction in the ability to access as wide a range of categories as controls or to sample as widely within chosen categories.

The study by Miller (1984a) has raised a potential problem in the understanding of word fluency findings. A measure of verbal intelligence was also administered (based on the Wechsler Adult Intelligence Scale), and data from control subjects was used to derive a regression equation for predicting anticipated fluency scores on the basis of verbal intelligence. When this was employed with the demented group, their fluency scores were consistent with those predicted on the basis of their lowered verbal intelligence. However, in the group with frontal lesions, fluency still remained low even after correction for verbal intelligence. If Miller (1984a) is correct then fluency in dementia is only reduced in proportion to the decline in verbal intelligence. As Miller (1989) has argued, two views of this can be taken, depending on the model of intelligence that is adopted. If intelligence is seen as an overriding, superordinate function then lowered word fluency is adequately explained in terms of a decline in verbal intelligence. On the other hand, if a more fragmented view of intelligence is taken, with it consisting of a number of discrete functions that happen to intercorrelate only to a modest degree, then some other interpretation of the decline in function is required. If the latter is the case, work done so far offers little in the way of an explanation as to why word fluency is affected in dementia.

As it happens, further work has not entirely supported Miller (1984a). Hart *et al.* (1988b) used tests identical to those employed by Miller and found that a group with AD still had lowered fluency scores even after verbal IQ had been taken into account by using Miller's regression equation. Nevertheless, the use of this equation did reduce the level of the apparent impairment.

Regardless of whether the view of Miller (1984a) or that of Hart *et al.* (1988b) turns out to be closer to reality, this work illustrates a more general point. This is the degree to which impairments in specific functions like fluency can be accounted for by changes in other, more general abilities, such as intelligence. This is a basic point that complicates the study of any specific function in a condition that, like dementia, produces a wide range of impairments.

COMPREHENSION

There has been little work specifically looking at comprehension in dementia. Thompson (1987) included the Token Test in a battery of measures as an index of auditory comprehension. The Token Test (De Renzi & Vignolo, 1962) is widely regarded as one of the best tests of the comprehension of spoken language, in the context of work on aphasia. As might be expected, Thompson's demented subjects were impaired on this test, as were those of Faber-Langendoen *et al.* (1988). Unfortunately, performance on the Token Test, as with many other tests of comprehension, could be affected by other types of impairment, for example in memory or general intellectual functioning, as well as comprehension difficulties. For this reason, the findings of Thompson (1987) and Faber-Langendoen *et al.* (1988) need to be treated with caution.

Similarly, impairments in reading comprehension have also been claimed. Cummings, Houlihan & Hill (1986) started by demonstrating that subjects with AD could read words even when these were obscured by superimposed diagonal lines. This implies that any apparent difficulty in the comprehension of written material cannot readily be explained as difficulties in visual perception. It also appeared that the comprehension of written commands was adversely affected. Many could read out commands that they were unable to perform. Evidence of difficulties in written comprehension has also been reported by Thompson (1987) and Faber-Langendoen *et al.* (1988). Schwartz, Marin & Sffran (1979) examined a single case of dementia as well as three with Broca's aphasia. The aphasics appeared to have difficulty with the syntactic aspects of the communications, whilst the demented subject had lexical difficulties in the face of a preserved understanding of syntax.

In another experiment, Kempler, Van Lancker & Read (1988) tested subjects in the comprehension of single words, familiar phrases (idioms and proverbs) and novel phrases. Subjects with probable Alzheimer's disease had particular difficulty in comprehending the familiar phrases and idioms (e.g. 'loud tie'). The authors conclude that this reflects a difficulty that such subjects have in interpreting abstract meanings.

Taken together, the evidence is certainly consistent with the notion that comprehension for both spoken and written information is affected by dementia. There is little further information as to the specific nature of these impairments, other than the evidence of Schwartz, Marin & Sffran (1979) implying that lexical problems may be paramount for the comprehension of written material at least and the identification by Kempler, Van Lancker & Read (1988) of particular problems with familiar idiomatic phrases.

WORD ASSOCIATION

A few investigators have considered word association in dementia. Associates supplied to a stimulus word can be categorised in a number of different ways. One distinction that can be made is between syntagmatic and paradigmatic responses. The former consist of words belonging to another part of speech that normally follow the stimulus word in speech (e.g. when 'tall' is followed by 'building' or 'ship'). Paradigmatic responses are in the same grammatical class as the stimulus (e.g. when 'large' is followed by 'big' or 'huge'). Two studies have found that dementia is associated with a reduction in paradigmatic responses, with no change in syntagmatic (Gewirth, Schindler & Hier, 1984; Pietro & Goldfarb, 1985). Both also reported an increase in idiosyncratic or unclassifiable responses, as when 'sick' is followed by the phrase 'when you are ill'.

PERSEVERATION

Perseveration is a feature of speech in dementia that has attracted special attention. Freeman & Gathercole (1966) described three types of perseveration which they named 'compulsive repetition' (as when an action or phrase is repeated over and over again), 'impairment of switching' (as when a response elicited by one stimulus is repeated inappropriately to another), and 'ideational perseveration' (where names and phrases crop up repeatedly in speech). These authors used a variety of different tasks designed to elicit these different forms of perseveration in an older group of subjects regarded as having dementia and in a younger group of schizophrenics. Both groups produced a similar total number of perseverations. However, the demented group exhibited more instances of impaired switching, whilst the schizophrenics showed an excess of compulsive repetition.

Bayles *et al.* (1985) also studied perseveration, using a modified version of Freeman and Gathercole's taxonomy of perseveration. They too found that demented subjects showed no increase in 'compulsive repetition', nor did subjects exhibit an increase in what Bayles *et al.* describe as 'carrier phrases' (e.g. 'well', 'let's see'). However, they did find that demented subjects were prone to perseverate ideas after an intervening response (e.g. when in describing a nail the subject says 'it's sharp, it's long, it's rather sharp'). It is possible that this type of perseveration is linked to a failure in memory, in that having gone on to list another characteristic of a nail after being sharp, the subject then returns to sharpness, forgetting that this has been mentioned before.

That subjects with dementia display an increased tendency to perseverate seems well established. Just what characterises this phenomenon and why it occurs remain to be established.

ORAL SPEECH

Spontaneous, or near spontaneous speech has been examined in a number of studies. Miller & Hague (1975) analysed samples of normal speech audiotaped from conversations with cases of AD. Statistical characteristics of the words used were examined in terms of such things as a possible tendency for demented subjects to rely on a smaller range of words that were used more frequently within samples of similar total word length. No differences between the experimental group and the controls were found. This implies that the total number of words available to demented subjects (the lexicon) remains intact, at least in relatively early cases. Combining this finding with the reduced word fluency established in another aspect of Miller's & Hague's (1975) study, led to the conclusion that, whilst the size of the lexicon may be relatively normal, access to words in the lexicon was either reduced or much slower, and that this reduction or slowness occurred to an equal degree across words, regardless of the frequency with which they are used in everyday speech.

Other investigators have used forms of discourse analysis. Hutchinson & Jensen (1980) analysed long conversations between an interviewer and demented elderly patients, as well as controls. The demented group produced fewer utterances. Looking at the nature of the utterances both groups were alike in that most utterances were statements of belief or assertions. The group with dementia differed in producing a higher rate of directives (utterances such as requests or questions that require the listener to do something). Those with dementia also initiated more topics in conversation, but these were largely as a part of what were considered to be violations of the ordinary rules of conversation. The description of these is not very adequate, but many of the newly initiated topics by the group with dementia may well have consisted of the introduction of irrelevances into the conversation. In turn, this might link to memory difficulties resulting in losing track of the conversation or in misunderstanding what the interviewer had just said.

A very similar experiment was reported by Ripich et al. (1991). Their subjects with AD spoke in shorter turns and used more nonverbal responses. The nature of their utterances displayed more requests and fewer assertions, with a higher proportion of unintelligible utterances.

In another investigation, Hier, Hagenlocker & Schindler (1985) showed that subjects with AD used fewer words, propositional phrases or subordinate clauses in speech, as well as producing more incomplete sentence fragments. They hypothesised that lexical defects occurred more frequently than syntactical deficits and that problems in accessing the lexicon increased with severity of dementia. Similar findings have also been reported by Kempler, Curtiss & Jackson (1987).

Nicholas *et al.* (1985) compared demented subjects with normal controls and patients with different types of aphasia in their oral descriptions of a picture. The group with dementia produced more empty phrases and conjunctions. In terms of the 'indices of empty speech' used in this analysis, the subjects with AD were most like people with anomic aphasia.

A number of descriptions of changes in oral speech now exist, but again there is little that could tie them all together in terms of an underlying or more fundamental impairment. It is clear that speech is more impoverished and fragmented in dementia. The evidence clearly points to abnormalities being more the result of inadequacies in lexical access than any problems with syntax.

WRITTEN LANGUAGE

Writing also changes in dementia. There is misspelling of simple words, letter reversal and poor letter formation (Pearce & Miller, 1973). Faber-Langendoen *et al.* (1988) report that written expression is one of the things that tends to be affected early in the course of dementia. Grafman *et al.* (1991) also found that when subjects with dementia are asked to write about events it is low-frequency occurrences (possibly described in low-frequency words) that are lost first. The presence or absence of agraphia has also been considered by some to be an important feature in arguing for distinct subtypes of dementia (Breitner & Folstein, 1984b; Seltzer & Sherwin, 1983).

Rapcsak *et al.* (1989) examined spelling in AD. In comparison with normal controls, their patient group was able to spell regular words (i.e. those like 'gate', which follow the straightforward rules of spelling) and regular non-words (i.e. non-words easily pronounceable on the basis of the normal spelling rules) quite satisfactorily. This group had particular difficulty with words whose spelling was irregular (e.g. 'tough'). Rapcsak *et al.* suggest that they have found an impairment of lexical spelling system somewhat akin to lexical agraphia with preservation of phonological spelling. An alternative explanation is that the words were too easy for the normal control group and, had they been more difficult, then the controls also might have shown a particular difficulty with irregularly spelled words.

MISCELLANEOUS DYSFUNCTIONS IN COMMUNICATION

Repetition (e.g. of phrases) has an important place in the study of aphasia but has largely been neglected in dementia. Rosen (1983) has shown that mildly demented subjects could repeat sentences containing high-frequency words with normal facility, but the ability to repeat sentences made up of low-frequency words was affected.

Kempler (1988) has studied pantomime abilities in subjects with AD; the subjects were asked to show how pictured objects (e.g. a telephone) were used. The findings suggested a parallel between pantomime representations and the lexical disturbances in production and recognition also found in this group. As far as this single investigation goes, the results are consistent with the presence of a common impairment in all forms of symbolic representation.

APHASIA ASSESSMENTS

The final set of studies of language impairment in dementia are different in nature from those described already. Rather than using a specific technique or a small set of techniques (e.g. naming or word association), they rely on the application of batteries of tests originally devised for the detection or examination of aphasia in patients with focal brain lesions. What emerges from investigations of this type is a description of the language impairment in dementia as if it were a type of aphasia. This begs the question as to whether those with dementia have language impairments that are truly of the same kind as those encountered in people who have focal lesions in the speech areas of the brain.

The first investigation of this type was reported by Ernst, Dalby & Dalby (1970) who used the system of the examination of aphasia described by Luria (1966). Whilst their subjects with dementia did not have normal language functioning, no clear pattern of impairment was established, but the authors claim that all showed poverty of vocabulary and that many had impairments in naming. On the other hand, studies using different batteries of tests and conducted by Cummings *et al.* (1985) and Murdoch *et al.* (1987) encountered patterns resembling transcortical sensory aphasia.

Kertesz and his colleagues (Appell, Kertesz & Fisman, 1982; Kertesz, Apell & Fisman, 1986) have used the Western Aphasia Battery and again found that all subjects with dementia have some degree of language impairment. The pattern of impairment was more varied than that described by some other authors (e.g. Cummings *et al.*, 1985). Pictures corresponding to transcortical sensory, Wernicke's and global aphasia were found. After examining the variations in severity of dementia in their sample, they concluded that there is a progression of language impairment in dementia. This starts with anomic aphasia and passes through transcortical sensory and Wernicke's aphasias before ultimately deteriorating into global aphasia. Whilst the notion of some progression of language impairment in dementia as the disease develops is not unreasonable, it should be noted that the Kertesz group's conclusions were only based on 25 subjects in a cross-sectional study. Longitudinal studies have yet to be conducted.

Bayles (1982) administered a large number of tests, some of which were similar to those used in aphasia assessments, to elderly patients with dementia and controls. There were strong indications of poor language functioning in the group with dementia, and it was the semantic aspects of language that emerged as being more liable to disruption than the phonological or syntactic. This is reasonably consistent with accounts of a tendency to produce the more posterior forms of aphasia (Appell, Kertesz & Fisman, 1982; Cummings *et al.*, 1985).

A final issue relating to aphasia-like patterns of deterioration in language is whether there may be distinct subtypes of those with AD who are particularly prone to developing language problems. It has been claimed that those with aphasic features tend to have an earlier onset, a more rapid progression of the disorder and stronger evidence of genetic transmission (Breitner & Folstein, 1984b; Faber-Langendoen *et al.*, 1988; Seltzer & Sherwin, 1983). Although this might be the generally accepted picture, it is important to note that these features do not emerge consistently in all relevant studies. For example, Bayles (1991) has reported evidence indicating that certain types of language impairment might be more prevalent in those with an older age of onset.

To summarise, it does seem that people with dementia do show language impairments on the types of test used to demonstrate aphasic disorders in those with focal brain lesions. In general, the pattern of impairment appears most commonly to resemble those forms of aphasia associated with more posterior lesions within the speech areas of the brain (e.g. transcortical sensory aphasia). As already indicated, this kind of work does carry the implicit assumption that the language impairments produced by dementia are like those found in aphasia due to focal lesions. The aphasia test batteries used would act to force the findings obtained from subjects with dementia into one of the standard aphasia patterns. It is quite possible that the pattern of language impairment resulting from dementia may be similar to that found in some forms of focal aphasia. Whether it is identical is more doubtful, especially as some reports have indicated differences between those with dementia and subjects with aphasia due to focal lesions (e.g. Code & Lodge, 1987; Rochford, 1971).

COMMENT

The evidence considered earlier in this chapter attests to the fact that not only is language affected by dementia but that this disturbance is manifested through a wide range of different aspects of language behaviour. Although some apparent language disturbances might be explicable in terms of other types of impairment, as when a failure to give a correct name for an object is attributable to a perceptual disability, it seems inherently unlikely that the whole range of language-related deficits could be explained as being secondary to other kinds of impairment. Indeed, it would also be rather surprising if dementia, which is known to affect almost all other aspects of functioning, should leave the cerebral processes underlying language entirely intact.

A number of further issues arise out of any consideration of language in dementia. One of these is the relation between the language changes in dementia and those associated with aphasia due to focal lesions. Some investigations based on batteries of tests designed specifically for the examination of aphasia (e.g. Appell, Kertesz & Fisman, 1982; Murdoch et al., 1987) have achieved some success in matching the language impairments in dementia to certain categories of aphasia. As has already been indicated, studies of this type are biased in this direction anyway. It does not follow from such work that dementia necessarily produces effects that are identical to those encountered in aphasia due to focal lesions. To resolve this issue it is necessary to compare subjects with dementia and those with aphasia on much more specific tasks. Those investigators who have done this have noted some indications that the two types of language impairment may not be identical (e.g. Code & Lodge, 1987; Rochford, 1971).

De Ajuriaguerra & Tissot (1975) have considered this issue, basing their arguments on their more clinically oriented observations of demented patients. They correctly draw attention to the fact that dementia affects a number of different functions. It is then hardly surprising if some of the phenomena which initially appear to be language related subsequently emerge as being at least partially the consequence of disturbances in other functions. Again, the indication that naming difficulties can be related to perceptual impairments offers an obvious example (Kirshner, Webb & Kelly, 1984; Rochford, 1971). One implication of this argument is that the different tasks used to study language in dementia (naming, word fluency, etc.) need to be carefully analysed from the perspective of whether other impairments, not related to language, might help to produce a breakdown in performance. Given that language-related tasks tend to be complex, the consequence is that it becomes virtually impossible to study language in isolation and without reference to other functions that might also be impaired.

A further issue of concern is to try to specify which aspects of language are most prone to disruption. Many investigations using different procedures point to the conclusion that phonology and the syntactic aspects of language remain relatively well preserved, at least until later on in the progress of the disease. It is the semantic and lexical aspects that are more liable to disturbance.

A potentially important point is that the dissociation between phonology and syntax, on the one hand, and the semantic and lexical aspects, on the other, may not really be as strong as the work so far implies. This is partly because more sensitive tests of phonology and syntax than those typically employed might produce more striking evidence of impairment in these aspects of language. Also, given the progressive and wide ranging effects of dementia, it is reasonable to expect that phonology and syntax might start to crumble later on in the course of the disease. If these qualifications are set aside, the evidence so far indicates that future attempts to further specify the nature of the language impairment in dementia need to concentrate on the semantic aspects of language and on lexical access.

Because dementia is a slowly progressive disorder, it is inevitable that the severity of the language impairment will change with time and possibly its nature will change as well. There appear to be no longitudinal studies of language, and few investigators using the cross-sectional method describe the stage of the disease process in their subjects with any degree of precision. As mentioned above, Kertesz, Apell & Fisman (1986) have attempted to comment on the progress of language impairment in dementia using a method that examined the pattern of impairment in relation to the length of illness. The only other study to try to relate impairment to severity of illness is that of Faber-Langendoen et al. (1988), and this is subject to the same limitations.

As was indicated in the introduction to this chapter, the study of language in dementia has been relatively atheoretical, with a concentration of attention on a number of fairly simple experimental paradigms like naming or word fluency. If work is to progress to examining such things as ease of lexical access, such theoretical neutrality becomes much less feasible. It then becomes necessary to have models that specify how the specific aspect of language at the focus of concern actually functions. There is therefore a need for work in this field to build links with psycholinguistic research in general, including work on normal linguistic processes.

Finally, another largely missing element in attempts to investigate language in dementia has been a concern with clinical issues. If people with dementia are to be helped to live as normal and as independent a life as possible, then the ability to communicate is of considerable importance. Just how this work on language might be employed to maintain or even enhance communicative skills remains to be explored.

CHAPTER 4   Other psychological impairments

As has been emphasised earlier in this book, dementia is a pervasive disturbance that affects all aspects of psychological functioning, or at least, all aspects that have been explored so far. Originally, the bulk of psychological work directed at exploring impairments in specific functions in dementia concentrated on memory, with appreciable interest having been shown more recently in language. Other psychological functions have received less sustained attention.

The present chapter aims to explore work concerned with aspects of functioning other than memory and language. This covers such things as attention and perception, spatial ability, and so on. However, the first section is devoted to the issue of intelligence.

INTELLIGENCE

Given the very meaning of the term 'dementia' it might be expected that changes in intelligence would occupy pride of place in any description of the psychological consequences of dementing illnesses. Indeed, many of the earlier psychological investigations of dementia made extensive use of intelligence tests, and there is an appreciable literature that could be cited related to changes in intelligence in people suffering from dementing illnesses.

In relation to the amount of work that has been reported, this section will be shorter than many of the others. This is for a number of reasons. Firstly, much of the work on intelligence test performance in dementia is not particularly recent and is therefore well described in a number of other sources (e.g. Miller, 1977;

Morris & McKiernan, 1993). There is little to be gained from rehearsing the same points in the same amount of detail. A summary would be more appropriate.

Secondly, picking up a point made above, there is little that is surprising in the fact that intelligence test performance declines in dementia. If performance on intelligence tests did not decline in dementia it would be an argument for re-examining the validity of the tests used, or the general concept of dementia, or even both. The interesting question is what the breakdown in intelligence test performance reveals about the underlying nature of the changes in intellectual ability produced by dementia.

From this point of view, work on the breakdown of intelligence has not been very illuminating. This may be due to two things. In the first place, intelligence tests, like the Wechsler scales, are deliberately developed so as to have high test–retest reliability (with coefficients often in excess of 0.90). Although high test–retest reliability is a great psychometric virtue in some contexts, it is also associated with a lack of sensitivity to change. This lack of sensitivity is partly due to the tendency for intelligence tests to concentrate on relatively overlearned or well-practised aspects of functioning. Well-practised skills are less prone to deteriorate in the face of cerebral pathology (Miller, 1984b). In looking at the impact of dementia on different aspects of intellectual functioning, some sensitivity to small amounts of deterioration in performance is useful. It might be useful to examine those aspects of functioning least prone to deteriorate, which will be less well detected by tests akin to intelligence tests, as well as those that are relatively likely to decline.

Also relevant to any consideration of the potential value of intelligence tests is the fact that many of them set out to sample a wide range of different domains of intellectual functioning without examining any single one of them in any detail. Any more extended analysis of patterns of decline in performance is therefore forced to use measures directed at specific abilities.

Leaving aside these limitations, the most extensively used intelligence tests are the various Wechsler scales. Work on these in relation to dementia has typically examined the subtest profiles in order to compare samples of subjects who have dementing illnesses with control groups. The use of the Wechsler Deterioration Index and related techniques for the estimation of intellectual decline (see Miller, 1980, and Chapter 6) implies that some subtests will differentiate those with dementia from normal subjects much better than others.

Christensen & MacKinnon (1992) have considered a very large number of studies that have provided such comparisons for the Wechsler Adult Intelligence Scale and have carried out a meta-analysis (Glass, McGaw & Smith, 1981) based on the published data from 21 reports. Their major finding was that whilst samples of patient with dementia performed worse than controls on all subtests, there was no discernible difference in the pattern of scores after the results of the different studies had been aggregated.

The results of the analysis by Christensen & MacKinnon (1992) run contrary to some previous reports (e.g. Pearce & Miller, 1973). Nevertheless, it is by no means the first paper to claim that there is no differential pattern of subtest decline (e.g. Larrabee, Largen & Levin, 1985). Given the variability in the samples used as well as the poor individual reliability of many of the Wechsler subtests, it would not be surprising if apparent differential patterns of decline were to be found from time to time on a purely chance basis. The meta-analytic results should offer a much greater level of reliability for the findings than is provided by any single study on its own and so the failure of Christensen & MacKinnon to find any differential pattern of subtest decline must be taken seriously. It suggests that further burrowing in the entrails of the Wechsler scales is unlikely to yield much of value.

Within the work on intelligence, some more specific notions have arisen. One example of this is based on the distinction that has been made between 'fluid' and 'crystallised' intelligence (Cattell, 1943). Crystallised intelligence consists of well laid down and established intellectual functions, such as the ability to define words in common use. In contrast, fluid intelligence refers to the ability to acquire new intellectual skills (and is a concept that shows some overlap with learning). The prediction is that in dementia it is fluid intelligence that suffers most. Despite Christensen's & MacKinnon's (1992) meta-analysis failing to give any support for such a notion, there are some much older investigations that could be interpreted as supporting a much bigger decline in fluid intelligence (Eysenck, 1945; Halstead, 1943). Unfortunately, choice of subject samples in these earlier investigations was not necessarily based on the same criteria as would be used in more recent work, which reduces the reliance that can be placed on these findings.

Overall, investigations based on the use of tests of intelligence have not proved very illuminating in terms of attempting to understand what is going on in dementia from a psychological perspective. It is necessary to look at much more specific functions rather than global concepts like 'intelligence'.

COGNITIVE SLOWING AND REACTION TIME

A reduction in the speed of processing information is a feature of dementia, with reduced reaction times on formal testing (Nebes, 1991). A central issue has been whether this slowing is uniform across different tasks and whether it can account for the pattern of cognitive decline associated with dementia. This view has been put forward in relation to cognitive changes associated with the normal elderly by Birren, Woods & Williams (1980), who propose that *all* cognitive operations are slowed to a similar extent. Attempts to examine this issue in dementia using a similar analysis have been conducted by Nebes & Brady (1992).

There are several examples where patients with dementia show particularly slow reaction times in comparison to normal subjects. For example, Ferris *et al.* (1976) found a larger difference between Alzheimer-type dementia (AD) patients and controls on a choice reaction-time task compared to a simple reaction-time task (in the first task the person has to choose between two response keys according to a particular stimulus, whilst in the second the person simply has to respond by pressing one key when a stimulus appears). Nebes & Brady (1989) required their AD patients to search an array of letters for a target letter. As the size of the array increased, from two, four and six letters, so did the difference in search time between the AD patients and control subjects. This was interpreted as a deficit in divided attention, with the larger array causing substantially increased search times because they divided the attention of the person.

Although divided attention appears to cause a much larger deficit, there is a question as to whether these effects are merely due to the increased difficulty of the task. In other words, patients may appear to do worse than normal on a divided attention task because they are operating at a different level of ability overall. A crucial point in interpreting these results is whether the *absolute* or *proportionate* difference in response time should be compared (Nebes, 1991). Salthouse & Somberg (1982) have argued convincingly that proportionate differences are relevant, because they take into account the baseline speed of response. Using this method of scoring the data, Nebes & Brady (1992) conducted a meta-analysis of several experiments with a variety of reaction-time measures. They found that the response times of young and old subjects were described by a simple linear function. In other words, as the difficulty of a task increases, causing normal subjects to take longer to respond, there is a simple proportionately increased slowing in patients with dementia. In the meta-analysis described by Nebes & Brady (1992) the function took the following form:

$$\text{Control RT} = A + B \times \text{Alzheimer's patient RT},$$

where A is a constant that varies according to the experiment, but B is a constant equal approximately to 2.2.

Overall, this result argues against inferring particular types of deficits (such as a deficit in divided attention) from a proportionate decrease in response speed on a particular task unless the decrease exceeds that predicted by the function established by Nebes & Brady (1992). It also may suggest that there is a generalised slowing in response speed across all tasks, but that more complex tasks exaggerate the decline. To some extent, however, this finding is of theoretical importance only, since the main result is that cognitive slowing will be increased in dementia when the task is made more complex.

SELECTIVE ATTENTION

The ability to focus attention on a particular aspect of incoming sensory information has long been recognised. Selective attention is a necessary feature of information processing because it limits the amount of sensory input that has to be processed at a higher level of cognitive functioning (Norman, 1976). A classic example is the 'cocktail party' phenomenon whereby a person can 'tune in' to one particular conversation in a crowded room. Several studies have investigated whether selective (or focused) attention is impaired in dementia (Bouma & Van Silfhout, 1989; Mohr *et al.*, 1990; Nebes & Brady, 1992).

Selective attention has been investigated experimentally in AD using the dichotic listening task. This task involves listening to two simultaneous auditory messages, one presented in each ear using earphones. The most common procedure is to use lists of words and require the subject to report back the two lists, with no instructions concerning which to report first. Normally, subjects (those who are right handed) spontaneously report the list presented to the right ear first and show greater accuracy with this list. Subjects can also focus their attention on a particular list and report it first if given the instructions. Mohr *et al.* (1990) tested a group of AD patients and elderly controls on this task, giving the subjects instructions to attend to the right or left ear. It was found that the AD patients did not respond to the instructions, and showed a right-ear superiority throughout. An almost identical pattern of performance has been found by Bouma & Van Silfhout (1989). An obvious interpretation of this result is that AD patients had difficulties in shifting their attention away from the right ear when given instructions to do so. They thus have a deficit in selective attention in relation to auditorily presented material.

In the visual domain, selective attention in AD has been studied by Nebes & Brady (1989) and by Freed *et al.* (1989). In a way similar to the processing of auditory information, it is possible to focus on a particular part of the visual field even if it is not in the direct line of gaze, hence the notion of an 'internal spotlight' proposed by Posner, Snyder & Davison (1980). There is some evidence that the mechanisms concerned with visual attention are preserved in dementia. Firstly, Nebes & Brady (1989) required subjects to scan an array of six letters for a particular letter. In some arrays all six letters were black, whilst in others only two were black and four were red. Normal subjects can identify the target letter more rapidly if there are only two letters coloured

red because their attention can be focused on only two letters that are relevant. Whilst AD patients were generally slower to identify the target letter, their speed of response with two black letters was increased to the same extent as elderly control subjects. This was interpreted as indicating that the ability to use the physical feature of colour to focus visual attention was normal in the AD patients.

Another method for exploring visual attention has been to use the task developed by Posner, Snyder & Davison (1980). The task involves pressing a response key when a target light appears on a visual display unit. The target might appear on the left or right of the screen, whilst the person observed a central fixation point. Before each trial the subjects were given a cue that might predict the location of the target. On most trials (80%) this cue was valid and pointed to where it would appear, but on other trials (20%) it was invalid and pointed away from the target. Normally, the valid cue speeds up the response, whilst the invalid cue slows it down because it directs attention away from the target. Freed *et al.* (1989) conducted this test on AD patients and found the pattern was the same.

Taken together, these studies show that AD patients have difficulty in shifting attention in the auditory domain, but no impairment in visual selective attention. This dissociation is not wholly unexpected, since different attentional mechanisms are involved in the two types of cognitive processes. However, it does have implications for clinical assessment and management of patients, indicating that patients will have difficulty in attending to different auditory inputs but less difficulty in orientating to visual stimuli.

VISUOSPATIAL FUNCTIONING

In terms of the behavioural manifestations of Alzheimer's disease, deficits in visuospatial functioning tend to be overlooked. This is partly because language and memory dysfunction appears more prominently in terms of neuropsychological impairment. There is some evidence, however, that visuoperceptual deficits lead directly to behavioural problems. For example, Henderson, Mack & Williams (1989) obtained ratings of how frequently patients with dementia became lost or spatially disorientated. This measure was correlated with performance on standard tests of neuropsychological functioning, including visuospatial ability, memory, language and attention. It was found that a combination of visuospatial and memory impairment provided a very strong predictor of spatial disorientation, but was not necessarily related to other factors, such as attention. Studies of visuospatial abilities have been conducted, albeit in a preliminary fashion, in a number of areas.

Low-level visual perception appears to be unimpaired in early Alzheimer's disease, at least in comparison to age-matched controls. Schlotterer, Moscovitch & Crapper-McLachlan (1983) report normal contrast sensitivity in patients who had to distinguish between alternating pairs of black and white regions (sinusoidal gratings) of differing spatial frequency. Visual acuity was also unimpaired, again in comparison to elderly control subjects. Similarly, Mendez et al. (1990) have found that AD patients and normal subjects performed at the same levels in tests of visual acuity and colour identification. One study has reported a deficit in low-level vision (Nissen et al., 1985), using a different method to that of Schlotterer, Moscovitch & Crapper-McLachlan (1983) to measure contrast sensitivity. In the Schlotterer, Moscovitch & Crapper-McLachlan (1983) task, the subject had to discriminate whether patterns were 'wide', 'medium' or 'fine', whilst the Nissen et al. (1985) study required the AD patients to detect stimuli of different frequency at threshold. The task demands of this experiment may account for the discrepancy, particularly if the AD patients found it more difficult to remember to respond appropriately to the absence of a stimulus, even when cued by the experimenter.

The relative preservation of low-level vision can be attributed to the lack of neurodegeneration of the striate cortex or decline in metabolic activity (measured using positron emission tomography scan) (Benson, Cummings & Kuhl, 1981). Despite this, the retention of incoming visual information for even very brief periods (iconic memory) is impaired. A preliminary study by Miller (1977a) used the backward masking technique in which an array of letters was presented tachistoscopically, followed immediately by a pattern of randomly arranged black and white squares. In comparison to control subjects, AD patients were able to report very few of the letters. An extension of this study by Schlotterer, Moscovitch & Crapper-McLachlan (1983) pinpoints the deficit at a more central level in processing of visual material. They used two types of pattern masking; the first was a homogenous noise field (a light flash), which is assumed to act at a very peripheral level of visual processing since it does not act dioptically (i.e. if presented to one eye, it limited perception of material by that eye only). The second type of mask consisted of fragments of letters and is known to have an effect on material presented to the contra-lateral eye, thus indicating a more central affect. Schlotterer, Moscovitch & Crapper-McLachlan (1983) found that the threshold exposure needed to identify single letters following this type of masking was very much greater for AD patients only when the letter-fragment mask was used.

The effect of this impairment on visual perception is unclear, although AD patients appear to perform poorly on a range of vis-uospatial tasks such as discriminating between random shapes, checkerboard patterns and spatially organised arrays of geometric shapes (Becker et al., 1988; Brouwers et al., 1984; Huff, Corkin & Growden, 1986). Alzheimer's disease patients are impaired on a variety of more complex perceptual tasks. Mendez et al. (1990) found that all their AD patients were impaired in figure-ground identification, in which patients are required to identify line draw-ings of objects where the contours overlap. As a variant of this test, patients are required to find a simple geometric shape hidden in a more complex shape. Capitani et al. (1988) found that AD patients were impaired on this task, with a proportion who were very substantially impaired. Identification of visual objects is also impaired and is one of the causes of difficulties in naming objects. For example, Kirshner, Webb & Kelly (1984) reported that AD pat-ients were more impaired in naming objects when they were shown as coloured photographs or as line drawings than when the actual objects were shown. They argued that the naming impairment is increased by perceptual misidentification (see Chapter 3 for a more detailed discussion of this issue).

One theory is that the deficit in visuospatial processing is caused by an impairment in the transformation of mental imagery or vis-ual material. This would explain, in particular, the substantial impairment across a range of tasks involving manipulation of visuospatial information, such as impairment on the Block Design Test requiring the manipulation of objects in three dimensions to produce a pattern (Storandt *et al.*, 1984). In order to test this hypothesis, Flicker *et al.* (1988) used a naming test, in which AD patients had to name objects that were presented normally or rotated, as a test of mental rotation. This task requires the rotation to be made in an allocentric fashion (i.e. not in relation to the person) and was contrasted with performance on the Money Road Map Test which requires the subject to mentally traverse through a route and decide whether left or right hand moves are made. Some of the turns in the route go back in the direction of the subject, and overall the task requires mental rotation in space relative to the person (egocentric rotation). As expected, the AD patients had more difficulty naming the objects, although there was no increased deficit with naming rotated objects. Nor was there extra difficulty in the rotated aspects of the Money Road Map Test. This result goes against the suggestion that there is a specific deficit in spatial transformation underlying the impairment in the two tasks.

It might be argued that the deficits across a range of visuospatial processing tasks are an inevitable result of a global impairment in cognition. There is evidence, however, that deficits in visuospatial abilities are dissociated in Alzheimer's disease. Eslinger & Benton (1983) compared AD patients on two visuoperceptual tasks that have been shown to be disrupted independently by different brain lesions, namely judgement of line orientation and face recognition. In the line orientation task the subject has to pick out a line of the same slope from an array of 11 lines that differ in angle of orientation, whilst in the face recognition task a target face has to be identified from an array of faces. Eslinger & Benton (1983) found that, overall, the AD patients were impaired on both tasks, but that some patients did much worse on one task and vice versa.

In relation to line drawing a similar type of dissociation has been observed by Moore & Wyke (1984), who provide a detailed breakdown of drawing errors by AD patients. Normally the pattern of drawing errors dissociates in terms of hemispheric damage, with left hemisphere lesions being associated with spatially organised drawing lacking in detail. Right hemisphere lesions are associated with spatial disorganisation and fragmentation (Warrington,

1969), leading to the notion that the left hemisphere is involved in the organisation and executive processing of drawing skills, whilst the right hemisphere is primarily concerned with the construction of parts of an object in space. Alzheimer's disease patients made both types of errors, but this was dissociated according to whether they were required to draw to command (drawing from memory) or copy a drawing. In drawing to command, the loss of detail was much more substantial than in patients with left hemisphere lesions. When copying, AD patients tended to place the components of the drawing in inappropriate positions. It is clear from these studies (Eslinger & Benton, 1983; Moore & Wyke, 1984) that visuospatial processing tends to dissociate in a more complex fashion, pointing towards a multifocal disorder rather than global deterioration.

The deterioration in visuospatial processing forms a central feature in the diagnosis of Alzheimer's disease and is clearly a prominent early symptom. A general feature is that central aspects of visuospatial processing are clearly impaired, whilst there is some evidence of preserved low-level visual processing. The significance of these findings in terms of behavioural change is unclear, partly because insufficient observational studies of visuospatial disturbance in AD patients have been carried out. Future studies relating performance on everyday tasks involving visuospatial processing may provide useful information with regard to this, but also there is the need to form a more detailed experimental analysis of visuospatial impairment in Alzheimer's disease.

NON-COGNITIVE CHANGES

The overwhelming emphasis in work on the psychological aspects of dementia has been on the deterioration that occurs in the various aspects of cognitive functioning. This does not give a complete picture. Although the end stages of a dementing illness can give the impression of a flat affect and almost absent personality, the earlier stages are characterised by a number of psychological changes in domains other than that of cognitive functioning.

There is a marked association between dementia and disturbances of affect, mainly depression. Both Teri & Wagner (1992) and

Wragg & Jeste (1989) have provided reviews dealing with depression. Teri & Wagner concluded that depression coexists with Alzheimer type dementia to a significant degree and that the prevalence of depression is appreciably higher than would be expected in samples of non-demented subjects of similar age.

In one detailed investigation of mood changes in dementia (Burns, Jaccoby & Levy, 1990c), almost two thirds of a large sample of presumed Alzheimer cases reported at least one depressive symptom. About 40% were reported by relatives to be depressed. In general, the findings support Teri's & Wagner's (1992) conclusion of an increased prevalence of depressive features in subjects with Alzheimer type dementia, as do the results of a number of other reports (e.g. Lazarus et al., 1987; Merriam et al., 1988; Rubin, 1990). One relationship noted by Burns, Jaccoby & Levy (1990c) was that it was those AD patients with the milder degrees of dementia who showed the most evidence of depression, which is consistent with the general clinical impression of flattened affect in the later stages of the disorder. In this sample, indications of elevated mood were rare, occurring in less than 5% of subjects.

A range of other psychiatric phenomena can be encountered in those with Alzheimer type dementia (Burns, Jaccoby & Levy, 1990a,b,d; Lopez et al., 1991; Rubin, 1990). These include delusions, hallucinations and behaviour disorders. In the 178 subjects with Alzheimer type dementia studied by Burns, Jaccoby & Levy, about 16% had suffered from delusions, mainly of a paranoid nature, and a slightly lower proportion had had hallucinations. Visual and auditory hallucinations were found more or less equally by Burns, Jaccoby & Levy, although Rubin (1990) found a predominance of visual hallucinations.

Recently attention has been drawn to 'disorders of behaviour' (e.g. Fairburn & Hope, 1988; Rubin, 1990). Burns, Jaccoby & Levy (1990d) reported that both aggression and wandering were present in about a fifth of their sample and binge eating in about 10%. Urinary incontinence occurred in almost half the sample. Sexual disinhibition, although something that can cause difficult problems in management, was only present in 7%.

The features of the classic Kluver–Bucy syndrome (Kluver & Bucy, 1937) identified in monkeys after bilateral temporal lobe removal were encountered quite commonly, although only one subject showed the complete syndrome. The features of the Kluver–Bucy syndrome are visual agnosia, strong tendencies to explore stimuli orally (including hyperphagia), excessive tendency to react to stimuli, and emotional changes (apathy and loss of fear or rage reactions). Features of this syndrome were especially associated with temporal lobe atrophy.

Behaviour problems of this type can be difficult in terms of every-day management but they typically represent complex forms of behaviour that might well be related to a number of different underlying cognitive impairments. For example, in some circum-stances, incontinence might be related to a loss of spatial orien-tation or memory for spatial relationships, which might make the lavatory difficult to find thus leading to 'accidents'.

Nevertheless, what the work briefly outlined in this section does emphasise is that a complete understanding of the psychology of dementia requires an examination of changes occurring in other domains than the cognitive, at least in so far as the latter is conven-tionally conceived. Psychiatric symptoms, such as hallucinations, delusions and especially depression, do occur. As emphasised by Teri & Wagner (1992), they add to the overall disability and are therefore of considerable practical as well as theoretical signifi-cance.

Two other issues arise. In the first place it is not always easy to see how some of the features discussed in this section link to, or interact with, the more extensively studied cognitive impairment. For example, forgetfulness may contribute to some psychiatric symptoms. It is not difficult to think of ways in which failures of memory might lead to suspiciousness or even to what might be regarded as paranoid delusions. Things may happen without apparent rhyme or reason to the afflicted individual simply because he or she has forgotten that certain decisions had been taken some hours or days previously.

The second problem is one of definition. To take mood changes as an example, estimates of the frequency of depressed mood in those with Alzheimer type dementia range from 0% to 87% (Knesevich et al., 1983; Merriam et al., 1988). Apart from possible sampling differences between studies, different criteria of lowered mood have also been employed. Not only may different criteria be used but information about mood may be obtained solely from patients themselves or from relatives or even from both (see Burke, Rubin & Morris, 1988; Lazarus *et al.*, 1987; Merriam *et al.*, 1988).

Limitations such as those just outlined make it difficult to reach any precise conclusions. However, it can be stated with some confidence that certain psychiatric features do appear to arise with greater frequency in Alzheimer type dementia. Exact figures, like those cited from the work of Burns, Jaccoby & Levy (1990a,b,c,d) have to be treated with some caution. The psychological mechanisms underlying these phenomena in subjects with dementia remain to be explored.

The other conclusion that is worth noting is that of Teri & Wagner (1992) to the effect that there is little evidence on the effectiveness of treating psychiatric symptoms in those with dementia. Not only do these features need to be recognised and understood, but their clinical management needs to be explored.

COMMENT

Taken together, the evidence described in both this and the preceding two chapters amply illustrates the claim that most aspects of functioning suffer deleterious effects in dementia and especially dementia of the Alzheimer type. This has a number of implications for trying to understand what is happening in dementia from a psychological point of view.

Given the impossibility of finding tasks that are entirely 'pure' in that they measure only one aspect of psychological functioning in total isolation from others, this then raises problems in the interpretation of findings. In other words, is poor performance of a task due solely to an impairment in the function that the task most obviously reflects? A clear example of this difficulty was described in the previous chapter (pp. 37–40), where the question arose as to whether impairments in naming tasks really reflected a linguistic difficulty as opposed to a problem in identification of the objects that were to be named.

Another implication is that it could be rather more interesting to find a task on which subjects with dementia produced a normal, or near normal, performance than tasks in which impairments were found. An example of normal, or near normal, performance being exploited for practical ends can be found in Chapter 7 (pp. 101–102). Here relatively preserved performance in the reading of words can be used as an estimate of premorbid levels of functioning.

Finally, the plethora of functions affected raises the issue as to whether certain groups of impairments might be viewed as examples of the malfunctioning of some more fundamental underlying ability. An obvious candidate for this is general intelligence. Could it be that poor performance on language, memory, information processing based tasks, etc., might reflect lowered general intelligence. The resolution of this issue involves a number of fundamental assumptions in psychology, such as that concerning the degree to which functions can be regarded as modular in the sense described by Fodor (1983). Any further discussion of this problem would involve a major excursion outside the useful boundaries of this book. Nevertheless, the fact that this fundamental question has arisen illustrates the general principle that applied psychology can relate quite closely to the most fundamental aspects of the discipline.

CHAPTER 5   Subcortical dementia

The idea of dementia-like features being associated with subcortical disease goes back at least to Naville (1922), and the term 'subcortical dementia' was coined by von Stockert in 1932 (for a historical account of the concept, see Mandell & Albert, 1990; Rogers, 1986). However, it was the report by Albert, Feldman & Willis (1974), dealing with an alleged form of dementia in progressive supranuclear palsy, that probably did most to bring the notion of subcortical dementia to the prominence that it now enjoys. Subcortical dementia is mainly claimed to be found in certain conditions having a predominantly subcortical pathology, such as Parkinson's disease, Huntington's chorea, Wilson's disease or progressive supranuclear palsy (the Steele–Richardson–Olszewski syndrome). There are of course a number of other diseases in which the cerebral pathology is subcortical and which might also be regarded as being associated with subcortical dementia. One commonly encountered example is multiple sclerosis.

The characteristic features of subcortical dementia have been summarised in a number of sources (e.g. Cummings, 1990a,b) and are set out in Table 5.1. The individual features will not be described further at this point since they will be picked up later in this chapter. In passing, it can be noted that subcortical dementia is typically described in contrast to 'cortical dementia', which is particularly exemplified by Alzheimer-type dementia. This convention is followed in Table 5.1.

The main question that arises is whether dementia-like features actually do arise in the group of conditions generally assumed to exhibit subcortical dementia. More particularly, do these features match the characteristics that are summarised in Table 5.1 and could they be otherwise explained as manifestations of some other

Table 5.1 Features of subcortical dementia as compared to those of Alzheimer's disease

Function	Subcortical dementia	Cortical dementia
Speed of cognitive processing	Slowed early	Normal until late in disease
Memory	Recall impaired, recognition normal or much better preserved	Recall and recognition both clearly impaired
Language	No aphasic features except when dementia very advanced	Aphasic features early
Speech	Dysarthria	Normal articulation
Visuospatial skills	Impaired	Impaired
Frontal symptoms	Disproportionately affected compared to other things	Impaired to degree consistent with other things
Other cortical dysfunctions (agnosia, apraxia, etc.)	Preserved until late in course of dementia	Impaired
Motor speed	Slowed	Normal
Neuropsychiatric manifestations (personality and mood change, etc.)	Present (apathetic, inert, depressed, etc.)	Not prominent; often patient is unconcerned

factor, such as depression, rather than as constituting a primary dementia?

If it is accepted that dementia-like features do occur in the relevant conditions with predominantly subcortical pathology, such as Parkinson's disease or Huntington's chorea, then a further issue needs to be tackled. Advocates of the concept of subcortical dementia mean something more than that pictures akin to dementia can be found in these conditions. There is the implication that subcortical dementia forms a distinct syndrome which can be differentiated from so-called cortical dementia. If this is the case, then the dementia-like features found in Parkinson's disease, Huntington's chorea, progressive supranuclear palsy, and so on, should show considerable similarity. Furthermore, it can be argued that, at the very least, these conditions should have more in common in the cognitive impairments that they produce than any of them considered individually have in common with a definite 'cortical dementia' such as Alzheimer's disease.

Before actually going on to consider these questions, a basic methodological point needs to be mentioned. As has been pointed out elsewhere (Brown & Marsden, 1987), it is quite possible that in their end stages all forms of dementia are going to appear similar, with extremely low performance on any measure that is considered. In consequence, in looking for distinctive features in particular types of dementia it is most appropriate to study subjects whose dementia is established but not yet severe. In addition, Brown & Marsden suggest that in studying an alleged condition, like subcortical dementia, which is progressive it is necessary to examine change in subjects over time. This is to avoid identifying spurious differences that may arise from comparing what is essentially the same deteriorating process but in different stages of its development. Unfortunately, very little published work actually does have a longitudinal component so as to deal with the development of impairments over time.

DO FEATURES OF DEMENTIA ARISE IN CONDITIONS WITH PREDOMINANTLY SUBCORTICAL PATHOLOGY?

The potentially relevant evidence that might be cited in this section is now extremely large. There will therefore be no attempt to provide an exhaustive coverage, but discussion will concentrate on the more important and critical work. In order to set out the very disparate sets of information in a coherent form, it has proved most convenient to subdivide the material according to the features set out in Table 5.1.

Before going on to look at the alleged features in detail, a general point can be briefly noted. Evidence that there is some form of intellectual deterioration that might, at least loosely, be described as 'dementia' in the various conditions associated with subcortical dementia is provided by a number of sources (e.g. Brown, 1991;

Brown & Marsden, 1984; Gibb, 1989; Maher, Smith & Lees, 1985). Since it is the analysis of the detailed characteristics that is important for present purposes, this general evidence will not be described any further. In any case, the more specific work that is cited below provides considerable evidence to support the notion of adverse changes in at least some aspects of cognitive functioning.

Bradyphrenia

The assumption is that those with subcortical dementia exhibit slowed mental functioning, or so-called bradyphrenia, somewhat reminiscent of the slowed motor functioning (bradykinesia) that is well described as a physical feature of Parkinson's disease (see Walton, 1985). It offers a good starting point for the examination of subcortical dementia because it is the one unique feature that is supposed to exist in subcortical dementia but not in cortical dementia. The notion of bradyphrenia was first put forward by Naville (1922) to describe the mental features of encephalitis lethargica, but it has been incorporated by more modern authorities as a key feature of subcortical dementia as it arises in a range of other conditions.

The concept of bradyphrenia presents a logical difficulty. This can most easily be discussed in terms of a fictitious example. Subjects thought to have some form of cerebral pathology may be required to carry out, say, a spatial task where they are asked to make judgements about spatial relationships. If a larger than normal number of incorrect responses are made, it is generally assumed that the subject has some form of impairment in spatial functioning. If subjects give a number of correct responses similar to normal controls but respond much more slowly, it might be tempting to say that they have normal spatial ability but slowed mental processing (bradyphrenia).

In fact a conclusion of this kind might be mistaken. In the first instance, subjects may have slowed mental processing rather than impaired spatial ability but compensate for this by trying to respond much more quickly than is compatible with accurate performance. This might result in a more-or-less normal speed of response but at the expense of an increased number of errors. In the second case, of slow but accurate performance, it could be that subjects have an impairment in spatial ability but compensate for this by taking much more time over each response thus reducing errors, possibly even to normal levels, but at the expense of a much slower response rate.

The point here is that a 'trade-off' can be established between speed of response and number of incorrect responses that will be accepted. This is so regardless of whether the basic fault lies in the level of underlying ability in the function being measured or in the rate at which mental processes can be executed. Bradyphrenia can only be reasonably claimed to have been demonstrated when evidence is derived from situations in which this potential 'trade-off' between accuracy and speed can be taken into account. Few claims to demonstrate bradyphrenia come close to meeting this criterion, and those that do not will be ignored in the present account.

One way of trying to get at bradyphrenia has been to compare simple with choice reaction time. If the subject has to make a response such as pressing as quickly as possible one of two buttons according to which of two lights comes on, then this experiment can be carried out with two variants or conditions. One condition is where the subject knows which light will come on next (simple reaction time), as opposed to the situation where no such information is provided and which light is lit is determined at random (choice reaction time). The additional time taken to respond in the latter condition reflects some additional, internal processing time involved in determining which response is required. It might be predicted that this internal processing time would be increased in subjects exhibiting bradyphrenia. Worcester-Drought & Hardcastle (1924) employed such a procedure and found no evidence of a greater increase in reaction time between simple and choice reaction times in patients exhibiting the long-term effects of encephalitis lethargica.

A more recent experiment by Evarts, Teravainen & Calne (1981) found that reaction times in patients with Parkinson's disease were slowed overall but, contrary to expectations based on the notion of bradyphrenia, Parkinsonian subjects showed a very much reduced tendency to increased reaction time in the two choice situation as compared with simple reaction time. This was interpreted as a difficulty for the Parkinsonian group in using the advance information in the simple reaction time situation to pre-programme the required movement, and this interpretation was confirmed by Sheridan & Flowers (1990). This links to claims of frontal impairments in subcortical dementia, which will be dis-cussed below.

A further, and more complex reaction time experiment by Stelmach, Worringham & Strand (1986) failed to yield any indi-cation of anything that would match the notion of bradyphrenia in Parkinson's disease. A similar finding to that of Stelmach, Wor-ringham & Strand (1986) was reported by Dubois *et al.* (1988) in relation to Parkinson's disease, although this latter investigation did find results compatible with bradyphrenia in progressive sup-ranuclear palsy.

A second relevant experimental paradigm has been based on the Sternberg (1975) memory scanning task. Here the subject is pre-sented with a string of digits of unpredictable length which is followed by a probe digit. The subject then has to indicate whether the probe digit appeared in the main string. The time to respond is a direct function of the number of digits in the string (i.e. the number to be scanned mentally). Again, the prediction is that bra-dyphrenia should result in slower mental scanning of the digits in the string.

The first experiment to use this technique generally found that subjects with Parkinson's disease appeared to scan at the same rate as normal controls (Wilson *et al.*, 1980). However, what appears to have been a *post hoc* analysis did find a relatively gre-ater increase in response time for each additional digit to be scanned for a subsample of the original Parkinsonian group aged over 65 years. A further experiment by Litvan *et al.* (1989), using patients with progressive supranuclear palsy, was unable to obtain any indication of bradyphrenia.

Finally, Rafal *et al.* (1984) argued that bradyphrenia in Parkinson-ian subjects could be modified by treatment, and therefore, using this paradigm, they compared Parkinsonian subjects both on and off drug treatment. Relative increases in reaction time with string length remained unaffected in the way that would have been expected if bradyphrenia had been present and had been manipulated by antiparkinsonian medication.

Other experimental procedures have been used to look for evidence of bradyphrenia, such as the switching of covert attention (e.g. Rafal *et al.*, 1984; Wright *et al.*, 1990). The relevant investigations do not significantly affect the picture given already. With very few exceptions, experimental studies have provided no really substantial confirmation that bradyphrenia exists, with the notable exceptions of Wilson, Kasniak & Fox (1980) for older parkinsonian subjects only and Dubois *et al.* (1988) for progressive supranuclear palsy. This may be because bradyphrenia does not exist other than as an erroneous clinical impression. Alternatively, it could be that the wrong kinds of task have been used, in that the experimental procedures employed have depended too much on the peripheral processing of information. It is possible that tasks based on deeper levels of cognitive functioning might show bradyphrenic effects. In addition, these might approximate more closely to the clinical concept of bradyphrenia since this implies slowed thought processes rather than slowed peripheral processing. Unfortunately, such studies do not yet appear to have been carried out. In addition, the present argument points to the fact that any further investigations designed to explore the possible occurrence of bradyphrenia need to be designed with considerably more methodological sophistication than has typically been the case so far.

Memory

Considerable evidence exists indicating that performance on memory-related tasks is impaired in people suffering from the conditions associated with subcortical dementia (e.g. Folstein, Brandt & Folstein, 1990; Freedman, 1990). The questions requiring attention here are whether the poor performance on memory related tasks is truly indicative of memory impairment, as opposed to being the consequence of other things like depression, and whether they match the alleged pattern in subcortical dementia of good recognition and impaired recall.

In Parkinson's disease any memory impairment tends to be small and definitely not as clear cut as is the case in, say, Alzheimer's disease or even Huntington's chorea. The possibility has therefore been raised that the apparent decline in memory performance in Parkinson's disease may reflect some factor other than a true memory loss. Thus Flowers, Pearce & Pearce (1984) argued that in most of the then previously published work, performance on the memory test used could have been adversely affected by poor attention, motivation, etc. These things might, in turn, be related to the depression that is also alleged to occur in Parkinson's disease. Flowers, Pearce & Pearce (1984) therefore opted for a procedure involving recognition testing, since this minimises the influence of such extraneous variables (e.g. forced-choice recognition testing eliminates the possibility inherent in recall testing that a poorly motivated or depressed subject might not bother to produce as many responses as he or she might have available). Using a number of different recognition tests, they found no evidence of memory impairment.

Another possibility is raised by Miller, Berrios & Politynska (1987). Their two measures of verbal memory, one involving recall and the other recognition, both gave evidence of memory impairment in Parkinsonian subjects. However, it was also found that memory performance in Parkinsonian subjects was significantly related to anticholinergic medication (benzhexol). This finding carries plausibility in view of the considerable evidence of the involvement of cholinergic systems in memory (e.g. Kopelman, 1986) and raises the possibility that poor memory performance in Parkinson's disease might be drug related. However, it should be noted that the use of anticholinergic medication in Parkinson's disease has largely been superseded, that most patients have been treated by levodopa-related preparations for some time and that Miller, Berrios & Politynska (1987) found no similar correlation between levodopa intake and memory performance. Use of anticholinergic medication is probably not a convincing explanation of all more recent reports of memory loss in Parkinson's disease.

Another group that has examined memory performance in Parkinson's disease is Riklan, Reynolds & Stellar (1989). Like Miller, Berrios & Politynska (1987), they found no association between memory and the dosage of a levodopa-based drug [Sinemet (co-careldopa)]. It is interesting that they did find a consistent negative correlation between various measures of memory and the degree of bradykinesia. As slowing of movement increased, so memory performance deteriorated.

In the case of Huntington's chorea, Wilson's disease and progressive supranuclear palsy, the question of apparent memory defects being artefacts consequent on some other factor has not been raised. Certainly as far as Huntington's chorea is concerned, the nature and size of the memory impairments reported make it unlikely that these are mere artefacts. It therefore seems appropriate to assume that memory impairments do occur in the conditions associated with subcortical dementia.

As far as the nature of the impairment is concerned, the common assertion summarised in Table 5.1 is that recall is affected but that recognition is either left intact or is relatively well preserved. Some evidence exists indicating relatively good recognition performance in Parkinson's disease. Flowers, Pearce & Pearce (1984) employed four different recognition tests based on different types of stimuli and found normal recognition in a Parkinsonian group. However, a somewhat similar experiment by Moss et al. (1986) showed some impairments in recognition memory in patients with Huntington's chorea. Papers by Sagar and his colleagues (Sagar et al., 1985, 1988; Sullivan & Sagar, 1989) as well as work by Helkala et al. (1988) have also shown either no recognition impairment or relatively better recognition performance in Parkinsonian subjects than subjects with Alzheimer's disease.

A number of studies have revealed evidence of poor recall in Parkinson's disease (e.g. Della Salla et al., 1986; Pirozzolo et al., 1982; Sagar et al., 1988). Unfortunately, as Flowers, Pearce & Pearce (1984) have pointed out, these are open to other interpretations. For example, poor motivation could result in poor recall in the absence of a true memory loss.

The general picture, despite some exceptions and qualifications, could be regarded as consistent with the notion of impaired recall in the presence of normal or near normal recognition, as far as Parkinson's disease is concerned. There is also a methodological problem that has to be taken into account in making any judgement about the significance of this evidence. It is well established in memory research with normal populations that recall testing gives a lower estimate of the amount of material remembered than recognition testing. It could therefore be that recall is a more sensitive measure of any form of memory decline. Should this be the case, it is not surprising if the relatively mild memory impairments in Parkinson's disease tend to be more readily manifest on recall rather than recognition testing.

Other forms of subcortical dementia tend to have more clear-cut memory impairments. Of these, Huntington's chorea has been the most extensively studied and will be singled out for special comment. Here also there is some evidence of relative sparing of recognition memory (e.g. Butters *et al.*, 1985), but there are also some suggestions of impairments in this aspect of memory (Moss *et al.*, 1986). Clear evidence of memory loss has come from other forms of testing (e.g. Caine, Ebert & Weingartner, 1977; Weingartner, Caine & Ebert, 1979). It is still possible that this pattern of relatively well-preserved recognition memory may also arise simply because recall testing is more sensitive to impairment. However, this explanation is less plausible than is the case with Parkinson's disease simply because the overall level of memory loss is generally much greater in Huntington's chorea than in Parkinson's disease.

Frontal impairments

The anatomical links which exist between the frontal lobes and basal ganglia add credence to the notion that impairments characteristic of those encountered in patients with frontal lesions may be found in Parkinson's disease and other manifestations of subcortical dementia. There are also a number of reports of investigations that offer some confirmation of such a view.

Lees & Smith (1983) employed a number of 'frontal tests'. These included the Wisconsin Card Sorting Test and a test of verbal fluency. The former requires subjects to switch between alternative responses in a situation in which the task can be carried out in more than one way. Patients with frontal lesions generally find it difficult to switch from one established pattern of responding to another. Patients with frontal lesions also do badly in verbal fluency tests that require them to produce as many words as they can belonging to a given category (in this case words beginning with certain letters) within a set time period. Subjects with Parkinson's disease gave some indication of more frontal types of performance on these tests, but the effects were weak. For example, using two alternative ways of scoring the Wisconsin Card Sorting Test, the frontal-type picture was present with one method of scoring but did not appear when employing the other.

Pillon *et al.* (1989) also employed the Wisconsin Card Sorting Test and showed that performance on this test was inversely correlated with severity of illness in Parkinson's disease, particularly as determined by motor rigidity. Again, this result is consistent with the idea that frontal-type impairments develop in Parkinson's disease.

A rather more elegant investigation of possible frontal impairments in Parkinson's disease has been reported by Flowers & Robertson (1985). Sets of 16 cards were used, each card containing three symbols. On each trial (a run through the 16 cards), subjects had to indicate which of the three symbols was the odd one out. The odd one out could be determined by one of two rules. On successive runs through the 16 cards, subjects had to alternate between the two rules. The results indicated that Parkinsonian subjects were less efficient in switching appropriately between the two rules, although they were not at all impaired in identifying the rules in the first place. This is reminiscent of the kinds of difficulty associated with frontal lesions.

A further interesting investigation has been reported by Piccirilli *et al.* (1989). They applied a number of frontal tests described by Luria (1966) to Parkinsonian subjects who allegedly exhibited no signs of intellectual impairment. This group was then split according to whether the tests revealed any indication of frontal impairment. At follow-up 4 years later, it was those subjects who showed frontal dysfunctions in the original assessment who also had the greatest evidence of more generalised intellectual impairment. The implication of this finding is that frontal impairments may be an early manifestation of dementia in this group.

However, it should be noted that not all studies which have attempted to detect frontal impairments in Parkinson's disease have been successful. Miller (1985) used a word-fluency test well established as being sensitive to the deleterious effects of frontal injury (see Miller, 1984a; Milner, 1964), and found no evidence of poor performance in a sample with Parkinson's disease. Despite this, the balance of evidence points towards the occurrence of impairments of the kind associated with frontal lobe lesions in subjects with Parkinson's disease.

Attempts to demonstrate frontal impairments in other conditions associated with subcortical dementia have been few. Maher, Smith & Lees (1985) claimed to find some evidence of frontal impairments in patients with progressive supranuclear palsy. Again, studying subjects with progressive supranuclear palsy, Grafman *et al.* (1990) found impairments in some tests linked to frontal functions, such as verbal fluency. This finding is difficult to interpret since their experimental group also performed worse than the controls on other cognitive tests. It may be that the poor performance on frontal tests was merely a manifestation of a much more general intellectual decline. As far as Huntington's chorea is concerned, Butters *et al.* (1978) reported the occurrence of deficits in verbal fluency in this condition.

Summarising all this evidence is difficult. There are some grounds for assuming that impairments of a frontal type do occur in most of the conditions linked to subcortical dementia. With a few exceptions most investigations give findings in support of this notion, but what is not as clear is whether frontal features are a particularly prominent feature of alleged subcortical dementia as opposed to being merely a manifestation of a much more general deterioration.

Other functions

As can be seen from Table 5.1 a number of other alleged characteristics of subcortical dementia remain to be discussed. These can be dealt with rather more expeditiously.

One central claim is that language remains unaffected in the subcortical dementias as opposed to the association of 'aphasia' with cortical dementia. Cortical dementias certainly do produce language impairments (discussed in Chapter 3), although whether they actually constitute aphasia of the type associated with focal lesions is more debatable.

Language has not as yet been well studied in relation to the subcortical dementias. The general clinical impression is that disorders like Parkinson's disease and Wilson's disease are often accompanied, and especially in the more advanced stages, by difficulties in articulation (dysarthria). The underlying language processes can appear to be relatively intact. Since detailed investigations have not been carried out, it would be premature to claim with any confidence that language impairments do not occur in the conditions associated with subcortical dementia. All that can be asserted is that, at least in the earlier stages, language impairments, if they do exist, appear to be relatively minor.

Another aspect of cognitive functioning that has been explored is spatial ability. There are a substantial number of reports claiming to demonstrate spatial impairments in Parkinson's disease (e.g. Boller et al., 1984; Della Salla et al., 1986; Levin et al., 1991). Similarly there have been reports of spatial impairments in Huntington's chorea (e.g. Brouwers et al., 1984; Potegal, 1971).

Some investigators have suggested that apparent spatial impairments may be secondary to some other factor. Stelmach, Phillips & Chau (1989) suggested that motor impairments might be at least partly responsible for poor performance on some spatial tests. This suggestion has some plausibility, since many tests of spatial functioning do require a motor response. On the other hand, at least two investigations have shown poor spatial performance in Parkinson's disease when using an untimed line orientation task that just requires the subject to express judgements about the angles at which lines are orientated (Boller et al., 1984; Goldenberg et al., 1986). It is difficult to see how motor impairments like the tremor, rigidity or bradykinesia in Parkinson's disease could have any appreciable effect on such a test.

Brown & Marsden (1986) have put forward an alternative explanation. They suggested that many of the tasks used in the study of visuospatial impairment in Parkinson's disease had possibly confounded two things. One was the need to make a spatial discrimination (e.g. a left–right judgement) and the other was a need for the subject to switch perspective from which such judgements were made from trial to trial. They carried out an experiment indicating that left–right discrimination per se was normal, whilst the switching of perspective could cause difficulties. The inability to change perspective with normal facility was lost and this could be related to frontal impairments rather than being regarded as purely spatial.

Two things go against Brown's & Marsden's analysis. The first is that the line orientation tasks used in the work mentioned above by Boller *et al.* (1984) and Goldenberg *et al.* (1986) do not require subjects to continually shift the perspective from which the spatial judgement is made. Yet spatial impairments were still found. Secondly, right–left judgements are a very simple form of spatial task, and the making of such judgements may not have been sensitive enough an index of any impairment to show any change in the Parkinsonian group. However, this leads to another relevant point raised by Brown & Marsden (1986), which is that spatial function is probably not a unitary entity (e.g. De Renzi, 1980). Attempts to specify spatial impairments in subcortical dementia need to be more careful in distinguishing between different types of spatial performance.

Motor symptoms are a prominent feature of conditions associated with subcortical dementia. These include the tremor, rigidity and bradykinesia of Parkinson's disease and the characteristic choreiform movements of Huntington's chorea. Motor disturbances also appear in Wilson's disease and progressive supranuclear palsy. In passing, it can be noted that these motor impairments are not always limited to the actual mechanics of executing movements. Even in Alzheimer-type dementia, mild Parkinsonian features have also been described (Pearce, 1984) There is evidence, at least in the case of Parkinson's disease, that the planning and preparation of movements might also be affected (e.g. Flowers, 1976).

Comment

As the above discussion has shown, there is a considerable amount of evidence to suggest that the conditions associated with subcortical dementia do exhibit many of the features described in Table 5.1. This is not to deny that there are some detailed findings which fail to match the claimed picture, of which possibly the most notable example is the failure so far to demonstrate clear evidence to support the notion of bradyphrenia. Apart from this, the balance of evidence so far runs generally in favour of the picture of subcortical dementia that has been put forward by those who have espoused the notion of subcortical dementia as a separate, identifiable form of dementia.

COMPARISON OF DIFFERENT FORMS

The questions relating to subcortical dementia go beyond the description offered in Table 5.1. Advocates of the concept of subcortical dementia want to claim that it has an independent existence and stands on its own as a separate and distinct form of dementia. For this to be the case, it is also necessary to show that the different conditions that allegedly exhibit subcortical dementia are generally alike in their psychological manifestations, and that any differences between these conditions are small in comparison with the differences between any one of them of the manifestations of cortical dementia as found in Alzheimer-type dementia.

Although the previous section concluded that, with some definite qualifications, the alleged features of subcortical dementia could be identified in people suffering from the relevant disorders, it is not at all clear that these disorders all exhibit the same features in the same way. For the most part, the work already considered has been dominated by the investigations of a single disorder, Parkinson's disease, with Huntington's chorea and progressive supranuclear palsy being less well represented. Very little work has been published on the psychological aspects of Wilson's disease.

It is logically elegant to look at similarities and differences within the conditions linked to subcortical dementia before going on to deal with the comparison between these things and cortical dementia. This approach will be followed in general, but there are difficulties. These exist because of the way that the work has developed, with Alzheimer's disease being the most commonly used reference group in any comparative studies. There is therefore very little work that has explored similarities and differences solely within the various manifestations of subcortical dementia.

Before discussing the actual findings, a major methodological issue needs to be mentioned. This essentially relates to the fact that groups with Parkinson's disease, Alzheimer-type dementia, Huntington's chorea, etc., generally differ in ways other than the nature of the disease process involved. The typical age of onset in Huntington's chorea is lower than that of Parkinson's disease and Alzheimer-type dementia. That of Wilson's disease is even lower still, with its presence often being recognised in childhood. Nevertheless, considerable overlaps can be found in the age ranges associated with the different conditions and so groups matched for age can be obtained, although this may be at the expense of letting length of illness vary. Even if age and length of illness can both be matched, say in comparisons of groups with Alzheimer's and Parkinson's diseases, then a third variable may exert a differential effect. Although empirical evidence is generally lacking on this point, the strong clinical impression is that the rate of intellectual deterioration is not the same in all groups. Patients with Huntington's chorea appear to deteriorate faster than those with Parkinson's disease, for example. Making comparisons between the different conditions and controlling all these factors is likely to prove impossible. Longitudinal studies, if they existed in sufficient number, might be useful in helping to disentangle these variables but are unlikely to be wholly successful in doing this.

Possibly most important in comparisons is the need to match for overall degree of dementia. For example, the degree of dementia in Parkinson's disease is often quite small when compared to that in Alzheimer's disease. Any finding of an apparent differential pattern of impairment in these two conditions, as would be expected from Table 5.1, need not necessarily mean that they really do develop different types of dementia. It could be that the picture offered for subcortical dementia is, to some extent at least, merely that of an earlier stage in a common dementing process. The same process when further advanced might then result in the picture allegedly associated with cortical dementia.

The problem of matching for overall severity of dementia also arises within the conditions associated with subcortical dementia. Clinical impression suggests that the dementia encountered in Huntington's chorea can be more marked than that usually encountered in Parkinson's disease. In practice, the fact that groups of subjects representing the various conditions are likely to vary on a number of potentially relevant dimensions, e.g. age of onset, severity and rate of progression of dementia and length of illness, means that it is likely to be impossible to find groups matched for all the potentially confounding variables. Matching on one variable may inevitably push the others out of alignment.

Better evidence of real differences between groups may well come from demonstrating double dissociations. This is by showing that one group performs well on measure A but poorly on measure B, whilst another group has the reverse pattern of performance. Such dissociations are rather more difficult to explain in terms of the effects of confounding variables such as different degrees of dementia. Nevertheless, it still has to be recognised that, whilst double dissociations can offer a powerful methodology under some circumstances, they do have limitations (e.g. Dunn & Kirstner, 1988; Miller, 1993; Weiskrantz, 1968) and need not always imply that qualitative differences between the groups do exist.

This brief discussion of methodology by no means exhausts the issues involved in comparing the various relevant pathological conditions. It goes far enough to indicate that such comparisons are no simple matter and that the results of studies that compare a group with one or more other groups necessarily need to be interpreted with caution.

The evidence

Only a very small number of investigations have concentrated on comparisons within the conditions associated with subcortical dementia and without involving Alzheimer's disease as well. The experiment of Dubois et al. (1988), based on the use of reaction times of increasing complexity, has already been mentioned in discussing evidence relating to the concept of bradyphrenia (p. 73). It will be recalled that it was only subjects with progressive supranuclear palsy and not those with Parkinson's disease who showed evidence of relatively increased central processing times with choice as opposed to simple reaction times.

Massman et al. (1990) looked at both Parkinson's disease and

Huntington's chorea in relation to various measures of verbal learning and memory. The two groups were similar on some measures, but the group with Huntington's chorea differed from that with Parkinson's disease on others, including exhibition of poorer free recall and less improvement across learning trials.

Multiple sclerosis has also been considered by some authorities to produce a subcortical dementia, and Caine et al. (1986) compared subjects with both Huntington's chorea and multiple sclerosis, as well as controls, on a large battery of neuropsychological tests. The two patient groups showed some similarities, but those with Huntington's chorea had greater deficits in verbal and non-verbal memory.

Especially in the light of the methodological difficulties mentioned above, these investigations are not very convincing. They point to the conclusion that the different conditions studied do have some similarities but also some differences. It is difficult to say whether better matching of the groups on potentially contaminating variables, like degree of dementia, would have tended to eliminate or to exacerbate the differences. All that can be concluded is that, whilst a common pattern of subcortical dementia cannot be excluded, it is far from being proven.

There is a much larger range of work in which the various conditions linked to subcortical dementia have been compared either singly or severally with the archetypical cortical dementia (Alzheimer's disease). It is this work that will now become the focus of attention, and it is easiest to describe the studies in terms of the nature of the dependent variables that have been employed.

Some investigators have relied on scales or batteries of tests that might purport to offer a wide coverage of different aspects of cognitive functioning. Huber and his colleagues (Huber et al., 1986; Huber, Shuttleworth & Freidenberg, 1989) used Parkinsonian and Alzheimer groups. In the first of these a battery of different neuropsychological tests was administered, with the Parkinsonian group performing worse than normal control subjects on some measures and the Alzheimer group worse on all. The Alzheimer group was also consistently worse than the group with Parkinson's disease. Huber et al. (1986) regard the results as confirming the distinction between cortical and subcortical dementia, but an alternative explanation is that the differences merely reflect the greater degree of dementia in the Alzheimer group. The authors appeal to the pattern of impairments as confirming the distinction, but this is debatable. For example, the Parkinsonian group should, in theory, be impaired on frontal tests. On the one test used which is known to be sensitive to frontal impairments, verbal fluency, it was only the Alzheimer group that showed a significant impairment as compared to the normal control group.

In the second of these papers, Huber, Shuttleworth & Freidenberg (1989) present results of similar groups of Parkinsonian and Alzheimer subjects matched for overall level of dementia on the Mini-Mental State Examination (Folstein, Folstein & McHugh, 1975). Here the Parkinsonian group did worse than the Alzheimer group on verbal fluency. The differential pattern of impairments in the two patient groups matched more closely the subcortical/cortical dementia distinction than in the earlier report, but again there was a potential mismatch. Just why the Parkinsonian group should do worse than those with Alzheimer's disease on Raven's Progressive Matrices, regarded by Huber, Shuttleworth & Freidenberg (1989) as a test of visuospatial ability, is not clear. Disturbed visuospatial ability is more linked to cortical impairments. Again, with this exception disregarded, the general pattern is one of poorer performance in the Alzheimer group.

The Mini-Mental State Examination was also used by Mayeux (1983) in comparing Parkinson's disease and Huntington's chorea with Alzheimer's disease. The authors matched subjects for the three groups for overall severity on this scale and then looked at different patterns of performance. They could find no real evidence of the distinguishable patterns of performance that might be expected on the basis of the distinction between cortical and subcortical dementia.

Salmon et al. (1989) compared cases of Huntington's chorea and Alzheimer's disease on a dementia rating scale with a number of subtests. The Alzheimer group were more impaired on the memory subtest whilst the Huntington group did worse on the 'initiation subtest', which included such things as fluency, alternating movements and copying figures. The Huntington's chorea group could have performed less well on this subtest simply because of their associated movement disorder rather than any differential pattern of cognitive performance.

The final instance of an investigation based on a battery of tests has been provided by Pillon *et al.* (1991). They used four patient groups, consisting of subjects with Parkinson's disease, Huntington's chorea and progressive supranuclear palsy as well as Alzheimer's disease. After matching for level of intellectual impairment they concluded that Alzheimer's disease was characterised by remote memory and linguistic disorders, progressive supranuclear palsy by frontal lobe abnormalities and Huntington's chorea by concentration and acquisition deficits. They found no consistent pattern in Parkinson's disease. This study is of particular interest because it used several different patient groups and also endeavoured to match for overall level of dementia. On the balance of the evidence as provided by this particular investigation, the authors' conclusion that subcortical dementia is not a homogeneous entity appears fully justified. In addition, the three alleged examples of subcortical dementia appeared to have little or nothing more in common with one another than each had separately with the Alzheimer group.

Investigations like those described immediately above, in which a range of measures sampling different aspects of cognitive functioning have been employed, are the most interesting for present purposes. Most other potentially relevant work has been confined to examining different aspects of memory and mainly involves comparisons between groups with Parkinson's and Alzheimer's diseases. Because they contribute less critical evidence to the question of different types of dementia, these studies can be covered briefly and much more selectively.

Helkala *et al.* (1989) gave a variety of memory tests, dealing with both episodic and semantic memory, to groups of subjects with both Parkinson's and Alzheimer's diseases as well as to control subjects. They concluded that Alzheimer subjects appeared to perform badly because of an inability to inhibit irrelevant information and increased sensitivity to interference. In Parkinson's disease, poor memory allegedly reflected undue sensitivity to pro-active interference. In a rather similar and slightly more extensive report by Litvan *et al.* (1991), it was claimed that patients with Alzheimer's disease did worse on tests of memory, whilst those with

Parkinson's disease matched for degree of dementia were more impaired on so-called executive functions.

Both Sagar (1984) and Sahakian *et al.* (1988) have reported an interesting difference between the same two disorders. Using tasks requiring the matching or recognition after a delay of previously presented visual stimuli, both experiments found that retention declined fairly uniformly with delay interval in Alzheimer's disease. In Parkinson's disease, matching or recognition of the correct stimulus was actually worse after very short delays (of the order of 0–3 seconds) than it was after longer delays.

Potentially related to this work is a paper by Moss *et al.* (1986). They found that groups of subjects with Huntington's chorea and Alzheimer's disease were equally impaired in recall of words over a short delay (15 seconds). Over a longer delay (120 seconds) the Huntington group did much better than the Alzheimer and, unlike the latter, showed no decline in performance between 15 and 120 seconds. Further confirmation of differential delay effects in Parkinson's disease comes from Sullivan & Sagar (1989).

Yet another difference in memory-related performance between the same two conditions has been reported by Sagar *et al.* (1988). Subjects were examined for remote memory of public and personal events, both in terms of the content of these events and their dates. In both Parkinson's and Alzheimer's diseases retention of the content of remote events exhibited a gradient, with more remote events being better recalled. The degree of retrograde amnesia as assessed in this way was related to the severity of dementia. Compared to those with Alzheimer's disease, the Parkinsonian group was particularly impaired when it came to dating events, and the difficulty in dating was unrelated to the overall level of dementia, thus implying that dating capacity may be selectively impaired in Parkinson's disease, independently of any dementing process.

THE STATUS OF SUBCORTICAL DEMENTIA

What can be concluded about the status of the concept of subcortical dementia? Throughout this chapter a number of methodological problems have been identified. These will not be rehearsed again. What needs to be emphasised is that the research reported has almost invariably not dealt with the methodological issues satisfactorily. It is therefore difficult to draw conclusions with any certainty. The following comments are therefore tentative and made under the assumption that the methodological inadequacies of the work have not introduced any serious systematic bias.

What does seem to be the case is that the various conditions with marked subcortical pathology, such as Parkinson's disease and Huntington's chorea, do appear to exhibit intellectual impairments. These show some similarity to those claimed for subcortical dementia and summarised in Table 5.1. Nevertheless, it has to be noted that the match with the features listed in Table 5.1 is far from perfect. For example, evidence indicating the existence of bradyphrenia is far from wholly convincing. It is also the case that the majority of the available evidence relates to Parkinson's disease and that there has been little exploration of progressive supranuclear palsy and Wilson's disease. Whether all the conditions associated with subcortical dementia will match the picture given in Table 5.1 to the same degree as Parkinson's disease remains to be seen.

Studies that have compared different types of disorder have not so far managed to provide good evidence that there is marked consistency in the psychological changes produced by the different subcortical dementias. The evidence actually suggests that there might be significant differences between the various conditions linked with subcortical dementia. Similarly, it is far from being established that the different forms of subcortical dementia have more in common with one another than they do with Alzheimer-type dementia, which is usually taken as the archetypical 'cortical dementia'.

These views are very similar to those put forward by Brown (1991) in his evaluation of evidence relating to the comparative neuropsychology of dementia. Pillon et al. (1991) go slightly further than this in stating that subcortical dementia 'rather than being a homogeneous entity, should be subdivided into specific subtypes of cognitive impairment related to different underlying specific lesions of each disease'. The evidence that subcortical dementia is a homogeneous entity is certainly weak: that indicating that it is not a homogeneous entity is more compelling but still falls short of inducing complete conviction. Nevertheless, Pillon *et al.* (1991) could eventually turn out to be right, although the considerable methodological problems encountered in investigating this area mean that clear answers to the questions will remain extremely difficult to obtain.

CHAPTER 6   Assessment of dementia

The assessment of the person with a dementing illness or suspected dementia is an important practical issue arising in clinical
work. Within clinical psychology it was assessment that was originally the basis of professional practice. With the advent of more
extensive forms of psychological treatment, such as the behaviour
therapies, assessment tended to drop out of fashion with clinical
psychologists sometimes having been all too ready to abandon
assessment altogether. This was often on the grounds that assessment is unreliable and meaningless. The one area of clinical psychology where assessment issues have continued to attract substantial interest has been clinical neuropsychology, and
neuropsychological assessment procedures (see Lezak, 1983) have
considerable relevance in the examination of patients with possible dementing illnesses.

In fact, it is foolish to try to ignore assessment as a legitimate part
of clinical practice. This is simply because any decisions about
patients, such as what kinds of intervention to use, if any, and
determining whether the intervention has been useful, depend
upon some form of assessment. This is so whether that assessment
is based on traditional psychometric instruments or on other techniques, such as just interviewing clients about the nature of their
problems. The realisation that this is the case has led to a minor
resurgence in issues surrounding assessment, of which the book
by Peck & Shapiro (1990) is a recent example.

The essential point is not, therefore, whether assessment is an
important part of clinical practice, since it most certainly is. The
key issues in assessment evolve around questions such as what
kind of assessment, in what context, and with a view to achieving

what objectives. In terms of the assessment of the older person with a suspected dementing illness, a number of assessment goals can be identified:

1. The diagnosis or identification of people with dementing illnesses and discriminating between the different types of dementing illness.

2. The measurement of change.

3. The analysis of levels of functioning in order to better make decisions about management or disposal.

The diagnosis or identification of dementing illnesses can be difficult in the early stages. Diagnosis is important because whether an inadequately functioning individual is established as suffering from, say, an Alzheimer-like dementia as opposed to being depressed has considerable implications for treatment and prognosis. The measurement of change can be useful in determining rate of progression of the disorder as well as for determining the effectiveness of possible interventions, like reality orientation or the use of drugs alleged to enhance memory. Finally, if psychological interventions can be devised which are able to ameliorate some aspects of impaired functioning, then it is important to be able to analyse the present levels of functioning in order to target interventions appropriately. The bulk of the following discussion will consider the ways in which these different questions can be answered.

Before going further it is important to note that there is a considerable literature relevant to the subject matter of this chapter. The account given here cannot possibly describe all the possible instruments that might be used and their various advantages and disadvantages. Even if useful information could be given about a selection of the most useful or commonly used instruments, this would rapidly become outdated in the continuing flow of published work. This chapter will therefore take the rather different approach of describing the principles lying behind the assessment of the patient with possible dementia. Particular instruments will then be referred to as examples of their kind rather than as being anything like a comprehensive description of the range of instruments that the practising clinical psychologist might well be familiar with if working in this area. Reference to a wider range of techniques can be found in other sources dealing with the assessment of the elderly in general, or those with dementia in particular, as well as in other references dealing with more generalised aspects of assessment (e.g. Crawford, Parker & McKinlay, 1992; Gilleard & Christie, 1990; Kaszniak, 1990; Lezak, 1983; Miller, 1980; Morris & McKiernan, 1993).

GENERAL POINTS

There are a number of general points concerning the assessment of those with suspected dementia which are best considered first. For the most part, these relate to the fact that the individuals concerned are often elderly, since dementia is mainly an affliction of old age, and may have other handicaps. These things need to be taken into account in any assessment (see Miller, 1980; Morris & McKiernan, 1993).

Psychometric tests with good norms applicable to elderly populations are difficult to find. For example, the most recent version of the most commonly used intelligence test, the Wechsler Adult Intelligence Scale—Revised (WAIS—R), does not have norms which extend beyond the age of 74 years. This is by no means exceptional, and very few instruments have well-derived norms for elderly populations.

Secondly, older groups tend to have sensory handicaps and these can affect performance (e.g. O'Neill & Calhoun, 1975). Vision may be poor and hearing impaired. It is important at the outset to establish that sensory functioning, with appropriate correction with glasses or hearing aids, is adequate for the purposes of the assessment being carried out. Those whose memory is poor may not remember to bring their glasses with them. And when they do, it can be misleading to assume that these will be satisfactory, because some older people have experienced considerable change since their most recent glasses were prescribed. Various means exist to mitigate the effects of sensory impairment. For example, ensuring that where the subject has to read written stimuli the print is large and clear, and by trying to assess subjects with hearing loss in a room that has a minimum of distracting background noise.

Certain other health-related problems can also have an adverse effect on mental functioning. These include such things as cardiovascular disease, and it is a common observation that old people tend to be put on multiple drugs and can also therefore suffer from the toxic effects of overmedication (e.g. Abrahams & Birren, 1973; Hale *et al.*, 1992).

The very fact that those with dementia will have cognitive decline means that they may not be able to cope with the more intellectually demanding tests and are likely to have difficulty in following instructions. Particular attention needs to be given to giving instructions clearly and slowly, checking to ensure that the subject has fully understood. As intellectual decline progresses, the emphasis has to shift from such things as intelligence tests and tests of verbal memory to forms of assessment based upon ratings by carers and nurses and behavioural observations.

Finally, older people can be slower and may tire easily. They may also be upset and unwilling to continue the examination further if they experience obvious failure. This means that assessment sessions have to be taken more slowly and sometimes with frequent breaks. The judicious selection of instruments can often avoid the situation where the subject experiences repeated failure because the level of difficulty is too high. It is also possible to balance the order of administration of instruments so that the more difficult tests do not immediately follow one another. Similarly, if it is clinically useful to use a test that may prove difficult to the subject to such a degree that a refusal to continue testing may result, then this can be left until last so that the refusal does not prevent other information from being obtained. Careful explanation as to why the assessment is being carried out and, where possible, reassurance about the level of performance may help to avoid test refusal.

DIAGNOSTIC ASSESSMENT

Even the problem of determining whether an individual has a dementing illness is not as simple as it might seem. There is the problem of differentiating between those with generalised organic disease of the brain of the kind associated with dementing illnesses and both normal individuals of similar age and those with functional psychiatric disorders, such as depression. Depression is important in this context because not only is it frequently encountered amongst those in the older age ranges especially prone to dementia, but it can sometimes produce a clinical picture that is similar to dementia. Having determined that an individual has some form of dementing illness, there then arises the question as to its exact nature. For example, is it an Alzheimer type of process or a cerebrovascular form of dementia?

In terms of detecting evidence of some sort of widespread pathology of the brain, as occurs in dementia, a number of types of instrument have been found to have some value. In practice, the administration of tests of intelligence (like the WAIS—R) is not, by itself, of much value in this context, although it may be in combination with other instruments (see discussion of measurement of change, below). The reason for this is that measures of IQ tend to be relatively stable and therefore insensitive to small changes (see pp. 54–55 for a more extended discussion of this point). It is of course in the earliest stages of dementia that the diagnostic question is most acute. By the time that measured IQ, considered on its own, has clearly declined the patient is often readily identifiable as suffering from dementia as judged by other criteria.

A range of other instruments have been used and have some validity in this context. Amongst the methods most commonly used, especially by psychiatrists and geriatricians, are the various medically designed assessment scales. These include the dementia scale of Blessed, Tomlinson & Roth (1968), the Mini-Mental State Examination (MMSE) of Folstein, Folstein & McHugh (1975) and a number of similar instruments. These are quick and easy to administer and have some validity (e.g. Teng et al., 1987), although classification on the basis of their use is far from perfect. Quite a large literature exists on these scales, and the key items that appear to discriminate patients with dementia are those relating to memory and orientation (Orrell et al., 1992).

A number of more elaborate systems have been devised by psychiatrists including CAMDEX (Roth et al., 1986) and AGECAT

(Copeland, Dewey & Griffith-Jones, 1986). These may enhance validity, as compared with something like the MMSE, but at the expense of taking much longer to administer. They are probably best considered more as research instruments. In addition, American workers have developed detailed clinical criteria (e.g. McKhann *et al.*, 1984) and these are discussed in greater detail by Boller & Saxton (1990). There is now some evidence that carefully used clinical criteria can, in at least some settings, achieve useful levels of validity in the identification of dementia as determined by follow-up examination of cases 1 year later (Forette *et al.*, 1989).

The fact that memory declines in dementia offers the possibility of using tests of memory to detect those with dementing illnesses. A number of memory tests exist (see Gilleard & Christie, 1990; Lezak, 1983), all of them far from ideal and most implicitly based on outdated models of memory. Many show some discriminatory power in distinguishing subjects with dementia. Examples of tests in common use are the Wechsler Memory Scale—Revised (Wechsler, 1987), the Benton Visual Retention Test (Benton, 1963), the Rey Auditory–Verbal learning Test (see Lezak, 1983; Rosenberg, Ryan & Prifitera, 1984) and the Inglis Paired Associate Learning Test (Inglis, 1959). Many memory tests show appreciable ability to distinguish those with dementia from control subjects (e.g. Grober *et al.*, 1988; Miller, 1980; Zec, 1990).

Some memory tests, or instruments in which the testing of memory plays a major part, have been specifically designed for the diagnosis of dementia. A prominent example is the Kendrick Battery which is based both on a form of memory test (the Object Learning Test) coupled with a simple test of psychomotor speed. This battery showed quite impressive levels of validity in the diagnosis of dementia in more elderly samples in its initial validation (Kendrick, Gibson & Moyes, 1979), although later work has not yielded such outstanding results (Gibson, Moyes & Kendrick, 1980).

Memory is by no means the only psychological function that declines in dementia. As has been indicated elsewhere in this volume (see Chapters 2 and 3), such things as language and spatial ability decline. Tests of such functions, like naming tests (Stevens *et al.*, 1992), verbal fluency tests (Hart *et al.*, 1988b; Miller, 1984a) or the Benton Spatial Relations Test (Benton, Varney & Hamsher,

1978; Ska, Poissant & Joanette, 1990) may therefore make a contribution to diagnostic assessment. In fact the implication in the term 'cortical dementia' is that a whole range of functions that might be affected by cortical lesions can also suffer in Alzheimer type dementia.

One complication that arises in the diagnosis of dementia is the discrimination of those with dementia from people with depression, especially since depression can be associated both with complaints of memory loss and actual poor performance on formal testing of memory (Bolla *et al.*, 1991; Feehan, Knight & Partridge, 1991). For this reason, Kendrick, Gibson & Moyes (1979) standardised their diagnostic battery in terms of distinguishing dementia from depression. A significant feature of both the Bolla *et al.* (1991) and Feehan, Knight & Partridge (1991) studies was the demonstration that subjective memory complaint was found to be quite strongly linked to depression rather than dementia. In fact, the sample by Feehan *et al.* of elderly patients with dementia rated themselves as experiencing less in the way of cognitive failure than either those with depression or controls, and it was the depressed group who regarded themselves as the most cognitively impaired! In terms of objective test performance, it was of course those with dementia who did least well. Whilst people who present to clinics with a subjective memory complaint are much more likely to turn out to be depressed or to have some functional disorder other than a dementing illness, the prevalence of dementia in such patients may well be a little higher than it is in a comparable population of non-complainers (O'Brien *et al.*, 1992). In other words, subjective complaint of memory loss certainly does not rule out the presence of a dementing illness even though it is more commonly indicative of some other type of problem.

In passing, it should be noted that the discrimination between dementia and depression is further complicated by the fact that these are not mutually exclusive diagnoses. People can be encountered who are depressed as well as having a dementing illness, especially amongst those in the earlier stages of dementia (Teri & Wagner, 1992; Wragg & Jeste, 1989).

If there is evidence of some form of dementing illness, the question arises as to its nature. The two major groups of dementing illnesses for which there has been some systematic attempt to develop psychological methods of discrimination are those as a result of degenerative changes of the kind seen in Alzheimer's disease as opposed to those associated with cerebrovascular disease. In general, Alzheimer type dementia (AD) is slowly progressive, whereas cerebrovascular dementia is associated with a step-like progression whereby there is a series of small vascular episodes each one producing a small, sudden decrement in psychological performance.

From a psychological point of view, the pattern of impairment might be expected to be more even in AD, whereas more prominent focal features might be expected in cerebrovascular dementia, depending upon which parts of the brain had suffered vascular episodes. Unfortunately, this is not a very good guide in practice, partly because Alzheimer type dementias can have a predilection to affect certain parts of the brain first (see Neary et al., 1986; 1988).

Some reports have shown a degree of discriminative power in psychological measures in distinguishing between these types of dementia (e.g. Mendez & Ashla-Mendez, 1991; Perez et al., 1975a,b). Whilst differences may well exist, they are typically not good enough for reliable diagnostic use with a single case.

The question of the assessment of subcortical dementia also arises. This has been discussed in detail by Huber & Shuttleworth (1990). The question of diagnostic assessment by psychological means in relation to the subcortical dementias is not so critical as with the alleged cortical dementias. This is because other manifestations of the disease process give good clues as to diagnosis, for example, the different forms of extrapyramidal motor disorders encountered in Parkinson's disease and Huntington's chorea, the characteristic eye movements in progressive supranuclear palsy, the family history in Huntington's chorea, and so on. This is probably fortunate because the usually less severe manifestations of subcortical dementia make their reliable detection that more difficult, especially in the early stages when diagnostic questions are more relevant. Attempts to distinguish forms of subcortical dementia, such as Huntington's chorea, from AD run into the same problems as those involved in distinguishing the latter from cerebrovascular dementia (e.g. Salmon et al., 1989).

A number of methodological problems arise in relation to the use of diagnostic tests (see also Miller, 1980; Mitrushina & Fuld, 1990). In establishing the diagnostic validity of tests investigators, not surprisingly, prefer to use samples of subjects for whom the diagnosis is clear. In the case of subjects with dementia, this often means cases whose condition has progressed to some degree. Comparing such subjects with controls, whether normal controls or patients with other disorders like depression, is likely to overestimate the discriminative power of the test in comparison with its use for cases whose dementing illness is in an earlier stage of development and for whom the diagnosis is much less certain. It is with this latter category of cases that any diagnostic test will be of greatest use. One possible way round this problem is to validate further tests by applying them to a sample of subjects at the time of referral for the particular type of diagnostic assessment involved and then follow up the sample for some time to a point at which the diagnosis has become clear. The test can then be validated against later diagnostic status. Unfortunately this strategy has rarely, if ever, been followed.

Mitrushina & Fuld (1990) make a related point. The tests that are most sensitive to dementia in the earliest stages are not necessarily the same as those giving the best discrimination later in the course of the illness. Developing tests suitable for the identification of dementia by using clearly established cases of dementia will emphasise the use of the latter type of test rather than the former.

Another issue concerns base rates (Meehl & Rosen, 1955). This problem has been described in greater detail elsewhere (e.g. Miller, 1980). The base rate (or antecedent probability) is the frequency with which the particular diagnosis of concern arises in the sample with which the test is to be used. If patients referred for assessment are likely to have either dementia or depression, each with 50% probability, then a test which is 90% accurate can make a useful contribution to diagnosis. If, however, 90% turn out to be depressed and only 10% are true cases of dementia, then a 90% diagnostic accuracy can be achieved just by guessing that each individual has depression. Furthermore, the implications of the test indicating depression will not be the same as indicating dementia since, in the latter case, there would be a high risk of the individual labelled 'dementia' by the test being a true case of depression.

Base rates are therefore something that have to be taken into account in decision making. The one test battery for use in cases of possible dementia that explicitly takes base rates into account is that of Kendrick (1965). However, Kendrick's validation data assume that base rates occurring in other contexts will be the same as those in the unit where he developed the battery (i.e. that two cases of depression are encountered for every case of dementia). This assumption is unlikely to be true elsewhere. In addition, it does not take account of another possibility that needs to be considered in making this particular diagnostic discrimination. This is that dementia and depression are not mutually exclusive and both can occur in the same individual.

A final problem in diagnostic testing arises out of the fact that in clinical practice decisions are being made about individuals, whereas research into the validity of diagnostic instruments is based on groups and emphasises comparisons between group means (Mitrushina & Fuld, 1990). A potential diagnostic test may discriminate between, say, a group with early dementia and a group with depression at the $P < 0.001$ level. This appears very impressive, and it is tempting to assume that the test must therefore be very useful clinically. This conclusion is not necessarily valid because the conventional statistical comparison compares differences between the group means. It is still possible for a small but appreciable proportion of the subjects with dementia to score in the range associated with the depressed group and vice versa. In this way, a diagnostic decision made about an individual subject on the basis of this test could have an appreciable chance of being wrong despite the very impressive significance level.

MEASURING CHANGE

In the case of dementia, two aspects of measuring change arise. The first is the assessment of the degree of decline that has already taken place and the other is the measurement of ongoing change. The first is a further useful marker for diagnosis since, for the diagnosis of dementia to be valid, it is generally assumed that some degree of intellectual deterioration must have taken place. The second is of value in terms of determining the effects of any interventions and occasionally in making predictions. If intellectual decline is proving to be very rapid, this may well have important implications for management as opposed to a situation where the decline is relatively slow. Special programmes to help maintain as much independent functioning as possible may well be more feasible for the latter than the former.

Work on trying to measure the degree of change from the premorbid state has concentrated almost exclusively on intellectual decline. The assumption has been that it is possible to identify tests, or sets of tests, indicative of general intellectual functioning that are relatively resistant to decline in organic brain disease and others that readily show clear indications of decline. Comparing the estimate of intellectual functioning (e.g. IQ) obtained from a test resistant to change with that derived from one sensitive to change can then give an estimate of decline.

The assumptions underlying this general approach are, at best, imperfectly valid. This issue has been discussed in some detail in earlier publications (e.g. Miller, 1977b; 1980) and will not be covered in detail here. The earliest methods were based either on using vocabulary as an index of premorbid IQ, because of its alleged resistance to deterioration (see Miller, 1977b), or various versions of the Wechsler Deterioration Index. This latter is based on the assumption that scores on some Wechsler subtests are much more prone to decline than others. Without discussing these particular techniques any further, it can simply be stated that nothing has emerged to contradict Miller's (1977, 1980) conclusion that using methods of this type does not usually give results reliable enough for making decisions about individual patients. In fact, subsequent research has, if anything, strengthened this conclusion. For example, Christensen & MacKinnon's (1992) meta-analysis of comparisons between those with dementia and normal controls on the Wechsler Adult Intelligence Scales indicates that all Wechsler subtests are more-or-less sensitive to deterioration, thus directly refuting the assumptions underlying the various deterioration indices based on the Wechsler scales.

A more recent development employing the same general principle has given evidence of a level of accuracy in determining intellectual decline sufficient to give a useful indication in some contexts. Nelson & O'Connell (1978) noted that reading ability, and especially the ability to read single words, did not decline readily in dementia. They devised a reading test, now known as the National Adult Reading Test (NART). This is based on the subject reading out aloud 50 English words with irregular spelling (i.e. a native English reader unfamiliar with any of these words would have some difficulty in determining how the word should be pronounced). Using regression equations, the NART score is used to predict IQs based on the original WAIS. This predicted IQ can then be compared with the IQ actually obtained by formal administration of the test.

The NART does appear to have a useful degree of validity as an instrument for detecting decline in IQ (e.g. Crawford *et al.*, 1989; Grober & Sliwinski, 1991), although it is still not ideal when it comes to detecting relatively small changes. Evidence as to the validity of using the NART in relation to the more recent WAIS—R is also starting to appear (Grober & Sliwinski, 1991; Sharpe & O'Carroll, 1991). As already indicated, the demonstration of likely deterioration in IQ is indicative of cerebral pathology and the method might potentially be used to measure decline progressively.

Tests can also be applied on more than one occasion to determine the rate of decline of psychological functioning in someone known to have dementia or to confirm that an expected decline is occurring in a patient for whom the diagnosis has been uncertain. Tests of intelligence and other functions, such as memory or verbal ability, can be repeated on different occasions in order to do this.

From a methodological point of view, there are certain requirements when a test is used on more than one occasion and the resulting change in score used as an indication of change in the subject over the intervening time period. Changes in test score can occur on retesting due to factors other than a real change in the status of the subject. Even if no other factor were to be in operation, the appreciable standard error for many tests would ensure that the result obtained on second testing would rarely be the same as that originally found, merely as a result of chance variation.

The most important of these confounding variables is practice effects. Where test–retest data are available for psychometric tests, they sometimes show quite appreciable improvements in score purely as a result of previous exposure to the test (e.g. Guertin *et al.*, 1962). In intelligence tests, it is not unusual for practice gains on retesting to amount to more than half a standard deviation. Consider the circumstance of an individual with a possible progressively deteriorating condition who was tested on two occasions several months apart and gives more or less identical IQ scores. Does this mean that measured IQ has remained static or that the amount of intellectual deterioration over that period has almost exactly cancelled out the gain due to practice effects? In order to deal with difficulties in interpretation of this kind, it is highly advisable to use tests with test–retest characteristics that have already been established when trying to detect ongoing change. The relevant statistical procedures to use have been described by Payne & Jones (1957). Unfortunately, good test–retest data are available for very few instruments, especially in relation to older samples.

PREDICTING OUTCOME AND MAKING DECISIONS ABOUT MANAGEMENT

An important set of issues in relation to dealing with those suffering from dementing illnesses lies in predicting outcome and making decisions about management.

Psychological performance is related to mortality. As might be expected there is considerable evidence that those who do badly tend to die within a shorter time than those who do relatively well (e.g. Sanderson & Inglis, 1961). This trend, although established quite reliably in many studies, is not particularly strong, nor is predicting remaining length of life necessarily of great practical concern. Nevertheless, it may be of use in some circumstances, for example, in the case of relatives with limited financial resources who are finding it difficult to cope with an elderly relative with a dementing illness and who may need to provide financial support if the individual is to move from home into a nursing home; they may value having some indication as to whether their financial support could be required over a period of months, years or even as much as a decade.

Other practical decisions relating to management concern the extent to which the patient with early Alzheimer's disease can live independently. If patients are widowed or otherwise living alone, is it possible for them to return to live in their own home with occasional support from relatives and a community nurse? Alternatively, is admission to a residential unit the only viable option? The question of possibly enhancing the individual's functioning to make more independent living possible may also arise. Are there interventions that might assist in this way and, if so, what are these?

So far, the issues surrounding assessment designed to answer questions of this nature have not been widely addressed in relation to older people with dementing illnesses. The range of tried and tested methods is therefore limited. One approach would be to rely on the sort of 'activities of daily living' scales, especially developed by occupational therapists. There are large numbers of these (e.g. Kuriansky & Gurland, 1976) and some may have a place in the overall assessment of people with dementing illnesses. Nevertheless, many of these have not been systematically developed or validated, and they tend to rely solely on face validity.

One approach to assessment that would be of potential value in this context is that based on criterion-referenced measurement (see Popham & Musek, 1969; Ward, 1970). Criterion-referenced scales have mainly been used with children so far but have an obvious relevance to any situation where the aim is to examine client competency and to target areas for possible intervention.

Criterion-referenced measurement differs from the conventional psychometric approach in that, instead of asking how well the subject performs on some task (e.g. defining words in a vocabulary scale) in relation to a normative population, the various items assess whether the subject can achieve certain things to an acceptable standard of performance. A major item in a criterion-referenced scale may thus relate to whether the subject can dress him or herself in ordinary indoor clothing within a certain length of time and without making errors such as putting a garment on back to front or failing to do up fastenings. If this item is failed, a set of lower-level items then typically deals with aspects of the overall skill, such as can the subject do up buttons or other fastenings, put on certain specific garments, and so on. A well-designed criterion, referenced scale therefore enables the examiner to not only determine whether important practical tasks can be achieved accurately but, where this cannot be done, to identify where performance breaks down in a way that could lead to ameliorative interventions. These interventions might consist of special training or retraining programmes. On the other hand, with groups likely to deteriorate or for whom retraining might be difficult, such as those with dementia or severely handicapping illnesses, the intervention might involve some appropriate adaptation of the task itself. For example, if doing up buttons and other small fastenings is the problem, then Velcro fastenings might be substituted. Alternatively, and especially in the case of women, using only garments which fasten at the front, where fastenings are more easily manipulated, might offer a satisfactory solution. It is unfortunate that criterion-referenced assessment has not been adequately exploited for handicapped adult groups.

Another general approach to assessment of value in this context is that of behavioural observation and behavioural assessment (e.g. Kazdin, 1975; Ciminero, Calhoun & Adams, 1978). These forms of assessment are not without their own technical problems (e.g. Kent & Foster, 1978) but have clear advantages in dealing with some problems where the client group involved, as with dementia, may have poor communication skills and may not be easy to assess on conventional psychometric tests. For example, incontinence as a problem often encountered in residents in units catering for elderly people with dementing illnesses. Incontinence is not necessarily an inevitable consequence of dementia, except in the more advanced stages (Sanford, 1975), and can have many causes, which vary from urinary tract infections to such things as not being able to reach the appropriate facility in time. A resident who is observed to set off from a chair in the day room but then wanders around until finally being found wet in a corridor suggests a problem in actually locating the right facility, possibly due to spatial difficulties or problems in discriminating which is the right door amongst many in a long corridor. This individual might benefit from having the location of the lavatory more clearly marked (e.g. by painting the door a prominent colour). Careful observation and recording might similarly identify the resident whose bladder sensation is dulled and whose slowed movement does not allow him or her to reach the lavatory in time. If this same individual also voids his/her bladder at fairly regular intervals or at more or less identifiable times, then a prompt from staff at key times might allow him or her to get to the lavatory in time and so preserve some independence and dignity that would otherwise have been lost. Experience attests to the fact that careful observation and recording of key aspects of behaviour can often reveal relationships that have not hitherto been suspected, in that problems most typically arise in certain contexts or at certain times, which can then suggest some form of ameliorative action.

In general terms, the need for assessment for decision making implies the use of techniques that are practically oriented in that they deal with what the individual can or cannot do in terms of everyday skills and functions. Although potential techniques exist, such as criterion-referenced measurement and behavioural assessment, their use has not been systematically explored or validated with this population. It is therefore typically necessary to rely to a considerable degree on the ingenuity of the investigator. Whilst all really good assessment requires some ingenuity, since no situation is exactly identical to any other, it would also be advantageous to have more in the way of tried and tested methods applicable to this population.

One cautionary point needs to be made in relation to assessment procedures based on direct observation of behaviour (including those where the direct observation feeds into criterion-referenced forms of assessment). What an individual may do or not do may be heavily dependent on the context. For example, one study of patients with multiple sclerosis (Lincoln, 1981) compared assessments of performance on everyday tasks (e.g. dressing, simple cooking) both in a rehabilitation unit and at home after the patient had been discharged. There were appreciable discrepancies between the two occasions. It is highly likely that patients with mild dementia would show similar variation, and so it is therefore sensible to assess functional competencies in the setting in which they would normally be carried out or a setting that is as near as possible to this ideal.

COMMENT

Assessment of the person with dementia or suspected dementia is not simple and varies considerably with the kind of question that needs to be resolved and the context in which the question arises. For this reason, no ideal standard assessment battery can be described which will cover all circumstances. Rather, it is up to whoever is conducting the assessment to think through the issues carefully and to select a set of procedures best designed to answer the identified problem.

Psychological assessment is often not carried out in isolation, and especially so in relation to persons with dementia or suspected dementia. The same person may also be seen by a psychiatrist, a geriatrician or even a neurologist. There may be formal or informal observations from nurses or social workers, and special medical investigations may have been ordered (e.g. some form of brain scan). It may also be feasible to get an account of the development of the problem from someone who knows the patient well, such as a spouse or other family member. It is foolish to waste valuable time in carrying out assessment procedures to answer questions that, in the context of that particular patient, have already been answered or which are more readily or more reliably answered by other means. Similarly, these other sources of information can feed into the psychologist's examination. In the case of a patient with known vascular disease and possible cerebrovascular dementia, a report by the spouse that the individual keeps on bumping into things on the left, such as door posts, might indicate the value of testing for visual neglect.

Some problems occur sufficiently often in assessment in the present context to merit some special discussion. As has already been indicated, there is a paucity of psychometric tests with adequate normative data extending into the older age ranges most associated with dementia, and the number of instruments specifically designed for use with elderly patients remains quite small. For this reason, the options available to the investigator may be more restricted than is the case for younger populations, and results from tests may sometimes need to be interpreted with greater caution.

Another factor complicating the assessment of older persons is that they may have multiple impairments. Sensory impairments, like deafness and impaired visual acuity, are common and their influence on performance can be difficult to gauge. It is often good practice to ensure that older people's sensory capacities, if necessary by correction by glasses or hearing aids, are sufficiently adequate not to adversely influence test performance. There is also a well-known tendency for older people to be prescribed different drugs for their various problems and so suffer the problems of mental confusion due to polypharmacy. Such a person can be erroneously regarded as suffering from dementia when a rationalisation of the drug intake might resolve the problem. It is of course not the psychologist's role to deal directly with medication, but it is important to be aware of the possible contaminating effects of medication on psychological performance.

A difficulty that occasionally arises in the assessment of older people is the patient who is often considered 'untestable'. By this is meant the individual who either cannot or will not cooperate with psychometric forms of assessment. Whilst some may be 'untestable' in this sense, there is no conscious person who cannot be assessed in some way or another, from a psychological point of view, using observational recording and ratings by those familiar with the patient. In the case of those unable to cooperate with formal psychometric testing, the main problems will concern management issues since diagnosis will usually have been already established. In this case, observational methods are particularly appropriate anyway.

Test refusal by subjects who probably could perform adequately on the instruments, but choose not to do so, is rather different. Such refusal can be minimised by taking care to establish a good rapport, explaining why the assessment is necessary and being sensitive to the anxieties that the person may feel about the assessment procedure. Administering tests that people find most acceptable first may also build up confidence and help reduce refusal. The relatively quick, simple and less threatening Object Learning Test of the revised Kendrick Battery (Kendrick, Gibson & Moyes, 1979) is much more acceptable than the more difficult Synonym Learning Test which it replaced (see Kendrick, 1965). Carrying out the assessment over several short sessions may also be more acceptable than trying to achieve the same results over one or two much longer sessions. Despite all these precautions, some test refusal is inevitable and it is possible then to fall back on methods that do not require the subject's active cooperation.

Assessment in relation to dementing illnesses is valuable in the overall clinical evaluation and management of a case where it is carried out carefully, thoughtfully and, sometimes, with ingenuity. The routine administration of a set of assessment procedures is typically less valuable and, where it is of some use, contributes most to diagnosis. In practice, clear diagnosis may not be possible and the crucial issue is the management of the problems that have been identified. Standard batteries have least to contribute in this latter context.

CHAPTER 7   Management of dementia

During the last 20 years there has been an important change in thinking about dependency in elderly people and dementia sufferers in particular. This has mainly taken place in day centres or residential care, where there is a move towards assessing the needs of dementia sufferers and designing interventions that will increase independent functioning. The approaches that have been developed have also been applied more recently in the community, where the immediate caregivers are now beginning to be offered training in specific procedures for dementia sufferers (see also Chapter 8 on psychosocial aspects of dementia). Psychological approaches tend to be presented as 'therapies' or 'treatments' (Woods, 1987), but in lay terms they can be seen as appropriate methods for overcoming the disabilities of a dementia sufferer and minimising behavioural problems that are associated with the more severe stages of the illness.

Attitudes to care are crucial in terms of the outcome of care giving procedures. Holden & Woods (1987) argue strongly that dementia sufferers are not always able to make the choices that they would if they did not have dementia, but that attitudes to care should always promote the person's individuality as an adult, providing dignity and self-respect. The implication of this approach, as outlined by Woods (1987) is as follows:

1. Dementia sufferers should be accorded full respect and dignity as people with human worth and rights.

2. Dementia sufferers should be treated appropriately for their actual age.

3. Dementia sufferers should be helped to participate in good social relationships in the ordinary community.

Attempts to achieve these goals present a major challenge to caregiving staff and carers alike. They imply an appropriate knowledge of dementia and psychological approaches that are individual-centred. This is a challenging area, given the range of disabilities of dementia sufferers and issues that arise, from deciding whether a person should continue to drive (Lucas-Blaustein *et al.*, 1988) to attempting to increase the activity levels of a severely demented person in residential care (Jenkins *et al.*, 1977).

INDIVIDUAL CARE PLANNING

Within this approach, individual care planning has enabled carers to address the needs of dementia sufferers more specifically. Each dementia sufferer is assessed in the broadest sense, identifying their resources and abilities. A care plan is then drawn up, indicating specific goals or 'targets' to be achieved by a person. For example, the goal for a disoriented dementia sufferer might be to find the way to the day room independently or to ask to be taken to the toilet.

Brody *et al.* (1974) have evaluated this approach with dementia sufferers and found it to be successful in terms of showing improvements in areas tackled directly by the caregiving programme. The approach is illustrated by Barrowclough & Fleming (1986), who evaluated the training of formal carers of dementia sufferers in 'goal-planning'. They cite the case of a dementia sufferer who was no longer having a bath since she lived alone and there was no one to remind her to do so. The goal was for her to have a bath and dry herself twice a week at the day centre with verbal prompting only. Table 7.1 shows how this was broken down into four specific stages to achieve the goal. Barrowclough and Fleming (1986) report a 30% success rate in goal plans after long-term follow-up, with success more likely if the stages were designed to be congruent with the amount of time available for working with the dementia sufferer.

BEHAVIOURAL APPROACHES

A feature of almost all psychological interventions is the assumption that a person can acquire new information and learn new

Table 7.1 An example of 'goal-planning' for a dementia sufferer (taken from Barrowclough & Fleming, 1986, with permission)

Present behaviour:	Sarah has good sight and hearing and is physically able to have a bath. Due to memory difficulties she is no longer having a bath/wash since she lives alone and there is no one to remind her. She understands simple verbal instructions and enjoys contact with staff. She is able to dress and undress herself.
Her 'goal':	Sarah will have a bath and dry herself twice a week at the day centre with verbal prompting only.
Step 1:	Sarah will have a bath with verbal prompting throughout all stages of washing and with verbal and physical prompting for running, emptying and getting out of the bath.
Step 2:	Sarah will have a bath with verbal prompting for running and emptying the bath and for drying herself. In addition, Sarah will be verbally prompted to start washing herself, but will complete this independently while staff leave the bathroom.
Step 3:	Sarah will have a bath with a maximum of two verbal prompts at each stage of running and emptying the bath and drying herself. She will wash herself independently and alone.
Step 4:	Sarah will have a bath with no more than one verbal prompt to initiate running and emptying the bath and drying herself. She will wash herself independently and alone.

skills. This is precisely the area in which dementia sufferers are most impaired, so it is not surprising that this has led to a therapeutic nihilism in some quarters. Nevertheless, both theoretical and applied research has shown that dementia sufferers are able to learn new information and show behavioural change with appropriate training, albeit at a slower rate.

Preserved learning abilities

Theoretical studies of learning in dementia have explored classical conditioning, operant learning, motor learning and verbal learning. They indicate preserved learning abilities in all four areas. In the classical conditioning paradigm, a puff of air has been applied to produce an eye-blink response in the patient. The air-puff is then combined with a buzzer so that eventually the buzzer alone is able to produce the eye-blink response. The rate of this 'classical conditioning' has been shown to be only slightly reduced in dementia patients by Brown, Gantt & Whitman (1960) and Solyom & Barik (1965).

A second type of learning, operant conditioning, has been explored using an apparatus akin to a fruit machine (Ankus & Quarrington, 1972). The person has to pull a lever on the apparatus and will receive a 'prize' (reward), either money or a drink. The prize is scheduled to be intermittent, but consistently given after a fixed number of lever pulls (this is termed a fixed-ratio schedule). Using this task, Ankus & Quarrington (1972) showed that the behaviour of the dementia patient can be conditioned successfully. It was noted that the success of training was dependent on individual preference for the reward, emphasising the need to explore the motivation of patients carefully in applying a training programme. A more recent study by Morris (1987b) has investigated simple discrimination learning using a 'matching-to-sample' task. The subject is presented with an object (in this case a coloured shape) and then later presented with the same object and another one. A limited set of coloured shapes are used interchangeably in a series of presentations in which the subject has to learn to choose the matching item consistently, based on feedback from the examiner. Patients with moderate to severe dementia are eventually able to learn to criterion on this task. Morris (1987b) also found that the patient's learned ability does not generalise to a novel set of coloured shapes, indicating that the original learning is based on 'stimulus–response' associations, rather than learning a specific matching rule. This supports the notion that moderately or severely impaired dementia sufferers may only be able to learn specific associations, rather than abstract conceptual information, through interacting with their environment.

A third area is skill learning (see also Chapter 2), the ability to learn a specific set of procedures brought to bear on a particular task. Skill memory has been investigated in Alzheimer's disease using the pursuit rotor task, in which the subject has to maintain a stylus in contact with a small metal target on a rotating disc. Evidence for learning is that the subject improves after several attempts at the task. Eslinger & Damasio (1986) required patients to attempt the pursuit rotor task over five learning trials, followed by another trial 20 minutes later. Although the baseline ability to keep the stylus on the target was lower in Alzheimer's disease, the rate of learning was the same as with normal subjects. A similar study by Heindel, Butters & Salmon (1988) repeated this experiment, but varied the rate of rotation to suit the abilities of each person, also finding that the rate of learning was the same.

A fourth area is verbal learning, which is frequently tested by giving the patient a series of word pairs (e.g. school–groceries), followed by the first word from each pair. The subject is required to produce the second word of the pair. By repeating the test several times using the same items, the efficiency of verbal learning can be determined. Patients with dementia have been found to do extremely poorly on this test, taking many trials to learn an association. However, if the word pairs are semantically related their performance is much improved (Whitehead, 1973, 1977). A more recent study by Little, Hemsley & Volans (1987) followed up patients with dementia and found that learning of semantically related word pairs remains relatively preserved over time, contrasting with a deterioration in the learning of unrelated word pairs.

These different aspects of learning, demonstrated using laboratory tasks, may predict the type of learning that dementia sufferers are capable of in everyday functioning. For example, preserved operant learning predicts success in approaches using behaviour modification to train dementia sufferers in particular tasks. Preserved procedural learning probably explains why dementia sufferers appear to learn new motor skills, such as how to operate the door in a new environment or institution. The relative preservation of verbal learning involving semantically related material may explain why certain aspects of reality orientation (see below) have been successful. For example, tasks that involve learning names of people in response to a specific cue (e.g. who is the current prime minister?) may involve strengthening existing semantic associations between the question and the response. As a caveat, success of training may depend on whether additional underlying neuropsychological abilities are intact. In the studies described above using the pursuit rotor task, the patients were not sufficiently dyspraxic to hinder their ability to learn. More severely impaired patients may not have had the perceptual motor skills to perform the basic task.

Self-care

A feature of most institutions that care for dementia sufferers is that they aim to maximise self-care (Baltes *et al.*, 1983). This is sometimes difficult to achieve because of the often quoted problem of it appearing to take longer to encourage a person to do a task than for the carer to do it themself. Institutions can be structured not so much to teach new skills but to facilitate the use of old ones. For example, Melin & Gotesdam (1981) report a hospital regime in which the dementia sufferers were given unlimited time to feed themselves with a large choice of food and accompaniments. This clearly led to an improvement in eating skills, compared to the old regime of limited choice and staff feeding the dementia sufferers if they took more than an allotted time. A more active form of intervention is described by Rinke *et al.* (1978) who targeted 'bathing' as a skill, breaking it down into five components, undressing, soaping, rinsing, drying and dressing. Each component was prompted verbally (a reminder) or physically (demonstrating what to do, or handing the resident an item such as soap). The dementia sufferers were also given praise and a wall chart for visual feedback of progress as a reward for appropriate responses to a certain level. This programme was sufficient to bring about a significant improvement in each component, in comparison to dementia sufferers who were not given the same regime. The study illustrates several aspects of behavioural approaches with dementia sufferers. Firstly, the approach is often to re-institute behaviours that may have existed in the past and may have been lost, perhaps when the dementia sufferer moved environments. Secondly, as indicated above, the outcome is dependent on basic skills being intact, for example appropriate dressing and undressing can only be instituted if the person is not dyspraxic.

Urinary incontinence is a condition with numerous psychological and medical implications for dementia sufferers. Estimates of prevalence range from 38 to 82% in long-term care settings, depending on the degree of functional disability displayed by patients (Burgio *et al.*, 1988). Behavioural techniques have been applied, adapting those used with children and people with learning difficulties (Foxx & Azrin, 1973). The goal of incontinence programmes has been to establish independent toileting behaviour. The main technique has been to check regularly for dryness and then to prompt the patient to go to the toilet when necessary. Gradually the prompts are faded until the person responds appropriately by visiting and using the toilet. For example, Sanavio (1981) reported the application of an independent toileting programme for a 61-year-old dementia sufferer. This person was previously incontinent day and night, but the programme produced independent toileting behaviour that was maintained after 8 weeks.

Independent toileting may be too high a goal in the case of dementia patients whose cognitive and physical disabilities are too severe. A complex set of skills is required, such as dressing/undressing, finding the toilet, mobility and planning ahead. For this reason, many programmes have concentrated on either teaching patients to request assistance from staff when the need to void exists or training staff to regularly toilet patients. Schnelle *et al.* (1983) used an hourly prompting technique that involved checking the patient's clothing and body to determine whether they were wet or dry and cueing the patient to request assistance to use the toilet (e.g. 'Mr X, do you need to go to the bathroom?'). Social approval, such as praising the patient in an adult manner, was given for dry checks or appropriate requests for assistance. Conversely, social disapproval, such as indicating disappointment, was given for wet checks. This increased the frequency of correct toileting by approximately 45% in a group of 11 dementia sufferers.

A critical aspect of establishing continence, however, is the degree to which staff members will assist patients in toileting. Schnelle *et al.* (1988) found that the care staff in the homes they studied assisted their patients an average of 0.49 times per day. Burgio *et al.* (1990) have found that nursing staff can be encouraged to use a prompted voiding procedure with patients by providing systematic feedback. For example, weekly summaries were collected by the staff managers, and the summary outcome of prompted voiding was reported back to the staff. Using this procedure, the staff had completed an average of 83% of the assigned prompted voidings, but it was found that without maintaining the feedback this dropped dramatically to 44%. Compliance with procedures may relate to the perceived cost efficacy, since Schnelle *et al.* (1988) have reported that 1- and 2-hour prompts generated higher costs than normal continence care.

A modification of the procedure of Schnelle *et al.* (1983) has been reported by Burgio *et al.* (1988) who argue that toileting more than every 2 hours is not practical within a nursing home and that even 2-hourly toileting may only be practical as an interim measure. Accordingly, over a period of 4 months they gradually increased the interval between prompts up to 4 hours, proceeding if the dementia sufferer improved. By 'thinning out' the schedule they were still able to increase dryness from 30% of clothes checks during a baseline period to 62% during the training phase.

Activity

Low levels of purposeful activity can be a feature of institutional care in the elderly, particularly for patients with dementia. The emphasis on physical care and activities of daily living is not always easy to match with alternative recreational or social activities. Jenkins *et al.* (1977) have found that increases in the level of interaction in old people's homes can be obtained by providing regular recreational sessions. During these sessions the residents are given the opportunity to use various extra recreational materials (for example, polish and varnish for shining up old coins). This approach has been applied specifically with dementia sufferers. For example, Melin & Gotesdam (1981) trained staff to use group activity sessions to encourage dementia sufferers to use recreational materials. They found, through direct observation of their behaviour, that the level of activity increased in the week following the sessions without further encouragement. A similar approach has been applied by Rothwell, Britton & Woods (1983), with an increase in activity levels among residents in residential care, the majority of whom had dementia.

Behavioural problems

Troublesome and disruptive behaviours are a very frequent component of dementia, concurrent with the intellectual impairments. These include physical and verbal aggression, paranoid thoughts, disordered sleep, wandering, and purposeless and repetitive activity (Swearer et al., 1988). Operant training techniques have been moderately successful at ameliorating these difficulties.

Hussian (1983) has used stimulus control and operant procedures to modify problem behaviours such as wandering and self-stimulatory behaviours. This involves identifying the environmental cues for the behaviour and providing a system of rewards for appropriate behaviour, mostly in the form of social reinforcement. For example, a major problem can be dementing patients absconding from a nursing home, thereby placing themselves at risk. Hussian & Brown (1987) describe a stimulus control procedure that reduces exit-seeking behaviour in dementia sufferers substantially. Likewise, bizarre verbalisations and communication deficits in dementia sufferers can be modified using behavioural techniques (Hoyer, 1973). Some of these approaches have been attempted in the community by training partners of dementia sufferers in simple behavioural procedures. Greene et al. (1982) taught carers to ignore their partners suspicious and accusatory verbalisations while reinforcing, through praise and touch, their appropriate verbalisations. In addition, the partner was trained to ask questions in order to encourage appropriate behaviour and then reinforce responses through touching, praising and smiling. These relatively simple procedures, when structured in this fashion, were able to change significantly the aversive behaviour of the dementia sufferer from a baseline level.

This approach, as indicated above, relies on careful targeting of specific behaviours, tailored to the individual. For example, using a multiple baseline design (tackling one specific behaviour at a time), Rosberger & Maclean (1983) were able to modify five of six target behaviours in a dementia sufferer. As indicated above, the problem of generalisation of appropriate behaviours can be over-come by directly training the care staff or carers in the procedures.

MEMORY MANAGEMENT

Memory rehabilitation

One of the main approaches used in neuropsychological rehabili-tation is memory management or memory retraining (Wilson, 1987). This approach, which consists of the systematic use of diary keeping or mnemonics has been found to be useful in patients with mild degrees of brain injury. The same techniques can be used with dementia sufferers at the early stages of their illness, when the degree of cognitive impairment is mild. For example, a dementia sufferer can be encouraged to use a diary to record daily events, telephone calls or appointments that someone without a memory disorder would not need to record. Hill et al. (1987) reported the use of imagery mnemonic training with a patient suffering from Alzheimer's disease. This consisted of the repeated presentation of yearbook photographs paired with the corre-sponding name. A mnemonic was used, which involved ident-ifying a prominent facial feature and creating a visual association with the name (e.g. a turtle for the last name 'Tuttle'). The patient was able to learn this mnemonic technique to improve memory performance. The technique works particularly well if the person is encouraged to draw the association (Wilson, 1987).

More impaired dementia sufferers cannot master these techniques or strategies, and would not remember when to use them. Hence the majority of rehabilitation approaches with dementia sufferers are pitched at a more basic level of cognitive functioning. Instead of training the person in a technique, either the environment is structured to decrease memory requirements, or the approach is directed to teaching information or changing the person's behav-iour, such as in reality orientation.

Reality Orientation—the basic approach

The origins of Reality Orientation (RO) go back to 1958 when Dr James Folsom instituted a programme of activity for elderly patients at the Veterans Administration Hospital in Topeka, Kansas, USA. It was developed as a means of orientating a person to their environment by means of continuous stimulation. In addition, a quasi-physiological explanation of the therapy was given, as a means of stimulating unused neurological pathways and compensating for organic brain damage. Those who use it tend to support RO on the pragmatic grounds that it improves the quality of life for dementia patients and has provided a coherent treatment package for caregiving staff.

Since 1958, RO has been used extensively and evaluated in full (Holden & Woods, 1987). Two main RO approaches have been developed, classroom RO and 24-hour RO.

Classroom Reality Orientation

Classroom RO involves three to five patients meeting for at least two sessions a week. Usually the sessions last for half an hour, depending on the abilities of the dementia sufferers. At a basic level, the group concentrates on learning each other's names through the use of verbal prompts and name badges. The group leader prompts the participants to provide basic information about the day, date and weather, tactfully giving the correct information where necessary. A 'Weather Board' is often used to focus the attention of the participants. With more able dementia sufferers, the approach is extended to include personal information about group members and compare features of the past and present. For example, a common theme is changes in coinage or prices. Comparison of the prices of food can be used to orientate the participants to current costs. Similarly, newspapers, slides, or a short film can all be used to stimulate discussion about the present. Holden & Woods (1987) have experimented with more advanced groups in which the group determines the activities, where possible, with basic orientation information extended towards awareness of world news and the local community. These groups operate at a much higher level and include cooking, shopping, outings and music. They are only recommended for dementia sufferers who are functioning fairly independently in the community.

24-Hour Reality Orientation

In contrast, 24-Hour RO is designed as a means of communicating with the dementia sufferer, used throughout the person's waking hours. The approach is two-fold, firstly to restructure the environment of a person to improve orientation, and secondly to enhance orientation by communicating directly with the dementia sufferer. In everyday conversation, the person is reminded of their name, where they are, the time of day, and current events in their surroundings. The aim is also to correct confused speech and actions and to prompt or encourage appropriate behaviours (Hanley, 1984). The approach is supplemented with changes in the physical environment to improve orientation, such as clocks, calendars, signs and pictures. For example, the staff ensure that there are signs that indicate where the dining rooms and toilets are, as well as a prominently placed information board. There is evidence that some patients may sometimes perceive symbols better than words, which suggests that both types of cues should be used.

Ward Orientation Training

Some have used a variation of 24-Hour RO, termed Ward Orientation Training (Hanley, McGuire & Boyd, 1981). This is a systematic attempt to combine the interpersonal and environmental approaches. In essence, the dementia sufferer is trained to use the environmental cues in a more active fashion. For example, large pictorial signposts may be placed round the ward which clearly label particular areas. The staff then accompany a dementia sufferer round the ward and train the patient to observe the signs.

Hanley (1986) describes the case of an 85-year-old female patient who was incontinent, despite the introduction of a 2-hour ing regime in which she was taken to the toilet. A pro was established in which the two ward toilets were clearly sign-posted with large symbol and word signs. The dementia sufferer was prompted hourly to use the toilet by asking her if she would like to use it, with minimal assistance given to help her find the toilet on her own. She was 'cued' where necessary, for example with the instruction 'actually it is just a bit across from the window.' This programme substantially reduced the frequency of incontinence and could be reduced to 2-hourly toileting reminders. Similarly, Lam & Woods (1986) identified eight target locations thought to be important for an 80-year-old female patient on a ward, including her bedroom, bathroom, toilet, day room, dining room and ward-orientation board. A simple training procedure was implemented in which the patient was required to move to the locations from a fixed starting point. Verbal prompts and physical prompts (showing the person where the location was) were given only if the dementia sufferer failed, but otherwise social reinforcement was given when the target was found. The success of this training had an interesting spin-off in that, when the dementia sufferer was relocated to a home, the staff were encouraged to implement a similar programme.

Reality Orientation—does it work?

The question 'does it work?' depends on 'what is it?' and 'what is it meant to achieve?' A summary of the different characteristics of RO compared to the other main approach, Reminiscence Therapy, is given in Table 7.2. Reports of adverse effects of RO (Dietch, Hewett & Jones, 1989) and doubts about the overall effectiveness (Powell-Proctor & Miller, 1982) have focused attention on evaluating the approach more fully. The different dimensions of RO complicate the issue since the various approaches do not always have the same aim. For example, Ward Orientation is tailored to suit specific patients, as described above, and has a very clear aim with an easily identifiable outcome. With Classroom and 24-hour RO, the aim is not so easily specified and various positive outcomes have been explored, including changes in cognitive functioning and mood and changes in the way staff interact with dementia sufferers. There are also questions as to how specific are the changes and how relevant are they to the needs of the dementia sufferer?

Table 7.2 Characteristics of Classroom Reality Orientation (RO) and Reminiscence Therapy in relation to dementia sufferers

Characteristic	RO	Reminiscence Therapy
Main focus of therapy	Encourage verbal orientation, improve cognition, verbal functioning, change staff attitudes	No clear focus; improve morale, interaction activity levels
Use of material	Used to focus attention and to improve orientation by 'past' and 'present' comparison	Used to elicit memories
Change in cognitive functioning	Improvements in information/orientation but no general cognitive changes	Improvements in information/orientation when combined with RO first (Baines *et al.*, 1987)
Change in mood	Negative changes in some patients	Generally thought to be enjoyable but some patients may be disturbed by recalling negative memories
Change in life satisfaction	No change found	No change found
Effect on staff/dementia sufferer interaction outside the group	Increase in staff interaction in some studies	Yes, but there is evidence that effect occurs where there is a low 'baseline' level (Head *et al.*, 1990)
Contraindications for use	Those whose confusion 'rambling' are too severe. Those with sensory deficits	Those whose confusion and rambling are too severe. Those with severe sensory deficits
	Where RO consistently produces negative emotions	Those who are likely to recall negative memories consistently

Changes in cognition

As indicated earlier in this chapter, there is evidence that dementia sufferers can learn new information, albeit at a slower rate, and show operant learning and classical conditioning of behaviour (Morris, 1987). Controlled trials of RO have explored changes in verbal orientation as the main form of investigating cognitive functioning. Patients are asked questions such as what day of the week it is and the name of their place of residence. In some cases, the questions concern current information, such as the name of the prime minister, as in Wood's (1979) use of the Information and Orientation section of the Wechsler Memory Scale (Wechsler, 1945). With the exception of one study, using an 18-item orientation questionnaire as their measure (Hogstel, 1979), all the reported controlled studies of RO have indicated a relative increase in verbal orientation (Baines, Saxby & Ehlert, 1987; Brook, Degun & Mather, 1975; Citrin & Dixon, 1977; Goldstein *et al.*, 1982; Hanley, McGuire & Boyd, 1981; Harris & Ivory, 1976; Johnson, McLaren & McPherson, 1981; Merchant & Saxby, 1981; Reeve & Ivison, 1985; Wallis, Baldwin & Higginbotham, 1983; Woods, 1979). This is a very consistent finding, given the range of experimental methods used in the different trials, and offers convincing evidence that dementia sufferers can increase their level of knowledge through RO, despite their dementing illness.

Changes in behaviour

A more rigorous test of the efficacy of RO is whether it changes the behaviour of dementia sufferers. Changes in verbal orientation may not improve the quality of life of a dementia sufferer or make the task of caregivers any easier. The outcome of controlled studies in terms of behavioural change has been more equivocal. In the first controlled trial of Classroom RO, Brook, Degun & Mather (1975) compared dementia patients given RO with a control group of patients who sat in an RO equipped room, but did not use the materials. Ratings were made fortnightly by nursing staff of their overall behaviour on the ward. These indicated that dementia sufferers improved in ratings of self-care, and socialisation, in comparison to the control group.

Subsequent studies were less encouraging, failing to provide evidence for changes in behaviour. These included a large scale study by Hanley, McGuire & Boyd (1981), who carried out RO sessions three times a week in both long-stay psychogeriatric hospital wards and an old people's home, over a 3-month period. No differences were observed on the Geriatric Rating Scale, despite an improvement in verbal orientation. Similarly, Zepelin, Wolfe & Kleinplatz (1981) conducted a trial incorporating classroom and 24-Hour RO over a 1-year period. Contrary to expectation, measures of social responsiveness, dressing skills, continence and mobility favoured an untreated control group rather than the patients administered RO. These early studies led Powell-Proctor & Miller (1982) to conclude, in a critical review, that the benefits were small and restricted in range.

In commenting on these negative outcomes, Holden & Woods (1987) have questioned whether some of the RO trials have been conducted in a setting that encouraged positive behaviour change, such as independent behaviour. If not, this would remove the chances of any carry-over effect of RO into the everyday living skills of dementia sufferers. 'Process' research, which looks at how RO has been conducted, is an important component of evaluation, since a positive outcome would not be expected if the approach is not used appropriately. Indeed Woods (1979) examined the degree to which care staff engaged in operationally defined behaviours associated with Classroom RO and found a significant increase in RO behaviour after training. In contrast, Hanley, McGuire & Boyd (1981) were unable to observe any change in the way staff interacted with patients following training in 24-Hour RO, despite the fact that the staff felt they were implementing RO. If RO is not being implemented properly it is not surprising that there is no behavioural change, but the paradox is that a change in verbal orientation would not be expected either.

More recent studies of RO have generally been more encouraging and may reflect a greater emphasis on motivating dementia sufferers and care staff. For example, Classroom RO is seen more as a social event rather than a dull monotonous routine, and 24-Hour RO has been seen as part of the ongoing development in the way a ward is run. In a psychogeriatric ward, Reeve & Ivison (1985) found improvements in communication and overall behavioural functioning after 4 weeks of Classroom RO, which was maintained after a further 8-week extension. Baines, Saxby & Ehlert (1987) (see below) found that RO followed by Reminiscence Therapy produced a significant decrease in problem behaviour and an increase in communication, measured using the Holden 5-point Communication Scale (Holden & Woods, 1987).

Discussion

In summary, RO may have suffered from becoming an institutional requirement and because the approach may involve groups of dementia sufferers and may be irrelevant to individual cases. The adverse affects of RO on individual cases have been documented, such as confronting a dementia sufferer with the death of a relative in an uncaring fashion (Dietch, Hewett & Jones, 1989). However these have to be balanced against other cases where skilled implementation of RO, such as Ward Orientation, has led to increased awareness of a person's surrounding, with a resulting increased level of independence, dignity (and continence) (Hanley, 1986). Critics of RO have tended to parody the basic approach as simplistic verbal learning that has no relevance to dementia sufferers. This ignores the fact that RO is a multifaceted approach that can be adapted to suit the particular setting in which it is applied, as indicated above. Those who promote RO emphasise basic attitudes that must be applied in implementing RO, such as respecting the individuality of dementia sufferers and maintaining their dignity and self respect. It is possible to tactfully remind a person of the time of year, without confronting them with failure and in a way that promotes activity and interest. In this respect 24-Hour RO is as much about changing the way the staff interact with the dementia sufferer as it is about specific techniques for increasing orientation.

More extensive evaluation is needed to establish the efficacy of this approach. Clearly, more attention should be given to the appropriateness of different approaches for individuals. Recently, Morris (1991) observed two female dementia sufferers who had recently lost their spouses. The first, who was mildly cognitively impaired, was able to learn through gentle reminding that her husband had died and helped to grieve over his death. The second was unable to retain this information, and when confronted with it would become very distressed each time. In this case, the Validation Therapy approach (see p. 130) was thought most appropriate when she asked questions about her husband's whereabouts.

REMINISCENCE

Increasingly, Reminiscence Therapy is being used as an alternative approach to RO for dementia sufferers. Reminiscence Therapy is usually conducted in a structured group setting and used to prompt memories from the past. This approach has some intuitive appeal with dementia sufferers because it focuses on the persons strength—their ability to use their remote memories as a way of communicating with other people (see Chapter 2). The approach was originally developed for elderly people without dementia and thought to provide an opportunity to review and reorganise events in their life (Butler, 1963). Specific procedures have been designed to elicit memories such as the *Recall* package (Help the Aged, 1981), which consists of six sets of slides with accompanying commentaries.

The *Recall* package has been used with dementia sufferers by Baines, Saxby & Ehlert (1987), in conjunction with old photographs of local scenes, personal photographs, books, magazines, newspapers and domestic articles. This material was used to encourage the dementia sufferers to think and talk about past experiences. A similar approach was used by Head, Portnoy & Woods (1990), in which three group leaders would use pictures of specific relevance to the members in order to cue memories from the past. For example, one member who had worked in a café was shown a picture of a waitress. They also used a technique called 'enactment' in which the person had to act out their past experiences, such as dancing, being a waiter/waitress or using a washboard. This technique was used to encourage enthusiasm and interest and minimised some of the difficulties associated with hearing problems and concentration difficulties. Another approach, used as a control condition in their evaluation study (see below), dispensed with a formal structure, but used memorabilia such as old kitchen equipment and articles of clothing to provoke responses and discussion. McKiernan & Bender (1990) decided on a theme for each session and focusing for 15 minutes on a variety of illustrative materials, including music, objects, pictures and slides. Both Head, Portnoy & Woods (1990) and McKiernan & Bender (1990) would break up the group into subgroups on occasions to increase the dementia sufferers' opportunity to speak to each other.

The approach is clearly popular amongst psychologists and occupational therapists who work with dementia sufferers. Part of this may be because it concentrates on the individual as a person and attempts to capitalise on preserved functioning. The approaches described above have all attempted to evaluate the efficacy of reminiscence therapy in this context. As with RO, the outcome of these studies depends on what the approach is trying to achieve, whether it is to improve cognition, produce a change in mood, or provide changes in the attitudes of the care staff towards the person. Baines, Saxby & Ehlert (1987) compared RO with Reminiscence Therapy using a cross-over design, using three cohorts of dementia sufferers. One received no therapy, another received reminiscence first and the final group RO first. The group with RO followed by Reminiscence showed a significant improvement on a range of behavioural and cognitive measures including the Holden Communication Scale and the Clifton Assessment Battery for the Elderly (Pattie & Gilleard, 1979). The other intervention group showed no such improvement on long-term follow up, after an initial improvement during the RO. This difference was interpreted as indicating that skills learned during RO, such as talking about current events and comparing the good and bad aspects of the past and present, enabled the dementia sufferers to benefit from the subsequent Reminiscence Therapy. It helped them to focus on positive past memories, avoiding potentially upsetting memories. This result, if replicated, may suggest that, to benefit from Reminiscence Therapy, patients and staff need to be given prior training or 'induction' into the procedures used. It was notable that whilst RO tended to decrease the life satisfaction of the dementia sufferers, Reminiscence tended to lead to an increase. The contrast can be drawn between confronting dementia sufferers with an unfavourable life situation and enabling them to enjoy memories concerning past experiences.

As with RO, another aim of Reminiscence has been to produce changes in the pattern of interaction between dementia sufferers and care staff. In a review of Reminiscence in general, Thornton & Brotchie (1987) suggest that one of the main purposes is to change staff attitudes towards the dementia sufferer. In relation to dementia, there is evidence that the therapy can increase the degree of staff–patient interaction and lead to the staff knowing more about the dementia sufferer. Baines, Saxby & Ehlert (1987) used the Personal Information Questionnaire (PIQ) (Hanley, 1982) to ask basic questions about the resident's family, former work roles, and past and present hobbies and interests. Following both RO and Reminiscence, the staff knew much more about the dementia sufferers than about patients who had not been included in therapy.

In both the Head, Portnoy & Woods (1990) and McKiernan & Bender (1990) studies, the level of interaction between participants in the group increased, a finding that is not particularly surprising given the structured nature of the therapy. There is evidence that much of the interaction is between staff members and dementia sufferers rather than between the dementia sufferers. In the study by Head, Portnoy & Woods (1990), Reminiscence increased the degree of interaction between staff and dementia sufferers *outside* the sessions, but only in the second group, where the quality of interaction had been much lower initially. This suggests that the gains made in a 'richer' and more interactive environment may be limited, because there is little room for improvement.

In summary, Reminiscence Therapy can be seen as an appropriate approach for dementia sufferers and has been shown to have beneficial effects. As with RO, there is the tension for care staff, between spending more time talking to residents and doing domestic activities and taking care of the physical needs of residents. Nevertheless, Reminiscence does seem to have the added advantage that many people, including care staff, perceive it as an enjoyable activity with a personal focus.

VALIDATION THERAPY

Validation Therapy arose out of a reaction to the insensitive use of RO. The creator Naomi Feil grew up in a residential home for the elderly in Cleveland Ohio, where her parents worked and where she saw some negative consequences of RO, such as dementia sufferers being confronted with the reality of their illness and situation. In response, she developed an alternative approach that involves listening with empathy to whatever dementia sufferers are trying to communicate about their current feelings (Feil, 1982). The aim is to 'validate' what is said, rather than correcting factual errors, in order to establish a dialogue with the dementia sufferer. For example, if an elderly dementia sufferer says that their mother (who has died several years previously) is coming soon, then the response is not to correct the person but to empathise with their feelings of loss and insecurity.

Validation Therapy has been widely used both as a way of communicating with dementia sufferers and more formally within a group setting (Bleathman & Morton, 1988; Morton & Bleathman, 1991). In a weekly group, the aim is to make the members feel as comfortable as possible. For example, Bleathman & Morton (1988) have run groups in which the members are welcomed, followed by a group song and then discussion on a topic. The group finishes with a ritual thanking of members, a closing song and refreshments. Such roles as 'song-leader', 'welcomer', 'host/ess' are encouraged within the group. The topics covered include those reflecting universal feelings such as anger, separation and loss, with the aim of allowing members to verbalise unresolved feelings and conflicts about their families or loss of role, home and faculties. Although the claims for Validation Therapy are remarkable (Feil, 1982) there has been only one evaluation study, conducted by Morton & Bleathman (1991). Their pilot study explored the amount of verbal interaction between five dementia sufferers who attended group Validation Therapy over a period of 20 weeks. Compared to a baseline level there was no overall increase in the degree of interaction between participants during Validation Therapy. However, it was noted that there was variability in the data, such that two showed a marked increase, and another two showed a marked decrease.

GENERAL DISCUSSION

The different psychological approaches to the management of dementia sufferers have been reviewed above. The different forms of management described apply mainly to dementia sufferers in institutional care or day centres or hospitals, but there is no reason why they should not be adapted by informal carers in the community. Indeed, Pinkston & Linsk (1984) describe how behavioural approaches have been applied in family settings, with training given by professionals. Other developments in relation to this are reviewed in Chapter 8.

The studies show that the behaviour of dementia sufferers can alter in a positive fashion in response to the correct type of intervention. However, an underlying theme is that changes, such as increased activity, orientation and self-care skills will only be maintained with a continued input from carers. Sometimes it takes extra effort to prevent problems developing later on. Thus the same amount of input, in terms of caregiving, if strategically placed can be used to produce a more desirable outcome. An example is implementing a programme to ensure toileting rather than reacting to incontinence by changing clothes. Another underlying theme is that approaches must be tailored to individual dementia sufferers who may or may not benefit from a particular approach. For example, Reality Orientation may make one person distressed, but be seen as pleasurable by another person. The same applies to Reminiscence Therapy, which might consistently stir up unpleasant memories, or alternatively provide a relaxing activity which adds to the dignity of a person. To this extent, the goal-planning approach, advocated by Barrowclough & Fleming (1986) will help to ensure that each dementia sufferer is treated as an individual. An additional consequence is that group studies of approaches with dementia sufferers may obscure the positive and negative effects of interventions, arguing for a single case study approach to evaluation. At the very least, it is important to understand what features of a person's background and abilities predict success for a particular approach. For example, in the case studies cited above, Morris (1991) found one patient at the early stages of dementia who benefited from a guided mourning, whilst another did not. The critical difference between these patients was that the second did not have a sufficiently good memory to recall that their spouse had died, so was not able to get past the initial reaction to loss. The second person gradually learned about the death of her husband and was able to grieve appropriately.

At present, approaches to improving the primary cognitive impairments in the various forms of dementia are severely limited. The studies indicate that positive changes in behaviour can occur through programmed intervention. This is contrary to the often negative view that learning is not possible, which can undermine cognitive and behavioural rehabilitation in the elderly. Developments in the management of dementia will occur through capitalising on the capacity for behavioural change and relating this to the needs of the dementia sufferer.

CHAPTER 8   Psychosocial aspects of dementia

The majority of dementia sufferers (five out of six) live in the community, and it has long been recognised that this would not be possible without the support of family and friends (Gilhooly, 1986). Thus the needs and experiences of informal carers are an important aspect in understanding the social impact of dementia. Caring for someone with dementia can stretch to the limit the resources of any individual and is held to cause a greater emotional burden than caring for a physically disabled older person. This is partly because of inevitable changes in the relationship with the dementia sufferer, but also having to cope with the behavioural changes associated with the illness.

Usually the responsibility for care falls on one person, with a 'cascade' effect in which each member of the family will take responsibility in turn, but not collectively. For this reason, this chapter focuses on the carer as an individual, outlining the stresses and strains experienced and what factors influence these. Often the carer copes with circumstances that otherwise might be thought to be intolerable, but there is much that can be provided by way of support and this is discussed at the end of the chapter.

BEHAVIOURAL CHANGES IN THE DEMENTIA SUFFERER

Many of the studies that have investigated the impact of caring have been influenced by the seminal work of Grad & Sainsbury (1965), which evaluated the burden placed on carers caused by transferring elderly psychiatric patients back into the community.

They introduced the distinction between *objective* and *subjective* burden in this context. The former refers to the behavioural changes of a dementia sufferer and some of the practical problems that follow, for example the need to constantly supervise someone who is at risk of leaving the house and becoming lost. In contrast, subjective burden refers to the emotional reaction of the carer, such as a lowering of morale and a build up of stress or strain. This distinction has remained a useful one; in addition, Gilleard (1984) has introduced the term 'daily hassles' to refer to the day-to-day stressors that impinge on the carer, and Poulshock & Deimling (1984) have used the term 'caregiving impact' to describe the social effect on the caregiver's daily life, such as changes in family employment and health.

The major behavioural problems experienced by carers have been elicited from carers using various forms of checklists. The cognitive impairments have been described in Chapters 2–4, but the main behavioural changes can be characterised as 'disinhibition, deficit, and adaptation' (Oppenheimer & Jaccoby, 1991). For example, the loss of the capacity to inhibit behavioural reactions in a proportion of sufferers may result in aggression or sexual misdemeanours. It is estimated that 18% of dementia sufferers become either verbally or physically aggressive, adding to the stresses and strain experienced by the carer (Burns, Jaccoby & Levy, 1990d). Neuropsychological deficits such as dyspraxia lead to problems with self-care skills, including dressing and feeding, which increases the physical burden of nursing care, whilst memory and learning problems result in an inability to adapt to new circumstances and remain orientated. It has been noted that personality changes can be the most distressing to close relatives, with the worst of these being loss of social skills or social control, and a tendency to be apathetic or egocentric in relation to the needs of other people (Gilleard, 1984). These problems tend to occur at the more severe stages of dementia, but even then the majority of sufferers continue to live in the community. Early on in the course of dementia the problems may be much less severe and more easily tolerated by supporters (Eagles *et al*, 1987).

Sanford (1975) required carers to list all the problems they encountered at home and then state which problems would have to be dealt with to make life tolerable. The main problems were nocturnal wandering and incontinence, an inability to dress or wash or feed unaided, immobility and dangerous behaviour, such as dealing with the gas cooker or heating appliances. Other studies have confirmed these findings, using problem checklists. Greene *et al* (1982) factor analysed the data from their study, deriving three problem dimensions that they termed 'apathy/withdrawal' 'behavioural disturbance' and 'mood disturbance'. Similarly, Gilleard, Boyd & Watt (1982) derived five factors labelled 'dependency', 'disturbance', 'disability', 'demand', and 'wandering'. More recently, Gilleard (1984) also required carers to rate the severity of elicited problems. The 'top ten' most frequent severe problems out of 34 are listed in Table 8.1. Having to be constantly with the dementia sufferer is a particular problem because it severely restricts the other activities of the carer, including recreation and social contact (George & Gwyther, 1986). Another major problem is when the dementia sufferer becomes restless and agitated and starts to wander within the home. The carer has to be constantly on the alert for what may be happening in a different room.

Table 8.1 Ten most frequent severe problems reported by carers of dementia sufferers (compiled from Gilleard, 1984)

Problems	Percentage of carers responding		
	No problem	Some problem	Great problem
Cannot be left alone even for 1 hour	0	32	68
Wanders about house	6	34	60
Unable to hold a sensible conversation	11	39	50
Not safe outside alone	13	39	49
Disrupts personal and social life	7	45	48
Unable to take part in family conversations	18	34	48
Unsteady on feet	10	44	46
Falling	8	50	42
Incontinent (wetting)	14	45	40
Unable to walk outside the home	18	42	40

These and other problems can literally wear down the carer, with a progressive adverse effect on emotional wellbeing and physical health (Pruchno & Resch, 1989).

THE PSYCHOLOGICAL WELLBEING OF CARERS

The psychological wellbeing of carers has been investigated in some detail (R. G. Morris, L. W. Morris & P. G. Britton, 1988). Many studies report a higher level of depression compared with what would be expected from a community sample. L. W. Morris, R. G. Morris & P. G. Britton (1988) found that 14% of their sample of carers reported clinically significant levels of depressive symptoms as measured by the Beck Depression Inventory. This result is consistent with a range of other studies indicating a moderately increased incidence of depression in carers (Fitting et al., 1986; George & Gwyther, 1986; Moritz, Kasl & Berkman, 1989; Pruchno & Resch, 1989). Even higher levels of depression have been found by Pagel, Becker & Coppel (1985), with 40% of their sample currently depressed according to the Research and Diagnostic Criteria (RDC; Spitzer, Endicott & Robins, 1978) and a further 41% having been depressed at some stage in caregiving.

Another major index of emotional disorder is the prevalence of probable 'caseness' of psychiatric disorder measured by global ratings. Here the findings have been more equivocal. Bergmann & Jaccoby (1983) estimated that 33% of their sample of carers had what could be considered psychiatric disorder according to the General Health Questionnaire (GHQ). Gilleard et al (1984) arrived at a much higher estimate with 68% of their sample exceeding the threshold value for caseness on the GHQ. A study by Anthony-Bergstone, Zarit & Gatz (1988) compared the scores of carers with normative data on different features of psychiatric symptomatology using the Brief Symptom Inventory (BSI). The largest amount of symptomatology was seen in elderly women carers, who differed significantly from normative scores on the obsessive–compulsive, depression, anxiety, hostility and psychoticism subscales. In contrast, some studies have reported very little change in emotional wellbeing in carers. Gilhooly (1986) reported that her mixed sample of mainly spouse and sibling carers were in 'good' mental health, and Eagles *et al.* (1987) found no difference in GHQ scores between co-resident carers of dementia sufferers and the relatives of non-dementing elderly. Perhaps one reason for the discrepancy is that some carers are well adjusted to their situation, particularly if they live in a supportive environment and if the dementia sufferer is at an early stage of the illness.

HEALTH OF CARERS

The level of objective burden is reflected in the health of carers. Haley, Brown & Levine (1987) found that their sample of 44 primary carers of dementia sufferers rated their health as poorer overall than a control group of non-carer subjects. Carers also had more chronic illness, assessed using the Health Status Questionnaire (HSQ), and reported a greater number of recent visits to physicians and greater use of prescribed medicines. It was notable that, in their sample, six were hospitalized around the time that they participated in the study, whilst none of the control sample were hospitalized. Similarly, Pruchno & Resch (1989) found that carers report higher levels of chronic conditions, with health problems such as hypertension and arthritis. In both cases, ill-health was attributed both to the stress of caring and also to the physically demanding task of nursing, often involving heavy lifting and complete responsibility for household chores. Haley, Brown & Levine (1987) cite the case of a carer who died of a heart attack following a period of excessive physical activity and emotional stress associated with caregiving. Commonly, the most vulnerable carer is looking after a dementia sufferer who requires a high level of nursing care as well as being frail and elderly him or herself.

FACTORS INFLUENCING STRESS AND STRAIN

The level of stress or strain is not necessarily related to the degree of behavioural disturbance in the dementia sufferer (R. G. Morris, L. W. Morris & P. G. Britton, 1988). It is clear that there are marked individual differences in the manner in which carers cope with their situation. For example, a sibling carer who occasionally has to provide help for a parent with mild dementia and is well supported by other siblings and friends may experience minimal levels of strain. In contrast, an elderly co-resident carer who is looking after someone with severe dementia and is isolated from other people is likely to be under severe strain. Factors such as the blood/role relationship, the coping strategies of the carer and the degree of informal and formal support all influence the outcome of caring.

Relationship factors

The degree of distance in the blood/role relationship has been confirmed as influencing the mental health of the carer. Generally, the greater the familial distance the less strain experienced by the carer (Cantor, 1983; George & Gwyther, 1986; Gilhooly, 1984). This is partly because spouses tend to be co-resident with dementia sufferers and thus more likely to play a greater part in day-to-day caregiving. Despite this, it has been found that spouse carers are less likely to consider long-term institutional care for their relative, with the result that they remain carers for a longer period (Gilhooly, 1986).

Another factor influencing strain is the *quality* of the relationship between the carer and dementia sufferer. Paradoxically, it has been suggested that the closer the emotional bond within the relationship, the less the strain for the carer. Horowitz & Shindelman (1983) found that carers who maintain positive feelings towards a frail elderly relative have a lower level of perceived strain and a greater commitment to caring. The quality of the past relationship has been found to correlate with the mental health of carers of dementia sufferers. It has been proposed that a poor previous relationship exacerbates resentments and hostility when one partner becomes dependent on the other. In contrast, the situation is better tolerated if the carer has felt a deep affection for the dementia sufferer and can take on the caregiving role with a desire to care for the person rather than out of a sense of obligation.

L. W. Morris, R. G. Morris & P. G. Britton (1988) studied the association between 'past' and 'present' levels of marital intimacy in spouse carers and the degree of strain or depression. The measure encompassed different facets of intimacy, including affection, cohesion, expressiveness, compatibility, conflict resolution and sexuality. As predicted, higher levels of intimacy in the past were associated with lowered strain and depression. In addition, they found that the decrease in intimacy following the onset of dementia was associated with increased levels of depression. Loss of intimacy occurs in a number of areas in the relationship, including the sharing of physical affection and the ability to share private thoughts, communicate about the relationship and resolve differences of opinion. These changes are likely to be perceived as loss, and result in anticipatory grief, which is often observed in carers.

Gender differences

There is now substantial evidence that female carers experience more strain than male carers, with increased levels of depression and lowered morale (Morris et al., 1991). This imbalance is over and above the higher level of emotional disturbance found in women in community studies (Pruchno & Potasnik, 1989). One major cause is thought to derive from the different life experiences and socialisation patterns that men and women experience, with female carers expected to take on the traditional role as carer (Finch & Groves, 1983). For example, Horowitz's (1985) study of son and daughter carers of the frail elderly found that women were much more likely to help their dependent parents with transportation, meal preparation, errands, shopping and personal care. Formal services tend to reflect this imbalance, with male carers in the UK more likely to be offered formal services such as meals on wheels, home helps, rehabilitation/assessment and long-term care (Charlesworth, Wilkin & Durie, 1984). Despite this, the caregiving role may be a source of conflict for many women. Eichorn et al. (1981) have proposed that elderly women become more instrumental and assertive as they grow older, whilst men can become more nurturant and expressive. Strain can be compounded for women who view their later years as a time for personal growth and opportunities and resent becoming the carers of their husbands (Zarit, Todd & Zarit, 1986). Similarly, daughter carers are mainly middle-aged and either have other roles as 'nurturers' or are in the process of relinquishing child-rearing responsibilities and planning to take more control of their lives. These conflicts may place many women at odds with a role that may be expected of them by other family members.

Coping strategies and attributional style

The manner in which carers respond to their experience varies enormously. Some carers feel a sense of bitterness and anger about what has happened, whilst others feel a sense of gratitude that their situation is not as bad as they perceive it to be for others. One of the difficulties in coming to terms with caring for someone with dementia is the insidious onset of the illness and the continual change that occurs. Often the behaviour of the dementia sufferer is misinterpreted, and carers can sometimes blame themselves for their relative's behaviour. At the same time, the increasing dependency of the dementia sufferer can lead to a sense of loss of control over the carer's own life.

Carers appear to experience less strain if they are able to maintain some sense of emotional distance, adopting a practical and instrumental approach to daily problems. This has been cited as the reason why husband carers are less prone to stress, because they more rapidly distance themselves emotionally from the problems (Zarit, Todd & Zarit, 1986). Generally, carers appear to cope in a more adaptive fashion if they concentrate their energies on solving management and financial problems (Barusch & Spaid, 1989). The manner in which the carer interprets the behaviour of the dementia sufferer can also influence the degree of strain. Miller (1987) has found that wife carers tend to explain their husbands behaviour in terms of a changing relationship with their spouse. Husband carers, in contrast, tend to refer to problems in the mind of their spouse as an explanation for behavioural change, attributing this specifically to the disease process.

More broadly, the attributional style of carers has been related to level of depression. Pagel, Becker & Coppel (1985) asked a sample of spouse carers to rate their perception of control and causal attributions for changes in the behaviour of the dementia sufferer, and their perceived control over the sufferer's current behaviour. For example, the carers were asked 'how much control do you feel you have over your spouse's [upsetting behaviour] in terms of being able to influence it within a certain range?' Perceived loss of control was associated with a higher level of depression, and carers tended to be more depressed if they blamed the spouse's behaviour on themselves. There was a general pattern for self-blame to be associated with anxiety and hostility, suggesting that this was a source of demoralisation and conflict. Using the same sample, Coppel *et al.* (1985) found that carers were more likely to be depressed if they felt that the dementia sufferer's upsetting behaviour affected all aspects of their lives and had become a permanent feature. Another significant finding was that carers who had higher expectations of being able to handle the behaviour of the dementia sufferer but experienced a lack of control were more likely to be depressed. More recently, Morris *et al.* (1989a) have confirmed that mitigating factors for psychological wellbeing are if strain and stress is thought to be shortlasting and if the behaviour of the dementia sufferer affects only limited aspects of the carer's life.

In summary, carers vary in terms of the amount of stress experienced, but tend to be more vulnerable if the behaviour disturbance of the dementia sufferer is particularly severe, or if the relationship has been poor in the past. The ability of the carer to cope depends in part on what attitudes are adopted, and whether the carer can gain a sense of control of the situation. These intrapersonal factors play their part, but equally important is the degree to which informal carers are supported by other people, including informal support and formal services.

Family and social support

The level of informal support is frequently considered by professionals working with carers. A negative aspect of caregiving is the degree of restriction from social activities and resulting increase in social isolation. This problem can be offset to some extent if the carer is well supported by other family members or their community (Niederehe & Fruge, 1984).

Studies of the role of social support in ameliorating carer burden indicate that it is the *quality* of 'support' not the *quantity* that is important. For example, both Gilleard *et al.* (1984) and Gilhooly

(1984) found that there was no association between the degree of contact and help received from family friends. In contrast, satisfaction with help from relatives appears to be associated with carer wellbeing (Gilhooly, 1984). More recently, Morris et al. (1989b) administered a measure of social support derived from the Californian Human Population Laboratory Questionnaire (Berkman, 1983). This measure looks in more detail at the emotional, instrumental and financial help received, and the web of social relationships that surround the carer. For example, carers would be asked the question 'If you can call on a relative or friend for help with a real problem, how often do you do so?' or 'When you need some extra help, can you count on anyone to help with daily tasks like shopping, cleaning, cooking or transport?' Carers who tended to respond positively to these questions were less depressed and felt less strain overall. Pearson, Verma & Nellett (1988) have also explored the types of help that carers most appreciate. These include social visits and being able to leave the dementia sufferer with a relative so that the carer could go out of the house for social or recreational activities.

EDUCATIONAL/SUPPORT GROUPS

An increasingly popular way of supporting carers is to bring them together for a series of meetings, either educational or support groups. The meetings can be professionally or peer led and can be time limited or continuous with members joining and leaving the group over time. The focus of these meetings varies substantially, providing education about dementia, training carers in how to manage the sufferer's disturbed behaviour and providing an opportunity for carers to be mutually supportive. It provides a vehicle for carers to express their hopes, fears, disappointments, worries and problems, and to share alternative methods of coping. In common with all successful groups, the meetings aim towards cohesiveness and should instil a sense of hope and common purpose in which the carers can learn from their experiences (Yalom, 1975).

Information

Information about dementia can be provided by professionals or experienced carers and supplemented by providing literature, such as *The 36-Hour Day* (Mace & Rabins, 1981). Areas that should be covered include the causes of illness, the effect of the illness on the sufferer's behaviour, and the types of help available from community resources (Zarit & Zarit, 1982). Morris *et al.* (1992) describe 'Information Groups' in which different professionals speak to the group in turn, each concentrating on their sphere of knowledge. These include a social worker, a community psychiatric nurse, a psychiatrist, a psychologist and a full-time worker from a voluntary organisation that supports carers.

Information about the *nature* of dementia is particularly important because it enables carers to make sense of the disturbing behaviour of the dementia sufferer. For example, repetitive questioning can be seen as an irritating habit or attempt to seek attention, rather than the result of impaired memory. Another example is interpreting the cause of the illness, where ignorance can lead to self-blame, such as blaming the onset of the dementia on a decision to move house (Morris, 1986). Carers also need to gain confidence in coping with problems, and in this sense professionals can affirm positive ways of managing and tactfully suggest alternative methods where necessary. Information about community resources can also be imparted by professionals, but often the experience of informal carers is equally useful, being the consumers of services. In this regard, it can help to have carers at the different stages of the caregiving process included in group meetings.

Enhancing coping strategies

Carers often express the need to feel that their role is recognised by other people and that their experiences are validated (Toseland, Rossiter & Labrecque, 1989). A way of facilitating this in a group is to encourage the passing on of management skills between the members of the group. The problem-solving approach provides a useful framework in which together carers can explore solutions to the problems that they are facing. This approach has been adapted specifically for carers of dementia sufferers by Zarit and his colleagues (Zarit & Zarit, 1982; Zarit, Orr & Zarit, 1985), and more recently in the UK by Morris *et al.* (1992). The basis for this approach is drawn from the work of D'Zurilla & Goldfried (1971) and involves enabling the carers to identify and describe specific problems, generate and evaluate a plan of intervention, and then implement and evaluate the plan. In a group setting, the participants can pool their knowledge and resources to provide ways of tackling problems, thus providing support for each other. For example, one problem for a carer was expressed as losing his temper when he became frustrated by his wife's interference with daily activities. This problem was identified as being more pervasive than originally thought, indicating a general heightening of stress associated with looking after his wife for long periods. Various solutions were explored by the group, including ways of reducing stress overall through stress management, employing a sitter who could distract his wife for a period, and arranging for day care. By exploring the problem in a group, the carer was helped to accept that he needed to elicit more support than he had hitherto recognised.

A specific course incorporating the problem-solving model is outlined in Table 8.2. A feature of the course is to apply problem-solving methods to specific aspects of caregiving, starting with identifying and managing problem behaviour, and proceeding to stress management techniques and ways of exploring the need for informal or formal support. The ideal size for groups of this type is approximately seven, allowing each member enough time to explore their own problems with the group as a whole. Specific problem-solving techniques are used by the facilitator, such as getting the group to list the 'pros' and 'cons' of a particular plan of action and encouraging members to try out solutions at home, reporting back at the next session. Each group member is debriefed individually by a course facilitator, in order to provide practical information that has been overlooked in the group. It also enables the facilitator to monitor levels of emotional strain and the development of coping strategies, as a way of evaluating the efficacy of the group. In practice, these types of groups appear

Table 8.2   Content of sessions used in the Morris *et al.* (1992) Carers'
Programme (Ways of Coping)

Session	Purpose
1. *Individual interview* of carer by professional	To assess the level of dependency of the dementia sufferer, the degree of stress or strain experienced by the carer. To explain the purpose of the group meetings.
2. *Group Meeting Theme:* 'Understanding Behaviour'	To introduce the carers to each other and enable them to explain their current situation. To describe the different stages of dementia To introduce methods for observing the behaviour of the dementia sufferer.

Material to take away: A record sheet for recording 'problem behaviours'.

| 3. *Group Meeting Theme:* 'Generating Solutions' | To discuss the use of the recording sheet and share problems encountered. To discuss ways of reframing problems. To introduce ways of coping with behavioural problems (e.g. wandering, aggression). To introduce ways of generating and evaluating solutions (e.g. 'pros' and 'cons' method). |

Material to take away: The carers are required to pick a particular problem and then to generate and evaluate different ways of tackling it.

| 4. *Group Meeting Theme:* 'Coping with stress' | To review ways of tackling problem behaviours. To introduce different ways that carers cope with stress and to evaluate positive and negative coping strategies. |

Material to take away: Participants would record a strategy that they had used to reduce stress and evaluate how successful it had been.

Continues

Table 8.2 Continued

Session	Purpose
5. *Group Meeting Theme:* 'Formal and informal support'	To review success of strategies for coping with stress. To describe what is available in terms of local community support.
Material to take away: The participants would identify areas where they might benefit from help and decide on strategies they might use.	
6. *Group Meeting Theme:* 'Conclusion'	To discuss the outcome of the task assignment from Meeting 5. To review the problem solving to improving coping strategies. To provide feedback from the participants in terms of their evaluation of the course.
7. *Individual interview* of carer by professional	To assess the level of strain and stress of the carer. To evaluate changes in coping strategies. To obtain the individual's evaluation of the course. To provide further information for the carer where necessary.
8. *Individual interview* of carer by professional	To repeat session 7 after a period of approximately 3 months.

to encourage carers to adopt new approaches and learn from the experiences of other participants.

A more intensive approach has been to use a highly structured 10-day residential programme for dementia sufferers together with their carers (Brodaty & Gresham, 1989). Up to four dementia sufferers and their respective carers are admitted into hospital at any one time. The dementia sufferers receive memory retraining whilst the carers are given intensive education, group therapy, training in management skills and extended family therapy sessions that involve other members of the dementia sufferer's social network. This programme has been noted to produce long-lasting increases in psychological wellbeing in the carers, over and above the waiting-list controls, and to reduce the level of admission of dementia sufferers into residential care. Such approaches may be costly in the short term, requiring more resources than running support groups, but in the long term they are justified by reducing the need for institutionalisation.

Psychotherapeutic orientation

One of the criticisms of groups that focus on management skills or coping strategies is that they ignore the emotional needs of carers. The main emotional adjustment stems from the losses associated with the onset of dementia, both in terms of loss of a relationship and loss of hitherto enjoyable and pleasurable activities. This loss can result in feelings of anger, frustration and guilt, as well as despair concerning the future. In addition, carers are often challenged with the need to redefine their role and adjust their own priorities, in order that caregiving be a time for 'personal growth'. Carers may need an emotionally supportive environment where they can share their feelings openly with other people.

Psychotherapeutically orientated groups have had mixed results, partly because carers within the group may be at different stages of adjustment. Barnes *et al.* (1981) describe carers in their group who refused to believe the diagnosis (and hence the prognosis) of their partner's illness. This was seen as a way of limiting the emotional impact of the diagnosis, but in the long term it was counterproductive because it interfered with appropriate planning for the future and fostered unrealistic expectations about the future. As the disease progressed many of their group members commonly felt a deep sense of loss and sadness, which they communicated with each other. Members were able to admit to wishes and fantasies for the dementia sufferer's early death, and that they found it hard to talk about or tolerate such feelings about a loved one.

The sharing of emotions and subsequent perceptions of support was felt to be beneficial overall in the groups run by Barnes *et al.* (1981). However, they found that individual expressions of anger and grief could have a negative effect on other group members, leading them to feel more depressed and less able to cope. This experience has been corroborated by Schmidt & Keyes (1985) and Wasow (1985), who warn that strong negative feelings that are expressed but not understood can overwhelm and threaten to destroy the cohesiveness of a group. To balance the increasing awareness or sense of despair created by the person's illness, Barnes *et al.* (1981) recommend that groups which explore emotions should still focus on curative factors such as support, education and inspiration of group members. There is also a case for screening out the more vulnerable carers, with low levels of psychological wellbeing, for individual counselling (Toseland & Smith, 1990).

Evaluations of groups

Formal evaluations of groups have tended to indicate positive results, both in terms of changes in carer emotional wellbeing and in high levels of consumer satisfaction. The results of intervention studies using formal measures, rather than clinical impressions, are summarised in Table 8.3. The earliest study, by Lazarus (1981), focused mainly on emotional support, and reported no changes in self-esteem, although carers felt an increased sense of control over their situation and felt that the group had helped them cope with specific problems. Subsequent studies by Gendron, Poitras & Engels (1986), Kahan *et al* (1985), Shibal-Champagne & Lapinska-Stachow (1985–1986), Zarit, Anthony & Boutselis (1987) and Whit-latch, Zarit & Von Eye (in press), show an increase in knowledge concerning dementia, and a decrease in either carer burden or improvements in levels of psychological wellbeing. These studies encompass a variety of approaches including 'support', provision and a skills training focus. Toseland, Rossiter & Labrecque (1989) report improvements in personal coping, in addition to other psychological changes. These included greater control over feelings of guilt about the quality of care that carers were providing and a greater balance between caregiving and other family responsibilities.

It is notable, however, that the improvements found by Zarit *et al.* (1985) for groups or individual counselling are no greater than for the waiting-list controls. These carers reported the same improvement in managing the dementia sufferer's behaviour and increased assistance in home-help and use of day care. It may be that the decision to seek help, combined with the initial interview by those conducting the study, was sufficient to produce the change observed in carers who attended the groups. Studies that did not report positive changes in psychological wellbeing nevertheless found high levels of satisfaction with the groups (Glosser & Wexler, 1985; Haley, 1989; Haley, Brown & Levine, 1987; Morris *et al*, 1992). Typical of aspects they found helpful were 'learning that the problems were not unique', and 'having the chance to meet people with similar problems', 'finding out how others are dealing with problems', 'learning about available community resources', and 'gaining information about medical aspects of dementia'. High levels of consumer satisfaction, in the absence of objective change in behaviour, may reflect the perceived usefulness of the groups but low impact in relation to other potent influences in the carers lives.

FORMAL SUPPORT

With the current emphasis on community care, more attention has been given to providing formal support to carers. A range of services has been implemented, including home helps, meals on wheels, laundry services, visits from District Nurses, and the provision of day care and respite care. These services are often vital to carers—enabling them to continue functioning, as well as improving the quality of life of the dementia sufferer. A social work study by Levin, Sinclair & Gorbach (1986) found that the build up of strain was less when greater formal support was provided, even though carers did not express complete satisfaction with the services. Gilhooly (1984) has also reported a positive association between the morale of the carer and home-help services or visits from a community nurse. In contrast, other studies indicate that the level of formal support is reactive to stress and strain in the carer. For example, Morris *et al.* (1989b) reported a paradoxical *positive* relationship between the amount of carer strain and formal support. It has often been argued that service

Table 8.3 Summary of the outcome of group intervention studies for carers of dementia sufferers (only studies using quantitative outcome measures are included)

Authors	Approach	Length	Outcome
Brodaty & Gresham (1989)	Intensive training versus staying on waiting list	Ten days, residential dementia sufferer less likely to be institutionalised	Increase in carer wellbeing
Chiverton & Caine (1989)	Education	3 sessions weekly; 2 hours	Increase in knowledge about dementia
Gendron et al. (1986)	Stress management	8 sessions weekly	Reduced anxiety, increased assertiveness
Glosser & Wexler (1985)	Education and support	8 sessions weekly; 2 hours	Positive ratings for perceived helplessness
Haley et al. (1987)	1. Support 2. Support and training 3. Waiting list control	10 sessions weekly; 1.5 hours	Positive ratings for perceived helpfulness but no difference between groups in carer wellbeing or coping strategies
Haley (1989)		Long-term follow-up	Confirmed outcome of previous study after approx. 2 years

Kahan et al. (1985)	Education and support	8 sessions weekly; 2 hours	Decrease in level of depression and perceived burden; increase in knowledge about dementia
Lazarus et al. (1981)	Support and therapy	10 sessions weekly; 1 hour	No change in self-esteem but increase in sense of locus of control
Morris et al. (1992)	1. Education 2. Training focus to improve coping strategies	5 sessions weekly; 1.5 hours	Positive ratings of helpfulness in both groups but no change in emotional wellbeing
Shibal-Champagne & Lapinska-Stachow (1985–1986)	Education and support	8 sessions weekly; 1.5 hours	Decrease in carer burden
Toseland et al. (1989)	1. Education and problem solving focus 2. Peer-led support focus	8 sessions weekly; 2 hours	Positive changes in psychological wellbeing in both groups
Zarit et al. (1987)	1. Education and support 2. Individual and family counselling 3. Waiting list control group	8 sessions weekly	Decrease in carer burden and frequency of emotional disorder, but equal change in all three groups

providers should work to promote the carer's own support system, such as their social network or family, rather than taking over responsibilities. There has been some success with programmes to coordinate professional and voluntary help for carers. Challis & Davies (1986) implemented a scheme in which local volunteers were recruited and funds were allocated for specific purposes concerning caregiving. This scheme was successful in maintaining approximately 50% of dementia sufferers in the community, in contrast to 23% in a control population.

Day care and respite relief has also been put forward as a way of enabling the carer to continue in their role for as long as possible. Day care provides temporary relief for the carer on a regular basis, freeing up their time to engage in other activities. There is some evidence that day care results in a significant decrease in emotional distress for the carer (Gilleard, 1987). Nevertheless, attendance may actually precipitate institutionalisation by bringing carers into greater contact with formal services (Bergmann & Jaccoby, 1983; Greene & Timbury, 1979). A similar pattern has been found with respite care. Carers using a respite programme reported improvements in their physical and mental health and increased confidence in their ability to continue caregiving (Burdz, Eaton & Bond, 1988; Scharlach & Frenzel, 1986). Nevertheless, people in respite care are far more likely to become institutionalised than those in the general population (Foundation for Long-term Care, 1983).

CONCLUSIONS

In conclusion, this chapter has focused on carers primarily because of their central role in supporting people with dementia. Carers have been shown to experience psychological burdens and emotional distress, but the stresses and strains of caring are influenced by a number of factors. These include the carer's premorbid relationship with the dementia sufferer, how caregiving is interpreted by the carer, and the degree of informal and formal support. The psychological burden of caring can be reduced by support from family and friends, but also by bolstering the carers coping abilities via educational and support groups. Formal services for dementia sufferers can be seen as supporting the carer in practical ways, and have been shown to reduce levels of strain. The psychosocial factors that impinge on caring for dementia sufferers in the community are complex and varied but equal in importance to understanding the psychological changes associated with the dementing illness.

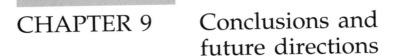

CHAPTER 9   Conclusions and future directions

Psychological approaches to dementia range from the cognitive approach to understanding mental impairment, to treatment and psychosocial issues. The development of knowledge in these areas parallels the very rapid developments in neurological and neuro-biological approaches during the last decade. The psychological aspects, although receiving less attention, are equally important in understanding and treating the different forms of dementia (Morris & MacKiernan, in press). For example, even if the neurobiological changes could be arrested completely, the problems of diagnosis and management would not go away. Indeed, a successful treatment for progressive dementia would place a premium on early diagnosis and screening, with a greater role for sophisticated neuropsychological assessment. In addition, the management problems of those people who had developed dementia would remain and may even require more systematic implementation over a longer period. Thus, both in the short term, where no substantially effective treatment is available, and in the longer term a psychological understanding of dementia will be needed.

Basic research into the neuropsychology of Alzheimer's disease has essentially mapped out the profile of cognitive impairment, and this approach is being extended to other forms of dementia. The growth of interest in *practice* as well as research in this area is encouraging and clearly the basic research has helped to shape treatment approaches. For example, knowledge of the working memory deficit in Alzheimer's disease (Morris & Baddeley, 1988) has direct implications for group approaches to therapy for dementia (see discussion below). Investigating the psychosocial aspects of dementia has isolated the factors that make a caregiver more at risk, in terms of psychological breakdown, and provide information about which approaches to support caregivers might be most beneficial (Morris & Morris, in press). Some of the more recent developments are outlined below, with a reflection on how the field might develop in the future.

NEUROPSYCHOLOGICAL IMPAIRMENT AND ASSESSMENT

In the early 1980s a Royal College of Physicians Report (1981) on organic mental impairment emphasised the need to refine the techniques for diagnosis of dementia, to improve detection and facilitate treatment. With respect to psychology, much has been achieved, with improved protocols for psychiatric and psychological assessment (see Chapter 6).The 1980s saw a plethora of studies of cognition in early Alzheimer's disease that has led to a much greater understanding of the pattern of impairment, including investigations of attention, memory and language processing. Prior to these investigations it was commonly assumed that all mental processes in dementia were equally impaired and therefore of no interest. Nevertheless, it has become clear that some aspects of cognition are selectively preserved (for example, the Articulatory Loop System of working memory, and aspects of selective attention and implicit memory), whilst other aspects are severely impaired (for example, episodic memory).

Knowledge of this pattern of deficits gives a clue as to how the underlying neurobiological changes affect cognition, and also helps in characterising different forms of dementia behaviourally. It is now known that even the basic subtypes of dementia, such as Alzheimer-type dementia (AD), fragment into smaller subtypes (Burns & Levy, in press). A cognitive neuropsychology of dementia will be needed to help differentiate between these groups. A number of recent studies have investigated the cognition of large groups of patients with dementia and used multivariate statistics to establish subtypes. For example, Becker (1988) and Becker & Lopez (1992) investigated 194 patients with AD and analysed their performance on measures of executive functioning and episodic memory. Patients dissociated into those with a specific dysexecutive syndrome and those with amnestic syndromes.

Allied to this, individual patients with relatively focal impairments could be studied in great depth using single-case study
methodology, for example the extensive investigation of semantic
memory in a single patient with AD, presented by Moss *et al.*
(1993).

In addition, the longitudinal study of cognitive functioning in
dementia may provide information as to how cognition breaks
down in different groups of patients and thus provide an indication of the 'natural history' of dementias. For example, there has
been controversy concerning whether aphasia is a good prognostic
indicator for AD. Berg *et al.* (1988) followed up 43 patients with
AD over 5 years and found that a measure of aphasia based on
subtests of the Boston Diagnostic Aphasia Evaluation Battery correlated with the degree of change on a clinical rating of dementia.
Another study, by Faber-Langendoen *et al.* (1988), assessed 150
AD patients and found that aphasic disturbances, particularly
impairments in comprehension and written expression, were
associated with a more rapid cognitive decline overall. In this
study, they also claim to have identified a subtype of AD with
more prominent aphasic disturbance, an earlier onset and more
rapid deterioration. Subsequent longitudinal observations suggest
that precipitous declines occur in language functions (object
naming) early in AD and declines on visuospatial tests occur later
in the illness (Rebok, Brandt & Folstein, 1990).

In terms of diagnosis, the incorporation of abbreviated neuropsychological assessment procedures such as the CAMDEX or
MEAMS (Golding, 1988; Roth *et al.*, 1986) is now well established.
A further development has been to explore the sensitivity and
specificity of neuropsychological measures more fully at the different stages of dementia. For example, various studies have
shown that performance on measures of recent memory differentiate cases of AD at the earliest stages from normal elderly control
subjects (Fuld *et al.*, 1990; Welsh *et al.*, 1991). The same studies,
however, indicate that not all measures of recent memory are
effective for this purpose, with the indication that impairment on
tests of delayed recall are particularly sensitive to early AD. In
addition, it was found that a combination of measures, including
fluency, praxis and recognition memory, best differentiated cases
with mild dementia from those with either moderate or severe

stages of the disease. Clearly, these approaches to validating traditional assessment procedures in this patient population needs to be integrated with the more experimental approaches described in this book.

One prime area for development is the use of computer-aided assessment procedures. Despite the potential use of computers, design of appropriate tests has been sporadic, one of the earlier commercially available systems for dementia being the Bexley–Maudsley Automated Psychological Screening (BMAPS) (Acker & Acker, 1982). This relates partially to the cognitive impairments associated with dementia which preclude cooperating with some assessment procedures. Nevertheless, some systems have proved successful, and have been used in evaluating the cognitive effects of drugs in dementia. For example, the Cognitive Drug Research Computerised Assessment System (COGDRAS) has recently been adapted for the assessment of patients with dementia and validated against more conventional tests (Simpson et al., 1991; Wesnes et al., 1987). The system includes a variety of tests of recognition memory, memory scanning, vigilance and choice reaction time, using the facility of a microcomputer to measure reaction times and present material in a precise manner. The validation study suggests that most of the patients found this test battery generally enjoyable.

A difficulty with the computerised approach is that many tests divide the attention of the patient between observing the visual display unit and responding, usually using response keys and buttons. The substantial difficulty in divided attention in patients with dementia can lead to very poor performance, perhaps accounting for the low scores of some of the dementia patients observed by Simpson et al. (1991) using the COGDRAS. A way round this problem is to use touch-sensitive screen technology which has the advantage of enabling the person to focus their attention in the same area of the visual field that they execute their response. This technique has been pioneered in dementia by Carr, Woods & Moore (1986), followed by the development of the Cambridge Automated Neuropsychological Test Battery (CANTAB) (Morris et al., 1987; Sahakian et al., 1988). This contains a series of tests tailored to suit early AD patients, including visual and verbal recognition memory, delayed response, and delayed matching to sample. The tests are all designed to minimise instruction, use visual stimuli presented on the visual display unit, and require a motoric output. Although this battery contains tests of dubious validity for this patient population, it has been used extensively on different groups of patients with cognitive impairment (Morris et al., 1987; Robbins et al., 1992; Sahakian et al., 1990) and in the evaluation of drug treatment (eg. Eagger et al., 1992). Proponents of the CANTAB tests (eg. Owen, in press) make claims about their greater sensitivity and acceptability than non-computerised approaches, but these have yet to be investigated fully.

Computerised tests have the advantage of being able to measure reaction times and also to make the test more interactive with the patient using the computer, to provide systematic feedback. In general, the 'gamelike' quality of the tests can make up for the lack of portability and 'human' interaction, and has been shown to motivate the patient as highly as alternative paper-and-pencil tests developed for this population. Advances in speech reception and production, allied to more powerful desk-top computers, should increase the range of possibilities in this area of assessment. The drawbacks of computer-aided assessment remain, however, and include lack of flexibility of use and the problem of rapidly outmoded technology which inhibits the validation and standardisation of new tests. All these factors are likely to be less important as the cost continues to decrease and the technology becomes more stable.

BEHAVIOURAL CHANGES

Behavioural assessment of dementia has long been established, mainly as a means of assessing the severity of dementia and determining the degree of dependency or disability (Jorm et al., 1991). The general approach has been to develop a scale that provides a global rating of dementia, perhaps with subscales assessing the level cognitive and social functioning (eg. The Clifton Assessment Battery for the Elderly; Pattie and Gilleard, 1979). Allied to this has been the use of psychiatric rating scales that are used to detect psychiatric symptomatology in patients with dementia (Burns, Jaccoby & Levy 1990c). A more recent departure has been the development of a greater variety of scales, which focus on particular aspects of cognition and behaviour, including memory, attention and personality. These scales may prove to be useful clinical instruments as well as providing more information about dementia, where self-assessment is not feasible. In addition, they provide information about everyday functioning that direct tests of cognition may not be able to predict.

One area is the use of informant's reports to measure memory impairment. This has been built into a number of behavioural rating scales, such as the Geriatric Evaluation by Relatives Rating Instrument (GERRI), which includes 21 items to measure cognitive functioning, most of which concern memory (Schwartz, 1983). Other scales have followed suit, including the CAMDEX, which includes five items covering memory (Roth *et al.*, 1986). More specialised procedures have included the Inpatient Memory Impairment Scale (IMIS) (Knight & Godfrey, 1984), designed to measure memory problems associated with dementia encountered in hospital settings. More recently, such scales have been used to investigate different aspects of memory functioning based on cognitive neuropsychological models. Thus the Informant Questionnaire on Cognitive Decline in the Elderly (IQCODE), developed by Jorm & Korten (1988), has been developed as a self-administered version for informants. The instrument has a number of subscales that map directly onto memory distinctions, such as episodic, semantic, remote memory and learning (see Chapter 2). Notably, however, Jorm *et al.* (1991) have found that in a study of geriatric patients the subscales all tend to correlate with objective measures of episodic memory. Jorm *et al.* (1991) also found that it correlates well with traditional brief measures of cognitive impairment, including the Mini-Mental State Examination, yet does not correlate with indicators of 'premorbid' abilities, including education (Jorm & Jacomb, 1989) and word-reading skill (Jorm *et al.*, 1991). The use of informant questionnaires adds 'ecological' validity to cognitive assessment, focusing on everyday memory problems. Clearly there is much scope for developing these questionnaires more fully in this population and relating them to the management of patients and evaluation of treatment.

Another intriguing attempt to obtain ecological validity in the measurement of behaviour is the conversational assessment task described by Alberoni *et al.* (1992). Their procedure was designed to explore the difficulty that patients with AD have in coordinating information from different sources, stemming from the deficit in working memory functioning (see Chapter 2). Patients were shown videotapes of conversations involving from two to five characters. After each tape, a statement from one of the characters was presented and the subject required to point to the person who had made the statement. The AD patients were significantly impaired on this task, particularly when the number of characters was greater than three. This finding has implications for assessment, and also shows that AD patients will have substantial difficulty in social situations that involve more than three participants, including the remedial therapies described in Chapter 7.

PERSONALITY

Much work has focused on the cognitive impairments associated with dementia. Despite this, it has been recognised that the development of psychiatric symptomatology and personality associated with dementia may be at least as important as the cognitive deficits (Burns, Jaccoby & Levy, 1990a–d). Changes in social interaction, including an increase in challenging behaviours and interpersonal conflicts, have been shown to be related to increased strain in the carer (Gilleard, Boyd & Watt, 1982). Increased apathy and withdrawal are also predictive of strain (Greene *et al.*, 1982).

Psychological studies of personality change in dementia have been limited, but this is clearly an area of substantial interest. The standard view has been that premorbid personality is accentuated, resulting in exaggerations of personality characteristics (eg. Adams & Victor, 1989). In non-pathological states, variability in personality has been thought to have a biological basis (Eysenck, 1967), with differences in the functional organisation of the central nervous system. If so, then the changes in the brains of patients with dementia, particularly the medial temporal, inferior parietal and frontal lobes, could be predicted to be accompanied by personality change, as is well known in other forms of neuropsychological or neuropsychiatric disorders (Lishman, 1987). Preliminary studies support the clinical impression of personality change, including the report by Bergmann, Manchee & Woods (1984), which explored maladaptive and adaptive traits in patients with dementia. Rubin, Morris & Berg (1987) investigated personality using open-ended questions, finding that passivity was increased in about two-thirds, with agitation and self-centredness each in a third. A different technique has been to use informant ratings. Petry et al. (1988; 1989) studied AD patients' position on bipolar continua (e.g. mature–childish; energetic–lifeless). A common pattern of increasing passivity, coarseness and decreased spontaneity was found which, incidentally, was unrelated to the severity of dementia.

Studies grounded in theories of normal personality structure are rare and would be of considerable theoretical and practical interest. Chatterjee et al. (1992) required the caregivers of AD patients to complete the NEO Personality Inventory (NEO-PI) (Costa & McRae, 1988), which assesses five major domains of personality: neuroticism, extroversion, openness, conscientiousness and agreeableness. They found persistent changes in all these personality traits and no reduction in the variability of personality, suggesting no convergence into a unified 'AD personality'. Of note, there was no exaggeration of previous personality traits, but all patients had a similar increase in traits (eg. neuroticism), irrespective of their premorbid personality. Clearly, studies of this type have the potential to relate changes in cortical pathology and brain neurochemistry in AD. One proposal by Chatterjee et al. (1992) is that as the AD population shifts away from the norm in terms of personality, they become more susceptible to developing categorical psychiatric symptoms, such as depressive symptoms or paranoid delusions.

NEUROIMAGING AND COGNITION

Advances in neuroimaging have improved substantially the possibility for relating brain damage to neuropsychological dysfunction in dementia *in vivo*. A variety of neuroimaging techniques have been developed and these will increase in range and sophistication in the future. Neuroimaging techniques divide into two main approaches, one that looks at structural changes in the brain, such as computed tomography (CT) and magnetic resonance imagining (MRI), and the other that measures brain activity, such as single photon emission tomography (SPET) and positron emission tomography (PET). Some of the methods have been developed further, to the extent that they are capable of both types of neuroimaging. For example, echoplanar imaging using MRI technology is capable of providing a measure of localised brain blood volume, an indirect index of brain activity in specific regions.

The link between neurobiological dysfunction and cognitive impairment has been explored using these techniques already. More recent examples include the use of MRI to investigate white matter changes, where significant associations with cognitive impairment has been found (Besson et al., 1990). In this case, there were significant associations between tests of visuospatial function and parieto-occipital changes. In relation to brain activity, SPET neuroimaging has found similar associations, for example, between amnesia and temporal hypoperfusion, between apraxia and decreased posterior parietal hypoperfusion, and between aphasia and hypoperfusion throughout the left hemisphere (see Burns et al., 1989). These findings are mirrored in the PET studies, which potentially provide a greater localisation of brain activity and have been used to explore changes at different stages of dementia. Regional cerebral metabolic rates for glucose (rCMR-glc) indicate that the fronto-parietal system may be dysfunctional at the early stages of AD (Grady et al., 1988). In addition, rCMR-glc rates show increased hemispheric asymmetry for association areas of the parietal temporal and frontal cortices, with the direction of asymmetry determining the relative severity of deficits in language and visuospatial dysfunction (Haxby et al., 1990). More 'fine-grained' analyses have been conducted, for example, Parasuraman et al. (1992) explored selective attention deficits and neural activity and found an association between right superior parietal lobe hypometabolism and the deficit in 'disengaging' attention in AD (see p. 59).

These studies are based on 'resting' measures of brain activity which are then correlated against neuropsychological performance. However, a more elaborate technique, facilitated mainly by PET, is to measure brain activity whilst the patient is performing a variety of tasks (Posner et al., 1988). This technique should reveal brain areas that remain inactive, in comparison to control subjects, when called up to support particular forms of mental activity. Such 'activation' studies are inevitably more complex but should provide a far greater integration between the cognitive neuropsychology of dementia and neuroimaging. In addition, functional neuroimaging may eventually provide a reliable way of splitting up the diseases causing dementia into subtypes *in vivo* (Chawluk *et al.*, 1990).

NEUROBIOLOGICAL APPROACHES TO TREATMENT

Drug studies have been a major focus of research into dementia, partly because of the commercial implications of finding a reliable treatment. Furthermore, accumulated knowledge concerning neurochemical deficits in AD have provided a rationale for many of the treatments under investigation (Collerton, 1985). Therapeutic drug treatments divide approximately into those which compensate for neurotransmitter deficiency, those which increase blood flow to affected areas through vasodilation, and those that are aimed at changing the metabolic functioning of cerebral tissue, the cerebroactive substances (Kendall, 1987). Successful treatment has a similar aim to those used with Parkinson's disease, where the underlying disease process is not inhibited but the effects are mitigated and delayed.

Of these treatments, the drugs aimed at improving neurotransmitter functioning have been the most promising, particularly those concerned with cholinergic activity. An example is the success of tacrine (tetrahydroamineoacridine, THA) in producing significant cognitive and behavioural changes in AD, equivalent to arresting the behavioural deterioration by 6 months (Eagger, Levy & Sahakian, 1991; Eagger *et al.*, 1992; Fitten & Ganzell, 1992). Another substance affecting the cholinergic system is nicotine, which has been shown to improve attention in AD, using subcutaneous administration (Sahakian *et al.*, 1989). A more recent study by R. Morris and co-workers at the Institute of Psychiatry, London, is attempting to replicate this result using nicotine patches to administer the drug extra-dermally and has found preliminary indications of improved attentional abilities in a pilot study. The potential success of psychopharmacological intervention makes it all the more crucial that cognitive and behavioural measures are available to detect changes in functioning, and that these procedures are carefully tailored for use with patients with dementia. Some of the principles in the development of tests have been outlined by Morris *et al.* (1987) and by Sahakian (1990).

A perhaps more futuristic treatment for dementia is to transplant neural tissue into the brains of patients with AD and thereby improve cognitive and behavioural functioning. Neural transplants have been proposed either as a means of replacing cholinergic neurones (or cells associated with other transmitter systems, such as serotonergic and noradrenergic neurones) or grafting in cells that induce recovery of damaged cortical neural circuitries by releasing nerve growth factor (NGF). In both cases there is some support, at least theoretically, for the notion that the effects of Alzheimer's disease could be ameliorated. Cholinergic grafts in the hippocampus or neocortex can reduce short-term memory deficits in aged animals (Dunnett *et al.*, 1988) and reverse the short-term memory deficits associated with basal forebrain lesions (Ikegami *et al.*, 1989) when transplanted into either the basal forebrain or into the neocortex. Transplantation of cells to deliver trophic factors has produced a remarkable recovery in cognitive functioning in rats with prefrontal cortical lesions (Stein *et al.*, 1988).

Neural grafting, therefore, may provide an effective means of reversing the cholinergic deficits in AD and improving cognition and memory functioning. Nevertheless, several issues have to be addressed before this form of treatment becomes a viable option. Firstly, it has been assumed that cortical damage may be secondary to basal forebrain lesions. Thus replacement of the basal forebrain cholinergic cells would be the obvious method of treatment. However, the evidence seems to support the notion that basal forebrain cell loss is a result of cortical degeneration, with a retrograde effect on the basal forebrain. This would make the task of cellular replacement more daunting, since the neocortex has a more complex columnar organisation and intricate efferent connectivity with other cortical and subcortical areas. It is unlikely that the precise internal reorganisation and connectivity of neocortical tissue can be restored by grafting in crude agglomerations of neurones. A second issue is that, currently, it is only feasible to transplant embryonic neurones, which raises ethical complications that might not be soluble on a wide scale. Although embryonic tissue has been used in the experimental treatment of Parkinson's disease, it is unlikely that it would be acceptable as a more widespread method of treatment.

Despite this, further development of neural transplantation techniques may provide different approaches in the future, particularly with a more fundamental understanding of the aetiology or primary neuropathology of Alzheimer's disease (Dunnett, 1991).

MANAGEMENT AND PSYCHOSOCIAL ISSUES

Kendall (1987) has made the point that neurobiological treatment of dementia is only a small part of the overall management and that the care and support given by doctors, nurses and other paramedical workers is vital. In this area, much progress has been made in understanding the social and family impact of dementia (Chapter 8) and in devising improved methods of patient management (Chapter 7). Innovations in this area have included an integration of different approaches, which recognise that dementia is a problem to work on at different levels. For example, the intensive 10-day residential programme used by Brodarty & Gresham (1989) involves admitting both the person with dementia and the carer into hospital. The patient is given a range of occupational activities and therapy, including memory retraining, whilst the carer is given intensive education, group therapy and training in management skills. Another example is the recent pilot study by Hinchliffe, Hyman & Blizard (1992) involving a multidisciplinary approach, including behavioural management and drug treatment to manage behavioural difficulties in patients with dementia. Of note was a clinically significant change in behaviour of the patients which matched an increase in the psychological wellbeing of the carer.

IN CONCLUSION

The approaches described are just some of the ways the field of dementia is developing, with a burgeoning interest in not only the neurobiological and cognitive aspects but also new approaches to management and the psychosocial issues. A psychological approach has the ability to span these different areas and thus convert the increased knowledge into new methods for diagnosis, management and treatment.

REFERENCES

Abrahams, J. T. & Birren, J. E. (1973). Reaction time as a function of age and behavioral predisposition to coronary heart disease. *Journal of Gerontology*, **28**, 471–478.

Acker, W. & Acker, C. F. (1982). *Bexley–Maudsley Automated Psychological Screening*. London: NFER-Nelson.

Adams, R. D. & Victor, M. (1989). *Principles of Neurology*, 4th Edn. New York: McGraw-Hill International.

Alberoni, M., Baddeley, A. D., Della Sala, S., Logie, R. H. & Spinnler, H. (1992). Keeping track of a conversation: impairments in Alzheimer's disease. *International Journal of Geriatric Psychiatry*, **7**, 639–646.

Albert, M. L., Feldman, R. G. & Willis, A. L. (1974). The 'subcortical dementia' of progressive supranuclear palsy. *Journal of Neurology, Neurosurgery and Psychiatry*, **37**, 121–130.

Anderson, J. R. (1983). A spreading activation theory of memory. *Journal of Verbal Learning and Verbal Behavior*, **22**, 261–295.

Ankus, M. & Quarrington, B. (1972). Operant behaviour in the memory disordered. *Journal of Gerontology*, **27**, 500–510.

Anthony-Bergstone, C., Zarit, S. H. & Gatz, M. (1988). Symptoms of psychological distress among caregivers of dementia patients. *Psychology and Aging*, **3**, 245–248.

Appell, J., Kertesz, A. & Fisman, M. (1982). A study of language functioning in Alzheimer patients. *Brain and Language*, **17**, 73–91.

Arendt, T., Bigl, V., Arendt, A. & Tennstedt, A. (1983). Loss of neurons in the nucleus basalis of Meynert in Alzheimer's disease, paralysis agitans and Korsakoff's disease. *Acta Neuropathologica*, **61**, 101–108.

Atkinson, R. C. & Shiffrin, R. M. (1968). Human memory: A proposed system and its control processes. In K. W. Spence & J. T. Spence (Eds). *The Psychology of Learning and Motivation: Advances in Research and Theory*, Vol. 2. New York: Academic Press, pp. 89–195.

Baddeley, A. D. (1986). *Working Memory*. Oxford: Oxford University Press.

Baddeley, A. D. (1990). *Human Memory: Theory and Practice*. Hillsdale, NJ: Lawrence Erlbaum.

Baddeley, A. D., Lewis, V. J. & Vallar, G. (1984). Exploring the articulatory loop. *Quarterly Journal of Experimental Psychology*, **26**, 233–252.

√ Baddeley, A. D. & Lieberman, K. (1980). Spatial working memory In R. Nickerson (Ed.). *Attention and Performance VIII*. Hillsdale, NJ: Lawrence Erlbaum, pp. 521–539.

Baddeley, A. D., Logie, R., Bressi, S., Della Sala, S. & Spinnler, H. (1986). Dementia and working memory. *Quarterly Journal of Experimental Psychology*, **36A**, 233–252.

Baddeley, A. D., Bressi, S., Della Salla, S., Logie, R. & Spinnler, H. (1991). The decline of working memory in Alzheimer's disease. *Brain*, **114**, 2521–2542.

√ Baines, S., Saxby, P. & Ehlert, K. (1987). Reality orientation and reminiscence therapy: a controlled crossover study of elderly confused people. *British Journal of Psychiatry*, **151**, 222–231.

Baltes, M. M., Honn, S., Barton, E. M., Orzech, M. & Lago, D. (1983). On the social ecology of dependence and independence in elderly nursing home residents: a replication and extension. *Journal of Gerontology*, **38**, 556–564.

Barker, M. G. & Lawson, J. S. (1968). Nominal aphasia in dementia. *British Journal of Psychiatry*, **114**, 1351–1356.

Barnes, R. F., Raskind, M. A., Scott, M. & Murphy, C. (1981). Problems of families caring for Alzheimer patients: the use of a support group. *Journal of the American Geriatrics Association*, **14**, 355–360.

Barrowclough, C. & Fleming, I. (1986). Training direct care staff in goal-planning with elderly people. *Behavioural Psychotherapy*, **14**, 192–209.

Barusch, A. S. & Spaid, W. M. (1989). Gender differences in caregiving: Why do wives report greater burden? *The Gerontologist*, **29**, 667–676.

Bayles, K. A. (1982). Language function in senile dementia. *Brain and Language*, **16**, 265–280.

Bayles, K. A. (1991). Age at onset of Alzheimer's disease: relation to language dysfunction. *Archives of Neurology*, **48**, 155–159.

Bayles, K. A. & Tomoeda, C. K. (1983). Confrontation naming in dementia. *Brain and Language*, **19**, 98–114.

Bayles, K. A., Tomoeda, C. K., Kaszniak, A. W., Stern, L. Z. & Eagens, L. K. (1985). Verbal perseveration of dementia patients. *Brain and Language*, **25**, 102–110.

Becker, J. T. (1988). Working memory and secondary memory deficits in Alzheimer's disease. *Journal of Clinical and Experimental Neuropsychology*, **6**, 739–653.

Becker, J. T., Huff, F. J., Neves, R. D., Holland, A. & Boller, F. (1988). Neuropsychological function in Alzheimer's disease: pattern of impairment and rates of progression. *Archives of Neurology*, **45**, 263–268.

Becker, J. T. & Lopez, O. L. (1992). Episodic memory in Alzheimer's disease: breakdown of multiple memory processes. In L. Backman (Ed.). *Memory Functioning in Dementia*. Amsterdam: Elsevier, pp. 27–43.

Benson, D. F., Cummings, J. L. & Kuhl, D. E. (1981). Dementia: cortical-subcortical. Paper presented at the 33rd Annual Meeting of the Academy of Neurology, Toronto. *Abstracts in Neurology, New York*, **31**, 101.

Benton, A. L. (1963). *The Revised Visual Retention Test*. Iowa City: State University of Iowa.

√ Benton, A. L., Varney, N. R. & Hamsher, K. (1978). Visuospatial judgment a clinical test. *Archives of Neurology*, **35**, 364–367.

Berg, L., Miller, J. P., Storandt, M., Duchek, J., Morris, J. C., Rubin, E. H., Burke, W. J. & Cohen, L. A. (1988). Mild senile dementia of the Alzheimer-type: 2. Longitudinal assessment. *Annals of Neurology*, **23**, 477–484.

Bergmann, K. & Jaccoby, R. (1983). The limitation and possibilities of community care for the elderly demented. In *Elderly People in the Community: Their Service Needs*. London: Her Majesty's Stationery Office.

Bergmann, K., Manchee, V. & Woods, R. T. (1984). Effect of family relationships on psychogeriatric patients. *Journal of the Royal Society of Medicine*, **77**, 840–844.

Berkman, L. F. (1983). The assessment of social networks and social support in the elderly. *Journal of the American Geriatrics Society*, **31**, 743–749.

Berrios, G. E. (1990). Memory and the cognitive paradigm of dementia during the 19th century. In R. M. Murray & T. H. Turner (Eds). *Lectures on the History of Psychiatry*. London: Gaskell.

Besson, J. A. O., Crawford, J. R., Parker, D. M. Ebmeier, Best, P. V., Gemmell, H. G., Sharp, P. F. & Smith, F. W. (1990). Multimodal imaging in Alzheimer's disease. The relationship between MRI, SPECT, cognitive and pathological changes. *British Journal of Psychiatry*, **157**, 216–220.

Birren, J. E., Woods, A. M. & Williams, M. V. (1980). Behavioral slowing with age: causes, organisation and consequences. In L. W. Poon (Ed.). *Aging in the 1980's*. Washington DC: American Psychological Association.

Bjork, R. A. (1975). Short-term storage: the ordered output of a central processor. In F. Restle, R. M. Shiffrin, N. J. Castellan, H. Lindman & D. B. Pisoni (Eds). *Cognitive Theory*, Vol. 1. Hillsdale, NJ: Lawrence Erlbaum.

Bleathman, C. & Morton, I. (1988). Validation therapy with the demented elderly. *Journal of Advanced Nursing*, **13**, 511–514.

Blessed, G., Tomlinson, B. E. & Roth, M. (1968). The association between quantitative measures of dementia and of senile change in the cerebral grey matter of elderly subjects. *British Journal of Psychiatry*, **114**, 797–811.

Bolla, K. I., Lindgren, K. N., Bonaccorsy, C. & Bleaker, M. I. (1991). Memory complaints in older adults: fact or fiction. *Archives of Neurology*, **48**, 61–64.

Boller, F., Passafiume, D., Keefe, N. C., Rogers, K., Morrow, L. & Kim, Y. (1984). Visuospatial impairment in Parkinson's disease: role of perceptual and motor factors. *Archives of Neurology*, **41**, 485–490.

Boller, F. & Saxton, J. (1990). Comparison of criteria for diagnosing Alzheimer's disease in the United States and Europe. In R. J. Wurtmann, S. Corkin, J. H. Growden & E. Ritter-Walker (Eds). *Advances in Neurology*, Vol. 15: *Alzheimer's Disease*. New York: Raven Press.

Bouma, A. & Van Silfhout, B. (1989). Dichotic listening in patients with Alzheimer's disease. *Journal of Clinical and Experimental Neuropsychology*, **11**, 369.

Bowen, D. M., Smith, C. B., White, P., Goodhardt, M., Spillane, J., Flack, J. A. & Davison, A. N. (1977). Chemical pathology of the organic dementias. *Brain*, **100**, 397–426.

Bowles, N. L., Obler, L. K. & Albert, M. L. (1987). Naming errors in healthy aging and dementia of the Alzheimer type. *Cortex*, **23**, 519–524.

Breitner, J. C. & Folstein, M. F. (1984a). Familial nature of Alzheimer's disease. *New England Journal of Medicine*, **311**, 192.

Breitner, J. C. S. & Folstein M. F. (1984b). Familial Alzheimer dementia: a prevalent disorder with specific clinical features. *Psychological Medicine*, **14**, 63–80.

Brodarty, H. & Gresham, M. (1989). Effects of a training programme to reduce stress in carers of patients with dementia. *British Journal of Medicine*, **299**, 1375–1379.

Brody, E. M., Kleban, M. H., Lawton, M. P. & Mos, M. (1974). A longitudinal look at excess disabilities in the mentally impaired aged. *Journal of Gerontology*, **11**, 124–133.

Brook, P. , Degun, G. & Mather, M. (1975). Reality orientation, a therapy for psychogeriatric patients: a controlled study. *British Journal of Psychiatry*, **127**, 42–45.

Brouwers, W., Cox, C., Martin, A., Chase, T. & Fedio, P. (1984). Differential perceptual–spatial impairment in Huntington's and Alzheimer's dementias. *Archives of Neurology*, **41**, 1073–1076.

Brown, C. C., Gantt, W. H. & Whitman, J. R. (1960). Measures of adaptability in senility. In P. H. Hoch & J. Zubin (Eds). *The Psychopathology of Aging*. New York: The American Psychopathological Association.

Brown, R. G. (1988). 'Subcortical dementia': the neuropsychological evidence. *Neuroscience*, **25**, 363–387.

Brown, R. G. (1991). Comparative neuropsychology of dementia. *Current Opinion in Psychiatry*, **4**, 106–111.

Brown, R. G. & Marsden, C. D. (1984). How common is dementia in Parkinson's disease? *The Lancet*, **2**, 1262–1265.

Brown, R. G. & Marsden, C. D. (1986). Visuospatial function in Parkinson's disease. *Brain*, **109**, 987–1002.

Brown, R. G. & Marsden, C. D. (1987). Neuropsychology and cognitive function in Parkinson's disease. In C. D. Marsden & S. Fahn (Eds). *Motor Disorders*, Vol. 2. London: Butterworth Scientific.

Burdz, M. P., Eaton, W. O. & Bond, J. B. (1988). Effect of respite care on dementia and nondementia patients and their caregivers. *Psychology and Aging*, **3**, 38–42.

Burgio, L. D., Engle, B. T., Hawkins, A., McCormick, K. & Scheve, A. (1990). A staff management system for maintaining improvements in continence with elderly nursing home residents. *Journal of Applied Behaviour Analysis*, **23**, 111–118.

Burgio, L. D., Engle, B., McCormick, K., Hawkins, A. & Scheve, A. (1988). Behavioral treatment for urinary incontinence in elderly inpatients: initial attempts to modify prompting and toileting procedures. *Behavior Therapy*, **19**, 345–357.

Burke, W., Rubin, E. & Morris, J. (1988). Symptoms of 'depression' in dementia of the Alzheimer's type. *Alzheimer's Disease and Associated Disorders*, **2**, 4356–4362.

Burns, A., Jaccoby, R. & Levy, R. (1990a). Psychiatric phenomena in Alzheimer's disease. 1. Disorders of thought content. *British Journal of Psychiatry*, **157**, 72–76.

Burns, A., Jaccoby, R. & Levy, R. (1990b). Psychiatric phenomena in Alzheimer's disease. 2. Disorders of perception. *British Journal of Psychiatry*, **157**, 76–81.

Burns, A., Jaccoby, R. & Levy, R. (1990c). Psychiatric phenomena in Alzheimer's disease. 3. Disorders of mood. *British Journal of Psychiatry*, **157**, 81–86.

Burns, A., Jaccoby, R. & Levy, R. (1990d). Psychiatric phenomena in Alzheimer's disease. 4. Disorders of behaviour. *British Journal of Psychiatry*, **157**, 86–94.

Burns, A. & Levy, R. (in press). *Dementia*. London: Chapman & Hall.

Burns, A., Tune, L., Steele, C. & Folstein, M. (1989). Positron emission tomography in dementia: a clinical review. *International Journal of Geriatric Psychiatry*, **4**, 67–72.

Butler, R. N. (1963). The life review: an interpretation of reminiscence in the aged. *Psychiatry*, **26**, 65–76.

Butters, N., Granholm, E., Salmon, D. P. & Grant, I. (1987). Episodic and semantic memory: a comparison of amnesic and demented patients. *Journal of Clinical and Experimental Neuropsychology*, **9**, 479–497.

Butters, N., Sax, D., Montgomery, K. & Tarlow, S. (1978). Comparison of the neuropsychological deficits associated with early and advanced Huntington's disease. *Archives of Neurology*, **35**, 585–589.

Butters, N., Wolfe, J., Martone, M., Granholm, E. & Cermak, L. S. (1985). Memory disorders associated with Huntington's disease: verbal recall, verbal recognition, and procedural memory. *Neuropsychologia*, **23**, 729–743.

Caine, E. D., Ebert, M. H. & Weingartner, H. (1977). An outline for the analysis of dementia: the memory disorder of Huntington's disease. *Neurology*, **27**, 1087–1092.

Caine, E. D., Bamford, K. A., Schiffer, R. B., Shoulson, I. & Levy, S. (1986). A controlled neuropsychological comparison of Huntington's disease and multiple sclerosis. *Archives of Neurology*, **43**, 249–254.

✓ Candy, J. M., Perry, R. H., Perry, E. K., Biggins, J. A. & Thomson, B. E. (1983). Pathological changes in the nucleus of Meynert in Alzheimer's and Parkinson's disease. *Journal of Neurological Science*, **59**, 277–289.

Cantone, G., Orsini, A., Grossi, D. & De Michele, G. (1978). Verbal and spatial memory span in dementia (an experimental study of 185 subjects). *Acta Neurologica (Naples)*, **33**, 175–185.

Cantor, M. H. (1983). Strain among caregivers: a study of experience in the United States. *The Gerontologist*, **23**, 597–604.

Capitani, E., Della Sala, S., Lucchelli, F., Soave, P. & Spinnler, H. (1988). Perceptual attention in aging and dementia measured by Gottschaldt's hidden figure test. *Journal of Gerontology*, **43**, 157–163.

Carr, A. C., Woods, R. T. & Moore, B. J. (1986). Automated cognitive assessment of elderly patients: a comparison of two types of response device. *British Journal of Clinical Psychology*, **25**, 305–306.

Cattell, R. B. (1943). The measurement of adult intelligence. *Psychological Bulletin*, **3**, 153–193.

Challis, D. & Davies, B. (1986). *Case Management in Community Care: An Evaluated Experiment in the Home Care of the Elderly*. Aldershot: Gower.

Charlesworth, A., Wilkin, D. & Durie, A. (1984). *Carers and Services: A Comparison of Men and Women Caring for Dependent Elderly People*. Manchester: Equal Opportunities Commission.

Chatterjee, A., Strauss, M. E., Smyth, K. A. & Whitehouse, P. J. (1992). Personality changes in Alzheimer's disease. *Archives of Neurology*, **49**, 486–491.

Chawluk, J. B., Grossman, M., Calcano-Perez, J. A., Alavi, A., Hurtig, H. I. & Reivich, M. (1990). Positron emission tomography studies of cerebral metabolism in Alzheimer's disease. In M. F. Schwartz (Ed.). *Modular Deficits in Alzheimer-type Dementia*. Cambridge: MIT Press.

Chiverton, P. & Caine, E. D. (1989). Education to assist spouses in coping with Alzheimer's disease: a controlled trial. *Journal of the American Geriatrics Society*, **37**, 593–598.

Christensen, H. & MacKinnon, A. (1992). Wechsler Intelligence Scale profiles in Alzheimer type dementia and healthy ageing. *International Journal of Geriatric Psychiatry*, **7**, 241–246.

Ciminero, A. R., Calhoun, K. S. & Adams, H. E. (1978). *Handbook of Behavioral Assessment*. New York: John Wiley.

Citrin, R. S. & Dixon, D. N. (1977). Reality orientation: a milieu therapy used in an institution for the aged. *The Gerontologist*, **17**, 39–43.

Code, C. & Lodge, B. (1987). Language in dementia of recent referral. *Age and Ageing*, **16**, 366–372.

Collerton, D. (1985). Rational drug treatment of dementia? *British Medical Journal*, **291**, 347–348.

Collins, A. M. & Loftus, E. F. (1975). A spreading-activation theory of semantic processing. *Psychological Review*, **82**, 407–428.

Copeland, J. R. M., Dewey, M. E. & Griffith-Jones, H. M. (1986). A computerised diagnostic system and case nomenclature for elderly subjects: GMS and AGECAT. *Psychological Medicine*, **16**, 89–99.

Coppel, D. B., Burton, C., Becker, J. & Fiore, J. (1985). Relationships of cognition associated with coping reactions to depression in spousal caregivers of Alzheimer's disease patients. *Cognitive Therapy and Research*, **9**, 253–266.

Corkin, S. (1982). Some relationships between global amnesias and the memory impairments in Alzheimer's disease. In S. Corkin, J. H. Growden, E. Usdin & R. J. Wurtman (Eds). *Alzheimer's Disease: A Report of Research in Progress*. New York: Raven Press.

Corkin, S., Growden, J. H., Nissen, M. J., Huff, F. J., Freed, D. M. & Sagar, H. J. (1984). Recent advances in the neuropsychological study of Alzheimer's disease. In R. J. Wurtman, S. Corkin & J. H. Growden (Eds). *Alzheimer's Disease: Advances in Basic Research and Therapies. Proceedings of the Third Meeting of the International Study Group: On the Treatment of Memory Disorders Associated with Aging*. Cambridge, MA: Centre for Brain Sciences and Metabolism Trust.

Costa, P. T. & McRae, R. R. (1988). Personality in adulthood: a six-year longitudinal study of self-reports and spouse ratings in the NEO Personality Inventory. *Journal of Personality and Social Psychology*, **54**, 853–863.

Cowburn, R. F., Hardy, J. A. & Roberts, P. J. (1989). Neurotransmitter defects in Alzheimer's disease. In D. C. Davies (Ed.). *Alzheimer's Disease: Towards an Understanding of the Aetiology and Pathogenesis*. London: John Libbey.

Craik, F. I. M., Morris, R. G. & Gick, M. (1990). Adult age differences in working memory. In G. Vallar & T. Shallice (Eds). *Neuropsychological Impairments of Short-term Memory*. Cambridge: Cambridge University Press.

Craik, F. I. M. & Tulving, E. (1975). Depth of processing and the retention of words in episodic memory. *Journal of Experimental Psychology: General*, **104**, 268–294.

Crawford, J. R., Parker, D. M. & McKinlay, W. W. (1992). *A Handbook of Neuropsychological Assessment*. Hove: Laurence Erlbaum.

Crawford, J. R., Parker, D. M., Stewart, L. E., Besson, J. A. O. & De Lacey, G. (1989). Prediction of WAIS IQ with the National Adult Reading Test: cross-validation and extension. *British Journal of Clinical Psychology*, **28**, 267–273.

✓ Cummings, J. L. (1990a). Clinical diagnosis of Alzheimer's disease. In J. L. Cummings & B. L. Miller (Eds). *Alzheimer's Disease: Treatment and Long-Term Management*. New York: Marcel Dekker.

Cummings, J. L. (1990). Introduction. In J. L. Cummings (Ed.). *Subcortical Dementia*. New York: Oxford University Press.

Cummings, J. L., Benson, D. F., Hill, M. A. & Read, S. (1985). Aphasia in dementia of the Alzheimer type. *Neurology*, **35**, 394–397.

Cummings, J. L., Houlihan, J. P. & Hill, M. A. (1986). The pattern of reading deterioration in dementia of the Alzheimer type: observation and implications. *Brain and Language*, **29**, 315–323.

Cummings, J. L., Miller, B., Hill, M. A. & Neshkes, R. (1987). Neuropsychiatric aspects of multi-infarct dementia and dementia of the Alzheimer-type. *Archives of Neurology*, **44**, 389–393.

D'Alessandro, R., Gamberini, G., Granieri, E., Benassi, G., Nacarrato, S. & Manzaroli, D. (1987). Prevalence of Parkinson's disease in the Republic of San Marino. *Neurology*, **37**, 1679–1682.

De Ajuriaguerra, J. & Tissot, R. (1975). Some aspects of language in various forms of senile dementia (comparisons with language in childhood). In E. H. & E. Lenneberg (Eds). *Foundations of Language Development*, Vol. 1. New York: Academic Press.

Deary, I. J., Wessely, S. & Farrell, M. (1985). Dementia and Mrs Thatcher. *British Medical Journal*, **291**, 1768.

Della Salla, S., Di Lorenzo, G., Giordano, A. & Spinnler, H. (1986). Is there a specific visuo-spatial impairment in Parkinsonians? *Journal of Neurology, Neurosurgery and Psychiatry*, **49**, 1258–1265.

De Renzi, E. (1980). *Disorders of Space Exploration and Cognition*. Chichester: John Wiley.

De Renzi, E. & Vignolo, L. A. (1962). The token test: a sensitive test to detect receptive disturbances in aphasics. *Brain*, **85**, 665–678.

Dietch, J. T., Hewett, L. J. & Jones, S. (1989). Adverse effects of reality orientation. *Journal of the American Geriatrics Society*, **37**, 974–976.

Downes, J. J. (1988). Memory for repetitions and word fragment completion in normal, depressed and demented elderly. In M. N. Gruneberg, P. E. Morris & R. N. Sykes (Eds). *Practical Aspects of Memory: Current Research and Issues*, Vol. 2. *Clinical and Educational Implications*. Chichester: John Wiley.

Dubois, B., Pillon, B., Legault, F., Agid, Y. & Lhermitte, F. (1988). Slowing of cognitive function in progressive supranuclear palsy: a comparison with Parkinson's disease. *Archives of Neurology, 45*, 1194–1199.

Dunn, J. C. & Kirsner, K. (1988). Discovering functionally independent mental processes. *Psychological Review, 95*, 91–101.

Dunnett, S. B. (1991). Neural transplants as a treatment for Alzheimer's disease? *Psychological Medicine, 21*, 825–830.

Dunnett, S. B., Badman, F., Rogers, D. C., Evenden, J. L. & Iversen, S. D. (1988). Cholinergic grafts in the neocortex or hippocampus of aged rats: reduction of delay-dependent deficits in the delayed non-matching to position task. *Experimental Neurology, 102*, 57–64.

D'Zurilla, T. J. & Goldfried, M. R. (1971). Problem solving and behaviour modification. *Journal of Abnormal Psychology, 78*, 107–126.

Eagger, S. A., Levy, R. & Sahakian, B. J. (1991). Tacrine in Alzheimer's disease. *The Lancet, 8748*, 989–992.

Eagger, S. A., Morant, N., Levy, R. & Sahakian, B. (1992). Tacrine in Alzheimer's disease: time course of changes in cognitive function and practice effects. *British Journal of Psychiatry, 160*, 36–40.

Eagles, J. M., Beattie, J. A. G., Blackwood, G. W., Restall, D. B. & Ashcroft, G. W. (1987). The mental health of elderly couples—I: The effects of the cognitively impaired spouse. *British Journal of Psychiatry, 150*, 293–298.

Eichorn, D. H., Clausen, J. A., Hann, N. (1981). *Present and Past Middle Life*. New York: Seadonic Press.

Ellis, H. D. & Young, A. W. (1990). Accounting for delusional misidentifications. *British Journal of Psychiatry, 157*, 239–248.

Ernst, B., Dalby, M. A. & Dalby, A. (1970). Aphasic disturbances in presenile dementia. *Acta Neurologica Scandinavica*, (suppl.) *43*, 571–576.

Esiri, M. M. (1989). Patterns of cortical and subcortical pathology in Alzheimer's disease. In D. C. Davies (Ed.). *Alzheimer's Disease: Towards an Understanding of the Aetiology and Pathogenesis*. London: John Libbey.

Eslinger, P. J. & Benton, A. L. (1983). Visuoperceptual performances in aging and dementia: clinical and theoretical implications. *Journal of Clinical Neuropsychology, 5*, 213–220.

Eslinger, P. & Damasio, A. R. (1986). Preserved motor learning in Alzheimer's disease: implications for anatomy and behavior. *The Journal of Neuroscience, 6*, 3006–3009.

Evarts, E. V., Teravainen, H. & Calne, D. B. (1981). Reaction time in Parkinson's disease. *Brain*, **104**, 167–186.

Eysenck, M. D. (1945). An exploratory study of mental organisation in senility. *Journal of Neurology and Psychiatry*, **8**, 15–21.

Eysenck, H. J. (1967). *The Biological Basis of Personality*. Springfield, IL: Charles C. Thomas.

Faber-Langendoen, K., Morris, J. C., Knesevich, J. W., LaBarge, E., Miller, J. P. & Berg, L. (1988). Aphasia in senile dementia of the Alzheimer type. *Annals of Neurology*, **23**, 365–370.

Fairburn, C. & Hope, R. (1988). Changes in behaviour in dementia: a neglected research area. *British Journal of Psychiatry*, **152**, 406–407.

Feehan, M., Knight, R. G. & Partridge, F. M. (1991). Cognitive complaint and test performance of elderly patients suffering from depression or dementia. *International Journal of Geriatric Psychiatry*, **6**, 287–293.

Feil, N. (1972). A new approach to group therapy, research findings. Unpublished paper presented at the 25th Meeting of the Gerontological Society in San Juan, Puerto Rico, December 1972.

Feil, N. (1982). *Validation: The Feil Method*. Cleveland, Ohio: Edward Feil Productions.

Ferris, S. H., Crook, T., Sathananthan, G. & Gershon, S. (1976). Reaction time as a diagnostic measure of cognitive impairment in senility. *Journal of the American Geriatrics Society*, **24**, 529–533.

Filley, C. M., Kelly, J. & Heaton, R. K. (1986). Neuropsychologic features of early- and late-onset Alzheimer's disease. *Archives of Neurology*, **43**, 571–576.

Finch, J. & Groves, D. (1983). *Labour of Love: Women, Work and Caring*. London: Routledge & Kegan Paul.

Fitten, L. J. & Ganzell, S. (1992). Spouse's assessments of Alzheimer patients's response to THA and lecithin. *American Journal of Psychiatry*, **149**, 575.

Fitting, M., Rabins, P., Lucas, M. J. & Eastham, J. (1986). Caregivers for demented patients: a comparison of husbands and wives. *The Gerontologist*, **26**, 248–252.

Flicker, C., Ferris, S. H., Crook, T. & Bartus, R. T. (1986). The effects of aging and dementia on an object-sorting task. *Developmental Neuropsychology*, **2**, 65–72.

Flicker, C., Ferris, S. H., Crook, T. & Bartus, R. T. (1987). Implications of memory and language dysfunction in the naming deficit of senile dementia. *Brain and Language*, **31**, 187–200.

Flicker, C., Ferris, S. H., Crook, T., Reisberg, B. & Bartus, R. T. (1988). Equivalent spatial-rotation deficits in normal aging and Alzheimer's disease. *Journal of Clinical and Experimental Neuropsychology*, **10**, 387–399.

Flowers, K. A. (1976). Visual 'closed loop' and 'open loop' characteristics of voluntary movement in patients with Parkinsonism and intention tremor. *Brain*, **99**, 269–310.

Flowers, K., Pearce, I. & Pearce, J. M. S. (1984). Recognition memory in Parkinson's disease. *Journal of Neurology, Neurosurgery and Psychiatry*, **47**, 1174–1181.

Flowers, K. & Robertson, C. (1985). The effect of Parkinson's disease on the ability to maintain a mental set. *Journal of Neurology, Neurosurgery and Psychiatry*, **48**, 517–529.

Fodor, J. A. (1983). *The Modularity of Mind*. Cambridge, MA: MIT Press.

Folstein, M. F., Folstein, S. E. & McHugh, P. R. (1975). 'Mini-Mental State': a potential method for grading the cognitive state of the patient for the clinician. *Journal of Psychiatric Research*, **12**, 189–198.

Folstein, S. E., Brandt, J. & Folstein, M. F. (1990). Huntington's disease. In J. J. Cummings (Ed.). *Subcortical Dementia*. New York: Oxford University Press.

Forette, F., Henry, J. F., Orgogozo, J. M., Dartigues, J. F., Pere, J. J., Hugonot, L., Israel, L., Luria, Y., Goulley, F., Lallemand, A. & Boller, F. (1989). Reliability of clinical criteria for the diagnosis of dementia: a longitudinal multicentre study. *Archives of Neurology*, **46**, 646–648.

Foundation for Long-Term Care (1983). *Respite Care for the Frail Elderly: A Summary Report on Institutional Respite Research*. New York: Centre for the Study of Aging.

Foxx, R. M. & Azrin, N. H. (1973). *Toilet Training in the Retarded*. Champaign, Illinois: Research Press.

Freed, D. M., Corkin, S., Growden, J. H. & Nissen, M. J. (1989). Selective attention in Alzheimer's disease: characterising cognitive subgroups of Alzheimer's disease. *Neuropsychologia*, **27**, 325–339.

Freedman, M. (1990). Parkinson's disease. In J. L. Cummings (Ed.). *Subcortical Dementia*. New York: Oxford University Press.

Freeman, T. & Gathercole, C. E. (1966). Perseveration—the clinical symptoms—in chronic schizophrenia and organic dementia. *British Journal of Psychiatry*, **112**, 27–32.

Fuld, P. A. (1983). Word intrusion as a diagnostic sign in Alzheimer's disease. *Geriatric Medicine Today*, **2**, 33–41.

Fuld, P. A., Katzman, R., Davies, P. & Terry, R. D. (1982). Intrusions as a sign of Alzheimer's dementia: chemical and pathological verification. *Annals of Neurology*, **11**, 155–159.

Fuld, P. A., Masur, D. M., Blau, A. D., Crystal, H. & Aronson, M. K. (1990). Object memory evaluation for prospective detection of dementia in normal functioning elderly: predictive and normative data. *Journal of Clinical and Experimental Neuropsychology*, **12**, 539–548.

Gendron, C. E. Poitras, L. R. & Engels, M. L. (1986). Skills training with supporters of the demented. *Journal of American Geriatrics Society*, **34**, 875–880.

George, L. K. & Gwyther, L. P. (1986). Caregiver well-being: a multidimensional examination of family caregivers of demented adults. *The Gerontologist*, **26**, 253–259.

Gewirth, L. R., Shindler, A. G. & Hier, D. B. (1984). Altered patterns of word association in dementia and aphasia. *Brain and Language*, **21**, 307–317.

Ghanbari, H. A., Miller, B. E., Haigler, H. J., Arato, M., Bissette, G., Davies, P., Nemeroff, C. B., Perry, E. K., Perry, R., Ravid, R., Swaab, D. F., Whetsell, W. D. & Zemlan, F. P. (1990). Biochemical assay of Alzheimer's disease-associated protein(s) in human brain tissue. *Journal of the American Medical Association*, **263**, 2907–2910.

Gibb, W. R. G. (1989). Dementia and Parkinson's disease. *British Journal of Psychiatry*, **154**, 596–614.

Gibson, A. J., Moyes, I. C. A. & Kendrick, D. C. (1980). Cognitive assessment of the elderly long-stay patient. *British Journal of Psychiatry*, **137**, 537–555.

Gilhooly, M. L. M. (1984). The impact of caregiving on caregivers: factors associated with the psychological well-being of people supporting a dementing relative in the community. *British Journal of Medical Psychology*, **57**, 35–44.

Gilhooly, M. L. M. (1986). Senile dementia: factors associated with caregiver's preference for institutional care. *British Journal of Medical Psychology*, **59**, 165–171.

Gilleard, C. J. (1984). *Living with Dementia: Community Care of the Elderly Mentally Infirm*. London: Croom Helm.

Gilleard, C. J. (1987). Influence of emotional distress among supporters on the outcome of psychogeriatric day care. *British Journal of Psychiatry*, **150**, 219–223.

Gilleard, C. J., Boyd, W. D. & Watt, G. (1982). Problems in caring for the elderly mentally infirm at home. *Archives of Gerontology and Geriatrics*, **1**, 151–158.

Gilleard, C. J., Belford, H., Gilleard, E., Whittick, J. E. & Gledhill, K. (1984). Emotional distress among the supporters of the elderly mentally infirm. *British Journal of Psychiatry*, **145**, 172–177.

Gilleard, C. J. & Christie, J. F. (1990). Behavioural and cognitive problems in the elderly. In D. F. Peck & C. M. Shapiro (Eds). *Measuring Human Problems*. Chichester: John Wiley.

Glass, G. V., McGaw, B. & Smith, M. L. (1981). *Meta-analysis in Social Research*. Beverly Hills: Sage.

Glosser, G. & Wexler, D. (1985). Participants' evaluation of educational/support groups for families of patients with Alzheimer's disease and other dementias. *The Gerontologist,* **25**, 232–236.

Goldenberg, G., Wimmer, A., Auff, E. & Schnaberth, G. (1986). Impairment of motor planning in patients with parkinson's disease: evidence from ideomotor apraxia testing. *Journal of Neurology, Neurosurgery and Psychiatry,* **49**, 1266–1272.

Golding, E. (1988). *The Middlesex Elderly Assessment of Mental State.* Fareham: Thames Valley Test Company.

Goldstein, G., Turner, S. M., Holzman, A., Kanagy, M., Elmore, S. & Barry, K. (1982). An evaluation of reality orientation therapy. *Journal of Behavioral Assessment,* **4**, 165–178.

Grad, J. & Sainsbury, P. (1965). An evaluation of the effects of caring for the aged at home. In *Psychiatric Disorders in the Aged. WPA Symposium.* Manchester: Geigy.

Grady, C. L., Haxby, J. V., Horwitz, B., Sundaram, M., Berg, G., Schapiro, M., Friedland, R. P. & Rapoport, S. I. (1988). A longitudinal study of the early neuropsychological and cerebral metabolic changes in dementia of the Alzheimer's type. *Journal of Clinical and Experimental Neuropsychology,* **10**, 576–596.

Graf, P. & Mandler, G. (1984). Activation makes words more accessible, but not necessarily more retrievable. *Journal of Verbal Learning and Verbal Behavior,* **23**, 553–568.

Grafman, J., Litvan, I., Gomez, C. & Chase, T. N. (1990). Frontal lobe function in progressive supranuclear palsy. *Archives of Neurology,* **47**, 553–558.

Grafman, J., Thompson, K., Weingartner, H., Martinez, R., Lawlor, B. A. & Sunderland, T. (1991). Script generation and an indicator of knowledge representation in patients with Alzheimer's disease. *Brain and Language,* **40**, 344–358.

Greene, J. G., Smith R., Gardiner, M. & Timbury, G. C. (1982). Measuring behavioural disturbance of elderly demented patients in the community and its effects on relatives: A factor analytic study. *Age and Ageing,* **11**, 121–126.

Greene, J. G. & Timbury, G. C. (1979). A geriatric psychiatry day hospital service: a five year review. *Age and Ageing,* **8**, 49–53.

Grober, E., Buschke, H., Crystal, H., Bang, S. & Dresner, R. (1988). Screening for dementia by memory testing. *Neurology,* **38**, 900–903.

Grober, E. & Sliwinski, M. (1991). Development and validation of a model for estimating premorbid verbal intelligence in the elderly. *Journal of Clinical and Experimental Neuropsychology,* **13**, 933–949.

Guertin, W. H., Rabin, A. L., Frank G. H. & Ladd, C. E. (1962). Research on the Wechsler Intelligence Scale for Adults, 1955–1966. *Psychological Bulletin,* **59**, 1–26.

Habot, B. & Libow, L. S. (1980). The interrelationship of mental and physical status and its assessment in the older adult: mind–body interaction. In J. E. Birren & R. B. Sloane (Eds). *Handbook of Mental Health and Aging*. Englewood Cliffs, NJ: Prentice-Hall.

Hale, W. E., Stewart, R. E., Moore, M. T. & Marks, R. G. (1992). Electrocardiographic changes and cognitive impairment in the elderly. *Journal of Clinical and Experimental Gerontology*, **14**, 91–102.

Haley, W. E., Brown, S. L. & Levine, E. G. (1987). Experimental evaluation of the effectiveness of group intervention for dementia caregivers. *The Gerontologist*, **27**, 376–382.

Haley, W. E. (1989). Group intervention for dementia family caregivers: a longitudinal perspective. *The Gerontologist*, **29**, 478–480.

Halstead, H. (1943). A psychometric study of senility. *Journal of Mental Science*, **89**, 863–873.

Hanley, I. G. (1982) *A Manual for the Modification of Confused Behaviour*. Lothian Regional Council, Scotland: Department of Social Work.

Hanley, I. G. (1984). Theoretical and practical considerations in Reality Orientation Training with the elderly. In I. G. Hanley & J. Hodge (Eds). *Psychological Approaches to the Care of the Elderly*. London: Croom Helm.

Hanley, I. G. (1986). Reality orientation in the care of the elderly patient with dementia—three case studies. In I. G. Hanley & M. Gilhooly (Eds). *Psychological Therapies for the Elderly*. London: Croom Helm.

Hanley, I. G., McGuire, R. J. & Boyd, W. D. (1981). Reality orientation and dementia: a controlled trial of two approaches. *British Journal of Psychiatry*, **138**, 10–14.

Hardy, J. A., Owen, J. M. & Groate, A. M. (1989). The genetics of Alzheimer's disease. In D. C. Davies (Ed.). *Alzheimer's Disease: Towards an Understanding of the Aetiology and Pathogenesis*. London: John Libbey.

Harris, C. S. & Ivory, P. B. C. B. (1976). An outcome evaluation of reality orientation therapy with geriatric patients in state mental hospitals. *The Gerontologist*, **16**, 496–503.

Hart, R. P., Kwentus, J. A., Harkins, S. W. & Taylor, J. R. (1988a). Rate of forgetting in mild Alzheimer's type dementia. *Brain and Cognition*, **7**, 31–38.

Hart, S., Smith, C. M. & Swash, M. (1988b). Word fluency in patients with early dementia of the Alzheimer type. *British Journal of Clinical Psychology*, **27**, 115–124.

Hartman, M. (1991). The use of semantic knowledge in Alzheimer's disease: evidence for impairments of attention. *Neuropsychologia*, **29**, 213–228.

Haxby, J. V., Grady, C. L., Koss, E., Horwitz, B., Heston, L., Shapiro, M., Friedland, R. P. & Rapoport, S. I. (1990). Longitudinal study of cerebral metabolic asymmetries and associated neuropsychological patterns in early dementia of the Alzheimer's type. *Archives of Neurology,* **47,** 753–760.

Head, D. M., Portnoy, S. & Woods, R. T. (1990). The impact of reminiscence groups in two different settings. *International Journal of Geriatric Psychiatry,* **5,** 295–302.

Heindel, W. C., Butters, N. & Salmon, D. P. (1988). Impaired learning of a motor skill in patients with Huntington's disease. *Behavioral Neuroscience,* **102,** 141–147.

Helkala, E.-L., Laulumaa, V., Soininen, H. & Riekkinen, P. J. (1988). Recall and recognition memory in patients with Alzheimer's and Parkinson's diseases. *Annals of Neurology,* **24,** 214–217.

Help the Aged (1981). *Recall, Audio-visual Presentation.* London: Help the Aged Education Department.

Henderson, V. W., Mack, W. & Williams, B. W. (1989). Spatial disorientation in Alzheimer's disease. *Archives of Neurology,* **46,** 391–394.

Hier, D. B., Hagenlocker, K. & Shindler, A. G. (1985). Language disintegration in dementia: effects of etiology and severity. *Brain and Language,* **25,** 117–133.

Hill, R. D., Evankovich, K. D., Sheikh, J. I. & Yesavage, J. A. (1987). Imagery mnemonic training in a patient with primary degenerative dementia. *Psychology and Aging,* **2,** 204–208.

Hinchliffe, A. C., Hyman, I. & Blizard, B. (1992). The impact on carers of behavioural difficulties in dementia: a pilot study on management. *International Journal of Geriatric Psychiatry,* **7,** 579–583.

Hodges, J. R., Salmon, D. P. & Butters, N. (1992). Semantic memory impairment in Alzheimer's disease. Failure of access or degraded knowledge? *Neuropsychologia,* **30,** 301–314.

Hogstel, M. O. (1979). Use of reality orientation with ageing confused patients. *Nursing Research,* **28,** 161–165.

Holden, U. P. & Woods, R. T. (1987). *Reality Orientation Psychological Approaches to the 'Confused' Elderly,* 2nd Edn. Edinburgh: Churchill Livingstone.

Horowitz, A. (1985). Sons and daughters as caregivers to older parents: differences in role performance and consequences. *The Gerontologist,* **25,** 612–617.

Horowitz, A. & Shindelman, L. W. (1983). Reciprocity and affection: past influences on current caregiving. *Journal of Gerontological Social Work,* **5,** 5–20.

Hoyer, W. J. (1973). Application of operant techniques for the modification of elderly behavior. *The Gerontologist,* **13,** 18–22.

Huber, S. J. & Shuttleworth, E. C. (1990). Neuropsychological assessment of subcortical dementia. In J. L. Cummings (Ed.). *Subcortical Dementia*. New York: Oxford University Press.

Huber, S. J., Shuttleworth, E. C. & Freidenberg, D. L. (1989). Neuropsychological differences between the dementias of Alzheimer's and Parkinson's diseases. *Archives of Neurology*, **46**, 1287–1291.

Huber, S. J., Shuttleworth, E. C., Paulson, G. W., Bellchambers, M. J. G. & Clapp, L. E. (1986). Cortical vs subcortical dementia: neuropsychological differences. *Archives of Neurology*, **43**, 392–394.

Huff, F. J., Corkin, S. & Growden, J. H. (1986). Semantic impairment and anomia in Alzheimer's disease. *Brain and Language*, **28**, 235–249.

Huppert, F. & Piercy, M. (1979). Normal and abnormal forgetting in amnesia: effect of locus of lesion. *Cortex*, **15**, 384–390.

Hussian, R. A. (1983). A combination of operant and cognitive therapy with geriatric patients. *International Journal of Behavioural Geriatrics*, **1**, 57–61.

Hussian, R. A. & Brown, D. C. (1987). Use of two-dimensional grid patterns to limit hazardous ambulation in demented patients. *Journal of Gerontology*, **42**, 558–560.

Hutchinson, J. M. & Jensen, M. (1980). A pragmatic evaluation of discourse communication in normal senile elderly in a nursing home. In L. K. Obler & M. L. Albert (Eds). *Language and Communication in the Elderly*. Lexington, MA: Lexington Books.

Hyman, B. T., VanHoesen, G. W., Damasio, A. R. & Barne, C. L. (1984). Alzheimer's disease: cell specific pathology isolates the hippocampal formation. *Science*, **225**, 1168–1170.

Ikegami, S., Nihonmatsu, I., Hatanaka, H., Takei, N. & Kawamura, H. (1989). Transplantation of septal cholinergic neurons to the hippocampus improves memory impairment of spatial learning in rats treated with AF64A. *Brain Research*, **496**, 321–326.

Inglis, J. (1959). A paired associate learning test for use with elderly psychiatric patients. *Journal of Mental Science*, **105**, 440–448.

Jenkins, J., Felce, D., Lunt, B. & Powell, L. (1977). Increasing engagement in activity of residents in old people's homes by providing recreational materials. *Behavioural Research and Therapy*, **15**, 429–434.

Johnson, C. M., McLaren, S. M. & McPherson, F. M. (1981). The comparative effectiveness of three versions of 'classroom' reality orientation. *Age and Ageing*, **10**, 33–35.

Jorm, A. F. & Jacomb, P. A. (1989). The informant questionnaire on cognitive decline in the elderly (IQCODE): Socio-demographic correlates, reliability, validity, and some norms. *Psychological Medicine*, **19**, 1015–1022.

Jorm, A. F. & Korten, A. E. (1988). Assessment of cognitive decline in the elderly by informant interview. *British Journal of Psychiatry*, **152**, 209–213.

Jorm, A. F., Scott, R., Cullen, J. S. & Mackinnon, A. J. (1991). Performance of the Informant Questionnaire on Cognitive Decline in the Elderly (IQCODE) as a screening test for dementia. *Psychological Medicine*, **21**, 785–790.

Inglis, J. (1959). A paired associate learning test for use with elderly psychiatric patients. *Journal of Mental Science*, **105**, 440–448.

Kahan, J., Kemp, B., Staples, F. R. & Brummel-Smith, K. (1985). Decreasing the burden in families caring for a relative with a dementing illness: a controlled study. *Journal of American Geriatrics Association*, **33**, 664–670.

Kaneko, Z. (1975). Care in Japan. In J. G. Howells (Ed.). *Modern Perspectives in the Psychiatry of Old Age*. New York: Brunner/Mazel.

Kaszniak, A. W. (1990). Psychological assessment of the aging individual. In J. E. Birren & K. W. Schaie (Eds). *Handbook of the Psychology of Aging*, 3rd Edn. New York: Academic Press.

Kay, D. W. K. & Bergmann, K. (1980). Epidemiology of mental disorders among the aged in the community. In J. E. Birren & R. B. Sloane (Eds). *Handbook of Mental Health and Aging*. Englewood Cliffs NJ: Prentice-Hall.

Kay D. W. K., Bergmann, K., Foster, E. M., McKechnie, A. H. & Roth, M. (1970). Mental illness and hospital usage in the elderly: a random sample followed-up. *Comprehensive Psychiatry*, **11**, 26–35.

Kazdin, A. E. (1975). *Behavior Modification in Applied Settings*. Homewood, Illinois: The Dorsey Press.

Kempler, D. (1988). Lexical and pantomime abilities in Alzheimer's disease. *Aphasiology*, **2**, 147–159.

Kempler, D., Curtiss, S. & Jackson, C. (1987). Syntactic preservation in Alzheimer's disease. *Journal of Speech and Hearing Research*, **30**, 343–350.

Kempler, D., Van Lancker, D. & Read, S. (1988). Proverb and idiom comprehension in Alzheimer's disease. *Alzheimer's Disease and Associated Disorders*, **2**, 38–49.

Kendall, M. (1987). Drugs for dementia. In B. Pitt (Ed.). *Dementia*. Edinburgh: Churchill Livingstone.

Kendrick, D. C. (1965). Speed and learning in the diagnosis of diffuse brain damage in elderly subjects: a Bayesian statistical approach. *British Journal of Social and Clinical Psychology*, **4**, 141–148.

Kendrick, D. C., Gibson, A. J. & Moyes, I. C. A. (1979). The revised Kendrick battery: clinical studies. *British Journal of Clinical Psychology*, **18**, 329–340.

Kent, R. N. & Foster, S. L. (1978). Direct observational procedures: methodological issues in naturalistic settings. In A. R. Cimenero, K. S. Calhoun & H. E. Adams (Eds). *Handbook of Behavioral Assessment*. New York: John Wiley.

Kertesz, A., Apell, J. & Fisman, M. (1986). The dissolution of language in Alzheimer's disease. *Canadian Journal of Neurological Science*, **13**, 415–418.

Kinsbourne, M. (1980). Attentional dysfunction in the elderly: the theoretical models and research perspectives. In L. W. Poon, J. L. Fozard, L. S. Cermak, D. Arnberg & L. W. Thompson (Eds). *New Directions in Memory and Aging: George A. Talland Memorial Conference*. Hillsdale, NJ: Lawrence Erlbaum, pp. 113–129.

Kirshner, H. S., Webb, W. G. & Kelly, M. P. (1984). The naming disorder of dementia. *Neuropsychologia*, **22**, 23–30.

Kluver, H. & Bucy, P. (1937). 'Psychic blindness' and other symptoms following bilateral temporal lobectomy in rhesus monkeys. *American Journal of Physiology*, **119**, 352.

Knesevich, J., Martin, R., Berg, L. & Danziger, W. (1983). Preliminary report on affective symptoms in the early stages of senile dementia of the Alzheimer type. *American Journal of Psychiatry*, **140**, 233–235.

Knight, R. G. & Godfrey H. P. D. (1984). Reliability and validity of a scale for rating memory impairment in hospitalized amnesics. *Journal of Consulting and Clinical Psychology*, **52**, 769–773.

Kokmen, M., Beard, M., Offord, K. P. & Kurland, L. T. (1989). Prevalence of medically diagnosed dementia in a defined United States population: Rochester, Minnesota, January 1, 1975. *Neurology*, **39**, 773–776.

Kolers, P. A. (1979). A pattern-analyzing basis of recognition. In L. S. Cermak & F. I. M. Craik (Eds). *Levels of Processing in Human Memory*. Hillsdale, NJ: Lawrence Erlbaum.

Kopelman, M. D. (1985). Rates of forgetting in Alzheimer-type dementia and Korsakoff's syndrome. *Neuropsychologia*, **23**, 62–638.

Kopelman, M. D. (1986). The cholinergic neurotransmitter system in human memory and dementia: a review. *Quarterly Journal of Experimental Psychology*, **38A**, 535–573.

Kopelman, M. D. (1987). Two types of confabulation. *Journal of Neurology, Neurosurgery and Psychiatry*, **50**, 1482–1487.

Kuriansky, J. B. & Gurland, B. J. (1976). The performance test of activities of daily living. *International Journal of Aging and Human Development*, **7**, 343–352.

Kurz, A., Haupt, M., Pollmann, S. & Romero, B. (1992). Alzheimer's disease: is there evidence of phenomenological subtypes? *Dementia*, **3**, 320–327.

Lam, D. H. & Woods, R. T. (1986). Ward orientation training in dementia: a single-case study. *International Journal of Geriatric Psychiatry*, **1**, 145–147.

Larrabee, G. J., Largen, J. W. & Levin, H. S. (1985). Sensitivity of age-decline resistant ('hold') WAIS subtests to Alzheimer's disease. *Journal of Clinical and Experimental Neuropsychology*, **7**, 497–504.

Lawson, J. S. & Barker, M. G. (1968). The assessment of nominal dysphasia in dementia. *British Journal of Medical Psychology*, **41**, 411–414.

Lazarus, R. S. (1981). The stress and coping paradigm. In C. Eisdorfer (Ed.). *Models of Clinical Psychopathology*. New York: Spectrum.

Lazarus, L. W., Stafford, B., Cooper, K., Cohler, B. & Dysken, M. (1981). A pilot study of an Alzheimer patient's relatives discussion group. *Gerontologist*, **21**, 353–358.

Lazarus, L., Newton, N., Cohler, B., Lesser, J. & Schwoen, C. (1987). Frequency in presentation of depressive symptoms in patients with primary degenerate dementia. *American Journal of Psychiatry*, **144**, 41–45.

Lees, A. & Smith, E. (1983). Cognitive deficits in the early stages of Parkinson's disease. *Brain*, **106**, 257–270.

Levin, B. E., Llabre, M. M., Reisman, S., Weiner, W. J., Sanchez-Rames, J., Singer, C. & Brown, M. C. (1991). Visuospatial impairment in Parkinson's disease. *Neurology*, **41**, 365–369.

Levin, E., Sinclair, I. & Gorbach, P. (1986). *The Supporters of Confused Elderly Persons at Home*. London: National Institute of Social Work.

Lezak, M. (1983). *Neuropsychological Assessment*, 2nd Edn. New York: Oxford University Press.

Lincoln, N. (1981). Discrepancies between capabilities and performance of activities of daily living in multiple sclerosis. *Rehabilitation Medicine*, **3**, 84–88.

Lishman, W. A. (1987). *Organic Psychiatry*, 2nd Edn. Oxford: Blackwell.

Little, A., Hemsley, D. & Volans, J. (1987). Comparison of current levels of performance and scores based on change as diagnostic discriminators among the elderly. *British Journal of Clinical Psychology*, **26**, 135–140.

Litvan, I. Grafman, J., Gomez, C. & Chase, T. N. (1989). Memory impairment in patients with progressive supranuclear palsy. *Archives of Neurology*, **46**, 765–767.

Litvan, I., Mohr, E., Williams, J., Gomez, C. & Chase, T. N. (1991). Differential recovery and executive functions in demented patients with Parkinson's and Alzheimer's diseases. *Journal of Neurology, Neurosurgery and Psychiatry*, **54**, 25–29.

Loftus, G. R. (1978). On interpretation of interactions. *Memory and Cognition*, **6**, 312–319.

Lopez, O. L., Becker, J. T., Brenner, R. F., Rosen, J., Bajulaiye, O. I. & Reynolds, C. F. (1991). Alzheimer's disease with delusions and hallucinations: neuropsychological and electroencephalographic correlates. *Neurology*, **41**, 906–912.

Lucas-Blaustein, M. J., Filipp, L., Dungan, C. & Tune, L. (1988). Driving in patients with dementia. *Journal of the American Geriatrics Society*, **36**, 1087–1091.

Luria, A. R. (1966). *Higher Cortical Functions in Man*. London: Tavistock.

McKhann, G., Drachman, D., Folstein, M., Katzman, R., Price, D. & Stadlan, E. M. (1984). Clinical diagnosis of Alzheimer's disease: report of the NINCDS/ADRDA work group under the auspices of the Department of Health and Human Services Task Force on Alzheimer's disease. *Neurology*, **34**, 939–944.

McKiernan, F. & Bender, M. (1990). Effects of reminiscence groups for elderly persons with severe dementia. Paper presented at the British Psychological Society Conference, London, December, 1990.

MacLachlan, D. R. C. (1986). Aluminium and Alzheimer's disease: a review. *Neurobiology of Aging*, **7**, 525–532.

Mace, N. L. & Rabins, P. V. (1981). *The 36 Hour Day*. Baltimore: Johns Hopkins University Press.

Maher, E. R., Smith, E. M. & Lees, A. J. (1985). Cognitive deficits in the Steele–Richardson–Olszewski syndrome (progressive supranuclear palsy). *Journal of Neurology, Neurosurgery and Psychiatry*, **48**, 1234–1239.

Mandell, A. M. & Albert, M. L. (1990). History of subcortical dementia. In J. L. Cummings (Ed.). *Subcortical Dementia*. New York: Oxford University Press.

Martin, A., Brouwers, P., Cox, C. & Fedio, P. (1985). On the nature of the verbal memory deficits in Alzheimer's disease. *Brain and Language*, **25**, 323–341.

Martin, A. & Fedio, P. (1983). Word production and comprehension in Alzheimer's disease: the breakdown of semantic knowledge. *Brain and Language*, **19**, 124–141.

Martyn, C. N., Barker, D. J. P., Osmond, C., Harris, E. C., Edwardson, J. A. & Lacey, R. F. (1989). Geographical relation between Alzheimer's disease and aluminium in the drinking water. *The Lancet*, **1**, 59–62.

Massman, P. J., Delis, D. C., Butters, N., Levin, B. E. & Salmon, D. P. (1990). Are all subcortical dementias alike?: verbal learning and memory in Parkinson's and Huntington's disease patients. *Journal of Clinical and Experimental Neuropsychology*, **12**, 729–744.

Mayeux, R. (1983). Depression and dementia in Parkinson's disease. In C. D. Marsden & S. Fahn (Eds). *Movement Disorders*. London: Butterworth Scientific.

Mayeux, R., Stern, Y., Rosen, J. & Benson, D. F. (1983). Is 'subcortical dementia' a recognisable clinical entity. *Annals of Neurology*, **14**, 278–283.

Meehl, P. E. & Rosen, A. (1955). Antecedent probabilities and the efficiency of psychometric signs, patterns or cutting scores. *Psychological Bulletin*, **52**, 194–216.

Melin, L. & Gotesdam, K. G. (1981). The effects of rearranging ward routines on communication and eating behaviours of psychogeriatric patients. *Journal of Applied Behavioural Analysis*, **14**, 47–51.

Mendez, M. F. & Ashla-Mendez, M. (1991). Difference between multi-infarct dementia and Alzheimer's disease on unstructured neuropsychological tests. *Journal of Clinical and Experimental Neuropsychology*, **13**, 923–932.

Mendez, M. F., Mendez, M. A., Martin, R. N., Smyth, K. A. & Whitehouse, P. J. (1990). Complex visual disturbance in Alzheimer's disease. *Neurology*, **40**, 439–443.

Merchant, M. & Saxby, P. (1981). Reality orientation: a way forward. *Nursing Times*, **77**, 1442–1445.

Merriam, A., Aronson, N., Gaston, P., Wey, J. L. & Katz, I. (1988). The psychiatric symptoms of Alzheimer's disease. *Journal of the American Geriatric Society*, **36**, 7–12.

Miller, B. (1987). Gender and control among spouses of the cognitively impaired: a research note. *The Gerontologist*, **27**, 447–453.

Miller, E. (1971). On the nature of the memory disorder in presenile dementia. *Neuropsychologia*, **9**, 75–81.

Miller, E. (1975). Impaired recall and the memory disturbance in presenile dementia. *British Journal of Experimental Psychology*, **14**, 73–79.

Miller, E. (1977). A note on visual information processing in presenile dementia: A preliminary report. *British Journal of Clinical Psychology*, **16**, 99–100.

Miller, E. (1977). *Abnormal Ageing*. Chichester: John Wiley.

Miller, E. (1979). Memory and ageing. In M. M. Gruenberg & P. E. Morris (Eds). *Applied Problems in Memory*. New York: Academic Press.

Miller, E. (1980). Cognitive assessment of the older adult. In J. E. Birren & R. B. Sloane (Eds). *Handbook of Mental Health and Aging*. Englewood Cliffs, NJ: Prentice-Hall.

Miller, E. (1984a). Verbal fluency as a function of a measure of verbal intelligence and in relation to different types of cerebral pathology. *British Journal of Clinical Psychology*, **23**, 53–57.

Miller, E. (1984b). *Recovery and Management of Neuropsychological Impairments*. Chichester: John Wiley.

Miller, E. (1985). Possible frontal impairments in Parkinson's disease: a test using a measure of verbal fluency. *British Journal of Clinical Psychology*, **24**, 211–212.

Miller, E. (1988). Methodological issues in abnormal psychology. In E. Miller & P. J. Copper (Eds). *Adult Abnormal Psychology*. Edinburgh: Churchill Livingstone.

Miller, E. (1989). Language impairment in Alzheimer type dementia. *Clinical Psychology Review*, **9**, 181–195.

Miller, E. (1992). Basic principles of neuropsychological assessment. In J. Crawford, W. McKinlay & D. Parker (Eds). *Practice and Principles of Neuropsychological Assessment*. London: Laurence Erlbaum.

Miller, E. (1993). Dissociating single cases in neuropsychology. *British Journal of Clinical Psychology*, **32**, 155–167.

Miller, E., Berrios, G. E. & Politynska, B. (1987). The adverse effects of benzhexol on memory. *Acta Neurologica Scandinavica*, **76**, 278–282.

Miller, E. & Hague, F. (1975). Some characteristics of verbal behaviour in presenile dementia. *Psychological Medicine*, **5**, 255–259.

Milner, B. (1964). Some effects of frontal lobectomy in man. In J. M. Warren & K. Akert (Eds). *The Frontal Granular Cortex and Behavior*. New York: McGraw-Hill.

Mishkin, M., Malamut, B. & Bachevalier, J. (1984). Memories and habits: Two neural systems. In G. Lynch, J. L., McGaugh & N. M. Weinberger (Eds). *Neurobiology of Learning and Memory*. New York: Guilford Press.

Mitrushina, M. & Fuld, P. A. (1990). Neuropsychological characteristics of early Alzheimer disease. In R. E. Becker & E. Giacobini (Eds). *Alzheimer's Disease: Current Research and Early Diagnosis*. New York: Taylor & Francis.

Mohr, E., Cox, C., Williams, J., Chase, T. N. & Fedio, P. (1990). Impairment of central auditory function in Alzheimer's disease. *Journal of Clinical and Experimental Neuropsychology*, **12**, 235–246.

Money, E. A., Kirk, R. C. & McNaughton, N. (1992). Alzheimer's dementia produces a loss of discrimination but not increase in memory decay in delayed matching to sample. *Neuropsychologia*, **30**, 133–142.

Moore, V. & Wyke, M. A. (1984). Drawing disability in patients with senile dementia. *Psychological Medicine*, **14**, 97–105.

Moritz, D. J., Kasl, S. V. & Berkman, L. F. (1989). The health impact of living with a cognitively impaired elderly spouse: depressive symptoms and social functioning. *Journal of Gerontology*, **14**, 517–527.

Morris, L. W. (1986). *The psychological factors affecting emotional wellbeing of the spouse caregivers of dementia sufferers*. Unpublished M. Sc. Thesis, University of Newcastle upon Tyne.

Morris, L. W., Morris, R. G. & Britton, P. G. (1988). The relationship between marital intimacy, perceived strain and depression in spouse carers of dementia sufferers. *British Journal of Medical Psychology*, **61**, 231–236.

Morris, L. W., Morris, R. G. & Britton, P. G. (1989a). Cognitive style and perceived control in spouse carers of dementia sufferers. *British Journal of Medical Psychology*, **62**, 173–179.

Morris, L. W., Morris, R. G. & Britton, P. G. (1989b). Social support networks and formal support as factors influencing the psychological adjustment of spouse caregivers of dementia sufferers. *International Journal of Geriatric Psychiatry*, **4**, 47–51.

Morris, R. G. (1984). Dementia and the functioning of the articulatory loop system. *Cognitive Neuropsychology*, **1**, 143–157.

Morris, R. G. (1986). Short-term forgetting in senile dementia of the Alzheimer's type. *Cognitive Neuropsychology*, **3**, 77–97.

Morris, R. G. (1987a). Articulatory rehearsal in Alzheimer-type dementia. *Brain and Language*, **30**, 351–362.

Morris, R. G. (1987b). Matching and oddity learning in moderate to severe dementia. *Quarterly Journal of Experimental Psychology*, **39**, 215–227.

Morris, R. G. (1991). A case of reduplicate amnesia complicated by the death of the real partner. Unpublished Manuscript.

Morris, R. G. & Baddeley, A. D. (1988). Primary and working memory in Alzheimer-type dementia. *Journal of Clinical and Experimental Neuropsychology*, **10**, 279–296.

Morris, R. G., Downes, J. J. & Robbins, T. W. (1990). The nature of the dysexecutive syndrome in Parkinson's disease. In K. J. Gilhooly, M. T. G. Keane, R. H. Logie & G. Erdos (Eds). *Lines of Thinking*, Vol. 2. Chichester: John Wiley.

Morris, R. G., Evenden, J. L., Sahakian, B. J. & Robbins, T. W. (1987). Computer-aided assessment of dementia: comparative studies of neuropsychological deficits in Alzheimer-type dementia and Parkinson's disease. In S. M. Stahl, S. D. Iversen & E. C. Goodman (Eds). *Cognitive Neurochemistry*. Oxford: Oxford University Press.

Morris, R. G. & McKiernan, F. (1993). Neuropsychological investigations of dementia. In R. Levy & A. Burns (Eds). *Dementia*. London: Chapman & Hall.

Morris, R. G. & Morris, L. W. (in press). Psychosocial aspects of caring for people with dementia: conceptual and methodological issues. In A. Burns (Ed). *Ageing and Dementia: A Methodological Perspective*. Sevenoaks: Edward Arnold.

Morris, R. G., Morris, L. W. & Britton, P. G. (1988). Factors affecting the emotional wellbeing of caregivers of dementia sufferers. *British Journal of Psychiatry*, **153**, 147–156.

Morris, R. G., Wheatley, J. & Britton, P. G. (1983). Retrieval from long-term memory in senile dementia: cued recall revisited. *British Journal of Clinical Psychology*, **22**, 141–142.

Morris, R. G., Woods, R. T., Davies, K. S. & Morris, L. W. (1991). Gender differences in carers of dementia sufferers. *British Journal of Psychiatry*, **158**, (suppl. 10), 69–74.

Morris, R. G., Woods, R. T., Davies, K. S., Berry, J. & Morris, L. W. (1992).

The use of a coping strategy focused support group for carers of dementia sufferers. *Counselling Psychology Quarterly*, **5**, 337–348.

Morton, I. & Bleathman, C. (1991). The effectiveness of validation therapy in dementia—a pilot study. *International Journal of Geriatric Psychiatry*, **6**, 327–330.

Moscovitch, M. (1982). A neuropsychological approach to perception and memory in normal and pathological aging. In F. I. M. Craik & S. Trehub (Eds). *Aging and Cognitive Processes*. New York: Plenum Press.

Moss, H., Tyler, L. K., Patterson, K. & Hodges, J. R. (1993). Preservation of detailed functional information in a case of semantic dementia: evidence from primed monitoring. Paper presented to Meeting of the British Neuropsychological Society.

Moss, M. B., Albert, M. S., Butters, N. & Payne, M. (1986). Differential patterns of memory loss among patients with Alzheimer's disease, Huntington's disease, and alcoholic Korsakoff's syndrome. *Archives of Neurology*, **43**, 239–246.

Murdock, B. B. Jr (1974). *Human Memory: Theory and Data*. Hillsdale, NJ: Lawrence Erlbaum.

Murdoch, B. E., Chenery, H. J., Wills, V. & Boyle, R. S. (1987). Language disorder in dementia of the Alzheimer type. *Brain and Language*, **31**, 122–137.

Naville, F. (1922). Etudes sur les complications et les sequelles mentales de l'encephalite epidemique. La bradyphrenie. *L'Encephale*, **17**, 369–375.

Neary, D. (1990). Dementia of the frontal lobe type. *Journal of the American Geriatric Society*, **38**, 71–72.

Neary, D., Snowden, J. S., Bowen, D. H., Sims, N. R., Mann, D. M. A., Benton, J. S., Northern, B., Yates, P. O. & Davison, A. N. (1986). Neuropsychological syndromes in presenile dementia due to cerebral atrophy. *Journal of Neurology, Neurosurgery and Psychiatry*, **49**, 163–174.

Neary, D., Snowden, J. S., Northern, R. & Goulding, P. (1988). Dementia of the frontal lobe type. *Journal of Neurology, Neurosurgery and Psychiatry*, **51**, 353–361.

Nebes, R. D. (1991). Cognitive dysfunction in Alzheimer's disease. In F. I. M. Craik & T. Salthouse (Eds). *Handbook of Cognitive Aging*. Englewood Cliffs, NJ: Prentice Hall.

Nebes, R. D., Boller, F. & Holland, A. (1986). Use of a semantic context by patients with Alzheimer's disease. *Psychology and Aging*, **1**, 261–269.

Nebes, R. D. & Brady, C. B. (1988). Integrity of semantic fields in Alzheimer's disease. *Cortex*, **24**, 291–299.

Nebes, R. D. & Brady, C. B. (1989). Focused and divided attention in Alzheimer's disease. *Cortex*, **25**, 305–315.

Nebes, R. D. & Brady, C. R. (1992). Generalised cognitive slowing and severity of dementia in Alzheimer's disease: implications for the interpretation of response-time data. *Journal of Clinical and Experimental Neuropsychology*, **14**, 317–326.

Nebes, R. D., Brady, C. B. & Huff, F. J. (1989). Automatic and attentional mechanisms of semantic priming in Alzheimer's disease. *Journal of Clinical and Experimental Neuropsychology*, **11**, 219–230.

Nebes, R. D., Martin, D. C. & Horn, L. C. (1984). Sparing of semantic memory in Alzheimer's disease. *Journal of Abnormal Psychology*, **93**, 321–330.

Nelson, H. & O'Connell, A. (1978). Dementia: the estimation of premorbid intelligence using the new adult reading test. *Cortex*, **14**, 234–244.

Nicholas, M., Obler, L. K., Albert, M. L. & Helm-Estabrooks, N. (1985). Empty speech in Alzheimer's disease and fluent aphasia. *Journal of Speech and Hearing Research*, **28**, 405–410.

Niederehe, G. & Fruge, E. (1984). Dementia and family dynamics: clinical research issues. *Journal of Geriatric Psychiatry*, **17**, 21–56.

Nielsen, J. (1962). Geronto-psychiatric period-prevalence investigation in a geographically delimited population. *Acta Psychiatrica Scandinavica*, **38**, 307–330.

Nissen, M. J., Corkin, S., Buonanno, F. S., Growden, J. H., Wray, S. H. & Bauer, J. (1985). Spatial vision in Alzheimer's disease: general findings and a case report. *Archives of Neurology*, **42**, 667–671.

Norman, D. A. (1976). *Memory and Attention*, 2nd Edn. New York: John Wiley.

Ober, B. A., Dronkers, N. F., Koss, E., Delis, D. C. & Friedland, R. P. (1986). Retrieval from semantic memory in Alzheimer-type dementia. *Journal of Clinical and Experimental Neuropsychology*, **8**, 75–92.

O'Brien, J. T., Beats, B., Hill, K., Howard, R., Sahakian, B. & Levy, R. (1992). Do subjective memory complaints precede dementia? A three-year follow-up of patients with supposed 'benign senescent forgetfulness'. *International Journal of Geriatric Psychiatry*, **7**, 481–486.

O'Neill, P. M. & Calhoun, K. S. (1975). Sensory deficits and behavioral deterioration in senescence. *Journal of Abnormal Psychology*, **84**, 579–582.

Oppenheimer, C. & Jaccoby, R. (1991). Assessment of the elderly patient: psychiatric examination. In R. Jaccoby & C. Oppenheimer (Eds). *Psychiatry in the Elderly*. Oxford: Oxford University Press.

Orrell, M., Howard, R., Payne, A., Bergmann, K., Woods, R., Everitt, B. S. & Levy, R. (1992). Differentiation between organic and functional psychiatric illness in the elderly: an evaluation of four cognitive tests. *International Journal of Geriatric Psychiatry*, **7**, 263–275.

Owen, A. (1993). Computerised assessment of dementia. In R. Levy & A. Burns (Eds). *Dementia*. London: Chapman & Hall.

Pagel, M. D., Becker, J. & Coppel, D. B. (1985). Loss of control, self-blame and depression: an investigation of spouse caregivers of Alzheimer's disease patients. *Journal of Abnormal Psychology,* **94,** 169–182.

Parasuraman, R., Greenwood, P. M., Haxby, J. V. & Grady, C. L. (1992). Visuospatial attention in dementia of the Alzheimer's type. *Brain,* **115,** 711–733.

Parry, G. & Watts, F. N. (1989). *Behavioural and Mental Health Research: A Handbook of Skills and Methods.* Hove, East Sussex: Lawrence Erlbaum.

Pattie A. & Gilleard, C. J. (1979). *Manual of the Clifton Assessment Procedures for the Elderly (CAPE).* Sevenoaks: Hodder and Stoughton.

Payne, R. W. & Jones, H. G. (1957). Statistics for the investigation of individual cases. *Journal of Clinical Psychology,* **13,** 117–121.

Pearce, J. M. S. (1984). *Dementia: A Clinical Approach.* Oxford: Blackwell.

Pearce, J. & Miller, E. (1973). *Clinical Aspects of Dementia.* London: Baillière Tindall.

Pearson, J., Verma, S. & Nellett, C. (1988). Elderly psychiatric patient status and caregiver perceptions as predictors of caregiver burden. *The Gerontologist,* **28,** 79–83.

Peck, D. F. & Shapiro, C. M. (1990). *Measuring Human Problems.* Chichester: John Wiley.

Pendleton, M. G., Heaton, R. K., Lehman, R. A. W. & Hulihan, D. (1982). Diagnostic utility of the Thurstone Word Fluency Test in neuropsychological evaluations. *Journal of Clinical Neuropsychology,* **4,** 307–317.

Peretz, J. A. & Cummings, J. L. (1988). Subcortical dementia. In U. Holden (Ed.). *Neuropsychology and Ageing.* London: Croom Helm.

Perez, F. I., Gay, J. R. A., Taylor, R. L. & Rivera, V. M. (1975a). Patterns of memory performance in the neurologically impaired aged. *Canadian Journal of Neurological Science,* **2,** 347–355.

Perez, F. I., Rivera, V. M., Myer, J. S., Gay, J. R. A., Taylor, R. L. & Matthew, N. T. (1975b). Analysis of intellectual and cognitive performance in patients with multi-infarct dementia, vertebrobasilar insufficiency with dementia and Alzheimer's disease. *Journal of Neurology, Neurosurgery and Psychiatry,* **38,** 533–540.

Perry, E. K., Gibson, P. H., Blessed, G., Perry, R. H. & Tomlinson, B. E. (1977). Neurotransmitter enzyme abnormalities in senile dementia. *Journal of Neurological Science,* **34,** 247–265.

Petry, S., Cummings, J. L., Hill, M. A. & Shapira, J. (1989). Personality alterations in dementia of the Alzheimer type. *Archives of Neurology,* **45,** 1187–1190.

Petry, S., Cummings, J. L., Hill, M. A. & Shapira, J. (1988). Personality alterations in dementia of the Alzheimer type: a three-year follow-up study. *Journal of Geriatric Psychiatry and Neurology,* **2,** 203–207.

Piccirilli, M., D'Alessandro, P., Finali, G., Piccinin, G. L. & Agostini, L.

(1989). Frontal lobe dysfunction in Parkinson's disease: prognostic value for dementia. *European Neurology*, **29**, 71–76.

Pietro, M. J. S. & Goldfarb, R. (1985). Characteristic patterns of word association responses in institutional elderly with and without senile dementia. *Brain and Language*, **26**, 230–243.

Pillon, B., Dubois, R., Bonnet, A.-M., Esteguy, M., Guimaraes, J., Vigouret, J.-M., Lhermitte, F. & Agid, Y. (1989). Cognitive slowing in Parkinson's disease fails to respond to levodopa treatment: the 15 objects test. *Neurology*, **39**, 762–768.

Pillon, B., Dubois, B., Ploska, A. & Agid, Y. (1991). Severity and specificity of cognitive impairment in Alzheimer's, Huntington's, and Parkinson's diseases and progressive supranuclear palsy. *Neurology*, **41**, 634–643.

Pinkston, E. M. & Linsk, N. L. (1984). Use of environmental manipulation and classroom and modified informal reality orientation with institutionalised, confused elderly patients. *Age and Ageing*, **14**, 119–121.

Pirozzolo, F. J., Hansch, E. C., Mortimer, J. A., Webster, D. D. & Kuskowski, M. A. (1982). Dementia in Parkinson's disease: a neuropsychological analysis. *Brain and Cognition*, **1**, 71–83.

Popham, W. J. & Musek, T. R. (1969). Implications of criterion referenced assessment. *Journal of Educational Measurement*, **6**, 1–9.

Posner, M. I., Petersen, S. E., Fox, P. T. & Raichle, M. E. (1988). Localisation of cognitive operations in the human brain. *Science*, **240**, 1627–1631.

Posner, M. I., Snyder, C. R. & Davison, B. J. (1980). Attention and the detection of signals. *Journal of Experimental Psychology: General*, **109**, 160–174.

Potegal, M. (1971). A note on spatial–motor deficits in patients with Huntington's disease: a test of a hypothesis. *Neuropsychologia*, **9**, 233–235.

Poulshock, S. W. & Deimling, G. T. (1984). Families caring for elders in residence: issues in the measurement of burden. *Journal of Gerontology*, **39**, 230–239.

Powell-Proctor, L. & Miller, E. (1982). Reality orientation: a critical appraisal. *British Journal of Psychiatry*, **140**, 457–463.

Pruchno, R. A. & Resch, N. L. (1989). Aberrant behaviors and Alzheimer's disease: mental health effects on spouse caregivers. *Journal of Gerontology*, **44**, 177–182.

Pruchno, R. A. & Potasnik, S. L. (1989). Caregiving spouses: physical and mental health in perspective. *Journal of the American Geriatrics Society*, **37**, 697–705.

Rafal, R. D., Posner, M. I., Walker, J. A. & Friedrich, F. J. (1984). Cognition and the basal ganglia: separating mental and motor components of performance in Parkinson's disease. *Brain*, **107**, 1083–1094.

Rapcsak, S. Z., Arthur, S. A., Bliklen, D. A. & Rubens, A. B. (1989). Lexical agraphia in Alzheimer's disease. *Archives of Neurology*, **46**, 65–68.

Rebok, G., Brandt, J. & Folstein, M. (1990). Longitudinal cognitive decline in patients with Alzheimer's disease. *Journal of Geriatric Psychiatry and Neurology*, **3**, 91–97.

Reeve, W. & Ivison, D. (1985). Use of environmental manipulation and classroom and modified informal reality orientation with institutionalised, confused elderly patients. *Age and Ageing*, **14**, 119–121.

Riklan, M., Reynolds, C. M. & Stellar, S. (1989). Correlates of memory in Parkinson's disease. *Journal of Nervous and Mental Disease*, **177**, 237–240.

Rinke, C. L., Williams, J. J., Lloyd, K. E. & Smith-Scott, W. (1978). The effects of prompting and reinforcement on self-bathing by elderly residents of a nursing home. *Behaviour Therapy*, **9**, 873–881.

Ripich, D. N., Vertes, D., Whitehouse, P., Fulton, S. & Ekelman, B. (1991). Turn-taking and speech act patterns in the discourse of senile dementia of the Alzheimer type. *Brain and Language*, **40**, 330–343.

Robbins, T. W., James, M., Lange, K. W., Owen, A. M., Quinn, N. P. & Marsden, C. D. (1992). Cognitive performance in multiple system atrophy. *Brain*, **115**, 271–291.

Rocca, W., Hofman, A., Brayne, C., Breteler, M., Clarke, M., Copeland, J., Dartigues, R., Engedal, K., Hagnell, O., Heeren, T., Jonker, C., Lindesay, J., Lobo, A., Mann, A., Molsa, P., Morgan, K., da Silva Droux, A., Sulkava, R., Kay, D. & Amaducci, L. (1991). Frequency and distribution of Alzheimer's disease in Europe: a collaborative study of 1980–1990 prevalence findings. *Annals of Neurology*, **30**, 381–390.

Rochford, G. (1971). A study of naming errors in dysphasic and demented patients. *Neuropsychologia*, **9**, 437–443.

Rogers, D. (1986). Bradyphrenia in parkinsonism: a historical review. *Psychological Medicine*, **16**, 257–265.

Rosberger, Z. & Maclean, J. (1983). Behavioral assessment and treatment of 'organic' behaviours in an institutionalised geriatric patient. *International Journal of Behavioural Geriatrics*, **1**, 33–46.

Rosen, W. G. (1980). Verbal fluency in aging and dementia. *Journal of Clinical Neuropsychology*, **2**, 135–146.

Rosen, W. A. (1983). Neuropsychological investigation of memory, visuoconstructional, visuoperceptual and language abilities in senile dementia of the Alzheimer type. In R. Mayeux & W. G. Rosen (Eds). *The Dementias*. New York: Raven Press.

Rosenberg, S. J., Ryan, J. J. & Prifitera, A. (1984). Rey's Auditory Verbal

Learning Test performance of patients with and without memory impairment. *Journal of Clinical Psychology*, **40**, 785–787.

Roth, M., Tym, E., Mountjoy, C. Q., Huppert, F. A., Hendrie, H., Verma, S. & Goddard, R. (1986). CAMDEX: a standardized instrument for the diagnosis of mental disorder in the elderly with special reference to the early detection of dementia. *British Journal of Psychiatry*, **149**, 698–709.

Rothwell, N., Britton, P. G. & Woods, R. T. (1983). The effects of group living in a residential home for the elderly. *British Journal of Social Work*, **13**, 639–643.

Royal College of Physicians Report (1981). Organic mental impairment in the elderly: implications for research, education and the provision of services. *Journal of the Royal College of Physicians of London*, **15**, 139–167.

Rubin, E. H. (1990). Psychopathology of senile dementia of the Alzheimer type. In R. J. Wurtman, S. Corkin, J. H. Growden & E. Ritter-Williams (Eds). *Advances in Neurology*. Vol. 51. *Alzheimer's disease*. New York: Raven Press.

Rubin, E. H., Morris, J. C. & Berg, L. (1987). The progression of personality changes in senile dementia of the Alzheimer-type. *Journal of the American Gerontological Society*, **35**, 721–725.

St. George-Hyslop, P. H., Tanzi, R. E., Polinsky, R. J., Haines, J. L., Nee, L., Watkins, P. C., Myers, R. H., Feldman, R. G., Pollen, D., Drachman, D., Growden, J., Bruni, A., Fancin, J. F., Samon, D., Frommelt, P., Amaducci, L., Sorbi, S., Piacentini, S., Stewart, G. D., Hobbs, W. J., Conneally, P. M., Gusella, J. F. (1987). The genetic defect causing familial Alzheimer's disease maps on chromosome 21. *Science*, **235**, 880–884.

Sagar, H. J. (1984). Clinical similarities and differences between Alzheimer's disease and Parkinson's disease. In R. J. Wurtman, S. H. Corkin & J. H. Growden (Eds). *Alzheimer's Disease: Advances in Basic Research and Therapies*. Cambridge, MA: Center for Brain Sciences and Metabolism Charitable Trust.

Sagar, H. J., Cohen, N. J., Sullivan, E. V., Corkin, S. & Growden, J. H. (1988). Remote memory function in Alzheimer's disease and Parkinson's disease. *Brain*, **111**, 185–206.

Sagar, H. J., Cohen, N. J., Corkin, S. & Growden, J. H. (1985). Dissociation among processes in remote memory. *Annals of the New York Academy of Sciences*, **444**, 533–535.

Sagar, H. J., Sullivan, E. V., Gabrieli, J. D., Corkin, S. & Growden, J. H. (1988). Temporal ordering and short-term memory deficits in Parkinson's disease. *Brain*, **111**, 525–539.

Sahakian, B. J. (1990). Computerised assessment of neuropsychological function in Alzheimer's disease and Parkinson's disease. *International Journal of Geriatric Psychiatry*, **5**, 211–213.

Sahakian, B. J., Jones, G., Levy, R., Gray, J. A. & Warburton, D. (1989). Nicotine treatment of dementia. *British Journal of Psychiatry*, **154**, 697–800.

Sahakian, B. J., Morris, R. G., Evenden, J. L., Heald, A., Levy, R., Philpott, M. & Robbins, T. (1988). A comparative study of visuospatial memory and learning in Alzheimer-type dementia and Parkinson's disease. *Brain*, **111**, 695–718.

Sahakian, B. J., Downes, J. J., Eagger, S., Evenden, J. L., Levy, R., Philpot, M. P., Roberts, A. C. & Robbins, T. W. (1990). Sparing of attentional relative to mnemonic function in a subgroup of patients with dementia of the Alzheimer type. *Neuropsychologia*, **28**, 1197–1213.

Sahgal, A. & Iverson, S. (1978). Categorisation and retrieval after selective inferotemporal lesions in monkeys. *Brain Research*, **146**, 341–350.

Salmon, D. P., Kwo-On-Yuen, P. F., Heindel, C., Butters, N. & Thal, L. J. (1989). Differentiation of Alzheimer's and Huntington's disease with the dementia rating scale. *Archives of Neurology*, **46**, 1204–1208.

Salthouse, T. A. & Somberg, B. L. (1982). Isolating the age effect in speeded performance. *Journal of Gerontology*, **37**, 59–63.

Sanavio, E. (1981). Toilet retraining psychogeriatric residents. *Behaviour Modification*, **5**, 417–427.

Sanderson, R. E. & Inglis, J. (1961). Learning and mortality in elderly psychiatric patients. *Journal of Gerontology*, **16**, 375–376.

Sanford, J. R. A. (1975). Tolerance of debility in elderly dependants by supporters at home: its significance for hospital practice. *British Medical Journal*, **3**, 471–475.

Schacter, D. L. (1989). On the relation between memory and consciousness: dissociable interactions and conscious experience. In H. L. Roediger & F. I. M. Craik (Eds). *Varieties of Memory and Consciousness*. Hillsdale, NJ: Lawrence Erlbaum.

Scharlach, A. & Frenzel, C. (1986). An evaluation of institution-based respite care. *The Gerontologist*, **26**, 77–82.

Schlotterer, G., Moscovitch, M. & Crapper-McLachlan, D. (1983). Visual processing deficits as assessed by spatial frequency contrast sensitivity and backward masking in normal ageing and Alzheimer's disease. *Brain*, **107**, 309–327.

Schmidt, G. L. & Keyes, B. (1985). Group psychotherapy with family caregivers of dementia patients. *The Gerontologist*, **25**, 347–350.

√ Schnelle, J. F., Traughber, B., Morgan, D. B., Embry, J. E. Binion, A. F. & Coleman, A. (1983). Management of geriatric incontinence in nursing homes. *Journal of Behavior Analysis*, **16**, 235–241.

Schnelle, J. F., Sowell, V. A., Hu, T. W. & Traughber, B. (1988). Reduction of urinary incontinence in nursing homes: does it reduce or increase costs? *Journal of the American Geriatrics Society*, **36**, 34–39.

Schoenberg, B. S., Anderson, D. W. & Haerer, A. F. (1985). Severe dementia: prevalence and clinical features in a biracial US population. *Archives of Neurology*, **42**, 740–743.

Schoenberg, B. S., Kokmen, E. & Okazaki, H. (1987). Alzheimer's disease and other dementing illnesses in a defined United States population: incidence rates and clinical features. *Annals of Neurology*, **22**, 724–729.

Schwartz, M. F., Marin, O. S. & Sffran, E. M. (1979). Dissociations in language function in dementia: a case study. *Brain and Language*, **7**, 277–306.

Schwartz, G. E. (1983). Development and validation of the Geriatric Evaluation by Relatives Rating Instrument (GERRI) *Psychological Reports*, **53**, 479–488.

Seltzer, B. & Sherwin, I. (1983). A comparison of clinical features in early- and late-onset primary degenerative dementia. *Archives of Neurology*, **40**, 143–146.

Shallice, T. (1988). *From Neuropsychology to Mental Structure*. Cambridge: Cambridge University Press.

Sharpe, K. & O'Carroll, R. E. (1991). Estimating premorbid intellectual level in dementia using the National Adult Reading Test. *British Journal of Clinical Psychology*, **30**, 381–384.

Sheridan, M. R. & Flowers, K. A. (1990). Movement variability and bradyphrenia in Parkinson's disease. *Brain*, **113**, 1149–1161.

Sheridan, M. R., Flowers, K. A. & Hurrell, J. (1987). Programming and execution of movement in Parkinson's disease. *Brain*, **110**, 1247–1271.

Shibal-Champagne, S. & Lapinska-Stachow, D. M. (1985–1986). Alzheimer's educational/support group: considerations for success—awareness of family tasks, pre-planning, and active professional facilitation. *Journal of Gerontological Social Work*, **9**, 41–48.

Shimamura, A. P., Slamon, D. P., Squire, L. R. & Butters, N. (1987). Memory dysfunction and word priming in dementia and amnesia. *Behavioral Neuroscience*, **101**, 347–351.

Simpson, P. M., Surmon, D. J., Wesnes, K. A. & Wilcok, G. K. (1991). The cognitive drug research computerised assessment system for demented patients: a validation study. *International Journal of Geriatric Psychiatry*, **6**, 95–102.

Sjögren, T., Sjögren, H. & Lindgren, A. G. H. (1952). Morbus Alzheimer and morbus Pick: a genetic, clinical and patho-anatomical study. *Acta Psychiatrica Scandinavica*, Supplementum 82.

Ska, B., Poissant, A. & Joanette, Y. (1990). Line orientation judgment in normal elderly and subjects with dementia of Alzheimer's type. *Journal of Clinical and Experimental Neuropsychology*, **12**, 695–702.

Skelton-Robinson, M. & Jones, S. (1984). Nominal dysphasia and severity of senile dementia. *British Journal of Psychiatry*, **145**, 168–171.

Solyom, L. & Barik, H. C. (1965). Conditioning in senescence and senility. *Journal of Gerontology*, **20**, 483–488.

Somberg, B. L. & Salthouse, T. A. (1982). Divided attention abilities in young and old adults. *Journal of Experimental Psychology: Human Perception and Performance*, **8**, 651–663.

Spinnler, H., Della Sala, S., Bandera, R. & Baddeley, A. D. (1988). Dementia, ageing and the structure of human memory. *Cognitive Neuropsychology*, **5**, 193–211.

Spitzer, R., Endicott, J. & Robins, E. (1978). *Research Diagnostic Criteria for a Selected Group of Functional Disorders*. New York: New York Psychiatric Institute.

Steele, J. C., Richardson, J. C. & Olszewski, J. (1964). Progressive supranuclear palsy. *Archives of Neurology*, **10**, 333–358.

Stein, D. G., Palatucci, C., Kahn, D. & Labbe, R. (1988). Temporal factors influence recovery of function after embryonic brain tissue transplants in adult rats with frontal cortex lesions. *Behavioural Neuroscience*, **102**, 260–267.

Stelmach, G. E., Phillips, J. G. & Chau, A. W. (1989). Visuo-spatial processing in Parkinsonians. *Neuropsychologia*, **27**, 485–493.

Stelmach, G. E., Worringham, C. J. & Strand, E. (1986). Movement preparation in Parkinson's disease: the use of advance information. *Brain*, **109**, 1179–1194.

Stengel, E. (1964). Psychopathology of dementia. *Proceedings of the Royal Society of Medicine*, **57**, 911–914.

Sternberg, S. (1975). Memory scanning: new findings and current controversies. *Quarterly Journal of Experimental Psychology*, **27**, 1–32.

Stevens, S. J., Pitt, B. M. N., Nicholl, C. G., Fletcher, A. E. & Palmer, A. (1992). Language assessment in a memory clinic. *International Journal of Geriatric Psychiatry*, **7**, 45–51.

Storandt, M., Botwinick, J., Danziger, W. L., Berg, L. & Hughes, C. P. (1984). Psychometric differentiations of mild senile dementia of the Alzheimer type. *Archives of Neurology*, **41**, 497–499.

Sullivan, E. V., Corkin, S. & Growden, J. H. (1986). Verbal and nonverbal short-term memory in patients with Alzheimer's disease and in healthy elderly subjects. *Developmental Neuropsychology*, **2**, 387–400.

Sullivan, E. V. & Sagar, H. J. (1989). Nonverbal recognition and recency discrimination deficits in Parkinson's disease and Alzheimer's disease. *Brain*, **112**, 1503–1517.

Swearer, J. M., Drachman, D. A., O'Donnell, B. F. & Mitchell, A. L. (1988). Troublesome and disruptive behaviours in dementia: relationships to diagnosis and disease severity. *Journal of the American Geriatrics Society*, **36**, 784–790.

Teng, E. L., Chui, H. C., Schneider, L. S. & Metzger, E. (1987). Alzheimer's dementia: performance on the Mini-Mental State Examination. *Journal of Consulting and Clinical Psychology*, **55**, 96–100.

Teri, L., Borson, S., Kiyak, H. A. & Yamagishi, M. (1989). Behavioural disturbance, cognitive dysfunction, and functional skill. *Journal of the American Geriatrics Society*, **37**, 109–116.

Teri, L. & Wagner, A. (1992). Alzheimer's disease and depression. *Journal of Consulting and Clinical Psychology*, **60**, 379–391.

Tomlinson, B. E., Blessed, G. & Roth, M. (1970). Observations on the brains of demented old people. *Journal of Neurological Science*, **7**, 205–242.

Thompson, I. M. (1987). Language in dementia. *International Journal of Geriatric Psychiatry*, **2**, 145–161.

Thornton, S. & Brotchie, J. (1987). Reminiscence: A critical review of the empirical literature. *British Journal of Clinical Psychology*, **26**, 93–111.

Toseland, T. W., Rossiter, C. M. & Labrecque, M. S. (1989). The effectiveness of peer-led groups to support family caregivers. *The Gerontologist*, **29**, 465–471.

Toseland, R. W. & Smith, G. C. (1990). Effectiveness of individual counseling by professional and peer helpers for family caregivers of the elderly. *Psychology and Aging*, **5**, 256–263.

Tulving, E. (1972). Episodic and semantic memory. In E. Tulving & W. Donaldson (Eds). *The Organisation of Memory*. New York: Academic Press.

Tulving, E. (1983). *Elements of Episodic Memory*. Oxford University Press.

Vallar, G. & Shallice, T. (1990). *Neuropsychological Impairments of Short-Term Memory*. Cambridge: Cambridge University Press.

von Stockert, F. G. (1932). Subcorticale demenz. *Archiv für Psychiatrie und Nervenkrankheiten*, **97**, 77–100.

Wallis, G. G., Baldwin, M. & Higginbotham, P. (1983). Reality orientation therapy: A controlled trial. *British Journal of Medical Psychology*, **56**, 271–278.

Walton, J. N. (1985). *Brain's Diseases of the Nervous System*. Oxford: Oxford University Press.

Ward, J. (1970). On the concept of criterion referenced assessment. *British Journal of Educational Psychology*, **40**, 314–325.

Warrington, E. K. (1969). Constructional apraxia. In P. J. Vinken & G. W. Bruyn (Eds). *Handbook of Clinical Neurology*, Vol. 4, *Disorders of speech, perception and symbolic behavior*. Amsterdam: North Holland Publishing Co.

Warrington, E. K. & Shallice, T. (1984). Category specific semantic impairments. *Brain,* **107**, 829–854.

Wasow, M. (1985). Support groups for family caregivers of patients with Alzheimer's disease. *Social Work,* **31**, 93–97.

Wechsler, D. (1945). A standardised memory scale for clinical use. *Journal of Psychology,* **19**, 87–95.

Wechsler, D. (1987). *Wechsler Memory Scale Revised.* New York: The Psychological Corporation.

Weingartner, H., Caine, E. D. & Ebert, M. H. (1979). Encoding processes, learning, and recall in Huntington's disease. In T. N. Chase, N. S. Wexler & A. Barbeau (Eds). *Advances in Neurology, Vol. 23: Huntington's Disease.* New York: Raven Press.

Weingartner, H., Kaye, W., Smallberg, S. A., Ebert, H., Gillin, J. C. & Sitaram, N. (1981). Memory failures in progressive idiopathic dementia. *Journal of Abnormal Psychology,* **90**, 187–196.

Weiskrantz, L. (1968). Some traps and pontifications. In L. Weiskrantz (Ed.). *Analysis of Behavioural Change.* New York: Harper & Row.

Welsh, K. A., Butters, N., Hughes, J., Mohs, R. & Heman, A. (1991). Detection of abnormal memory decline in mild cases of Alzheimer's disease using CERAD neuropsychological measures. *Archives of Neurology,* **48**, 278–281.

Wesnes, K., Simmons, D., Rook, M. & Simpson, P. (1987). A double blind placebo controlled trial of Tanakan in the treatment of idiopathic cognitive impairment in the elderly. *Human Psychopharmacology,* **2**, 159–171.

Whitehead, A. (1973). The pattern of WAIS performance in elderly psychiatric patients. *British Journal of Psychiatry,* **12**, 435–436.

Whitehead, A. (1977). The clinical psychologist's role in assessment and management. In A. D. Isaacs & F. Post (Eds). *Studies in Geriatric Psychiatry.* Chichester: John Wiley.

Whitehouse, P. J., Price, D. L., Struble, R. G. Coyle, J. I. & DeLong, M. R. (1982). Alzheimer's disease and senile dementia—loss of neurones in the basal forebrain. *Science,* **215**, 1237–1239.

Whitlatch, C. J., Zarit, S. H. & von Eye, A. (1991). Efficacy of interventions with carers: A reanalysis. *The Gerontologist,* **31**, 9–14.

Williams, L. & Miller, E. (1992). The effect of prolonged high aluminium intake on cognitive functioning. Paper presented to the London Conference of the British Psychological Society.

Wilson, B. (1987). *Rehabilitation of Memory.* New York: Guilford Press.

Wilson, R. S., Bacon, L. D., Fox, J. H. & Kaszniak, A. W. (1983). Primary memory and secondary memory in dementia of the Alzheimer-type. *Journal of Clinical Neuropsychology,* **5**, 337–344.

Wilson, R. S., Kaszniak, A. W., Bacon, L. D., Fox, J. H. & Kelly, M. P. (1982). Facial recognition memory in dementia. *Cortex*, **18**, 329–336.

Wilson, R. S., Kaszniak, A. W. & Fox, J. H. (1980). Depth of processing in dementia. Paper presented at the meeting of the American Psychological Association, Montreal, Canada.

Wilson, R. S., Kaszniak, A. W. & Fox, J. H. (1981). Remote memory in senile dementia. *Cortex*, **17**, 41–48.

Wilson, R. S., Kaszniak, A. W., Klawans, H. L. & Garron, D. C. (1980). High speed memory scanning in Parkinsonism. *Cortex*, **16**, 67–72.

Woods, R. T. (1979). Reality orientation and staff attention: a controlled study. *British Journal of Psychiatry*, **134**, 502–507.

Woods, R. T. (1987). Psychological management of dementia. In B. Pitt (Ed.). *Dementia*. Edinburgh: Churchill Livingstone.

Worcester-Drought, C. & Hardcastle, D. N. (1924). A contribution to the psychopathology of residual encephalitis lethargica. *Journal of Neurology and Psychopathology*, **5**, 146–150.

Wragg, R. E. & Jeste, D. V. (1989). Overview of depression and psychosis in Alzheimer's disease. *American Journal of Psychiatry*, **146**, 577–587.

Wright, M., Burns, R., Geffen, G. & Geffen, L. (1990). Covert orientation of visual attention in Parkinson's disease: an impairment in the maintenance of attention. *Neuropsychologia*, **28**, 151–159.

Yalom, I. D. (1975). *The Theory and Practice of Group Psychotherapy*. New York: Basic Books.

Zarit, S. H., Anthony, C. R. & Boutselis, M. (1987). Interventions with caregivers of dementia patients: comparison of two approaches. *Psychology and Aging*, **2**, 225–232.

Zarit, S. H., Orr, N. K. & Zarit, J. M. (1985). *The Hidden Victims of Alzheimer's Disease: Families under Stress*. New York: New York University Press.

Zarit, S. H., Todd, P. A. & Zarit, J. M. (1986). Subjective burden of husbands and wives as caregivers: a longitudinal study. *The Gerontologist*, **20**, 260–266.

Zarit, S. H. & Zarit, J. M. (1982). Families under stress: interventions for caregivers of senile dementia patients. *Psychotherapy: Theory Research and Practice*, **19**, 461–471.

Zec, R. F. (1990). Neuropsychology: normal aging versus early AD. In R. E. Becker & E. Giacobini (Eds). *Alzheimer's Disease: Current Research in Early Diagnosis*. New York: Taylor & Francis.

Zepelin, H., Wolfe, C. S. & Kleinplatz, F. (1981). Evaluation of a year-long reality orientation program. *Journal of Gerontology*, **36**, 70–77.

INDEX

Aluminium 5, 6
Alzheimer type dementia 4–6
Arteriosclerotic dementia, *see*
    Cerebrovascular dementia
Assessment 91–109, 155–163
    computer-aided 157, 158
    dementia scales 95
    depression 97
    diagnostic 98, 100, 155
        batteries 95, 96, 156
    goals of 92
    intelligence 95
    measuring change 100–103
    outcome prediction 103–106
    problems of 93, 94, 98–100
Attention 57–59

Behaviour disorders 64
Brain imaging 161–163

Cerebrovascular dementia 4, 5
Cognitive slowing 56, 57
Confabulation 18–19
Cortical dementia 4

Definitions 2–4
Delusions 19, 64, 65
Depression 63, 64
    assessment of 97
Drugs 163–165

Elderly 1
Epidemiology 8–10
    incidence 10
    prevalence 8, 9, 10

Genetics 10–12

Hallucinations 64
History of dementia 2
Huntington's chorea 7

Intelligence 41, 42, 53–56, 95
    assessment of decline in 101,
        102
Intrusions 18, 19

Kluver–Bucy syndrome 64, 65

Language 36, 52
    aphasia 47–50
    comprehension 42, 43
    naming 37–40
        linguistic aspects 39, 40
        perceptual difficulties in 37–
            39
    oral speech 45, 46
    perseveration 44
    subcortical dementia and 79,
        80
    word fluency 40–42
    written communication 46, 47

Management 110–132
    behavioural approaches 111–
        119
        activity 117, 118
        behaviour problems 118, 119
        learning abilities 113–115
        self-care 115–117
    individual care planning
    memory management 119–127
        general memory
            rehabilitation 119
        reality orientation 120–127

Management (*cont.*)
  classroom   120, 129
  effectiveness   122–126
  twenty-four hour   121
  ward orientation training
    121–122
  reminiscence   127–130
  validation therapy   130
Memory   16–35
  clinical description   16–17
  confabulation and   18, 19
  episodic   20–28
    articulatory rehearsal   22, 23
    dysexecutive syndrome   23,
      24
    encoding   26, 27
    fogetting   27, 28
    long-term   25–28
    retrieval   26
    short-term   21–25
    visuospatial   24, 25
  implicit   31–34
    priming   32, 33
    skills learning   31, 32
  intrusions   18, 19
  pathology   19, 20
  remote   28, 29
  semantic   29–31
  subcortical dementia and   74–
    77
Methodological issues   12–15, 36,
  37, 41, 70–72
Multi-infarct dementia, *see*
  Cerebrovascular dementia
Multiple sclerosis   5
  see also Subcortical dementia

Neuropathology   5, 19, 20
Neurotransmitters   5

Parkinson's disease   7, 10
  see also Subcortical dementia
Perseveration, *see* Language

Personality   160, 161
Presenile dementia   4
Progressive supranuclear palsy   7
  see also Subcortical dementia
Psychosocial aspects   133–153
  behavioural changes and   133
  formal support   149–152
  health of carers   137
  psychological well-being of
    carers   136, 137
  stress and strain   137–141
    coping strategies   140, 141
    gender   139, 140
    relationships and   138, 139
    support   141
  support groups
    coping methods   143–147
    evaluation   148, 149
    information   143
    psychotherapeutic
      orientation   147, 148

Reaction time   56, 57, 72, 73

Senile dementia   4
Social factors, *see* Psychosocial
  aspects
Spatial ability   59–63
  subcortical dementia and   80,
    81
Subcortical dementia
  bradyphrenia   71–74
  comparison of different forms
    82–88
  frontal impairments in   77–79
  language   79, 80
  memory   74–77
  spatial ability   80, 81

Treatment, *see* Management

Wilson's disease   7, 11
  see also Subcortical dementia